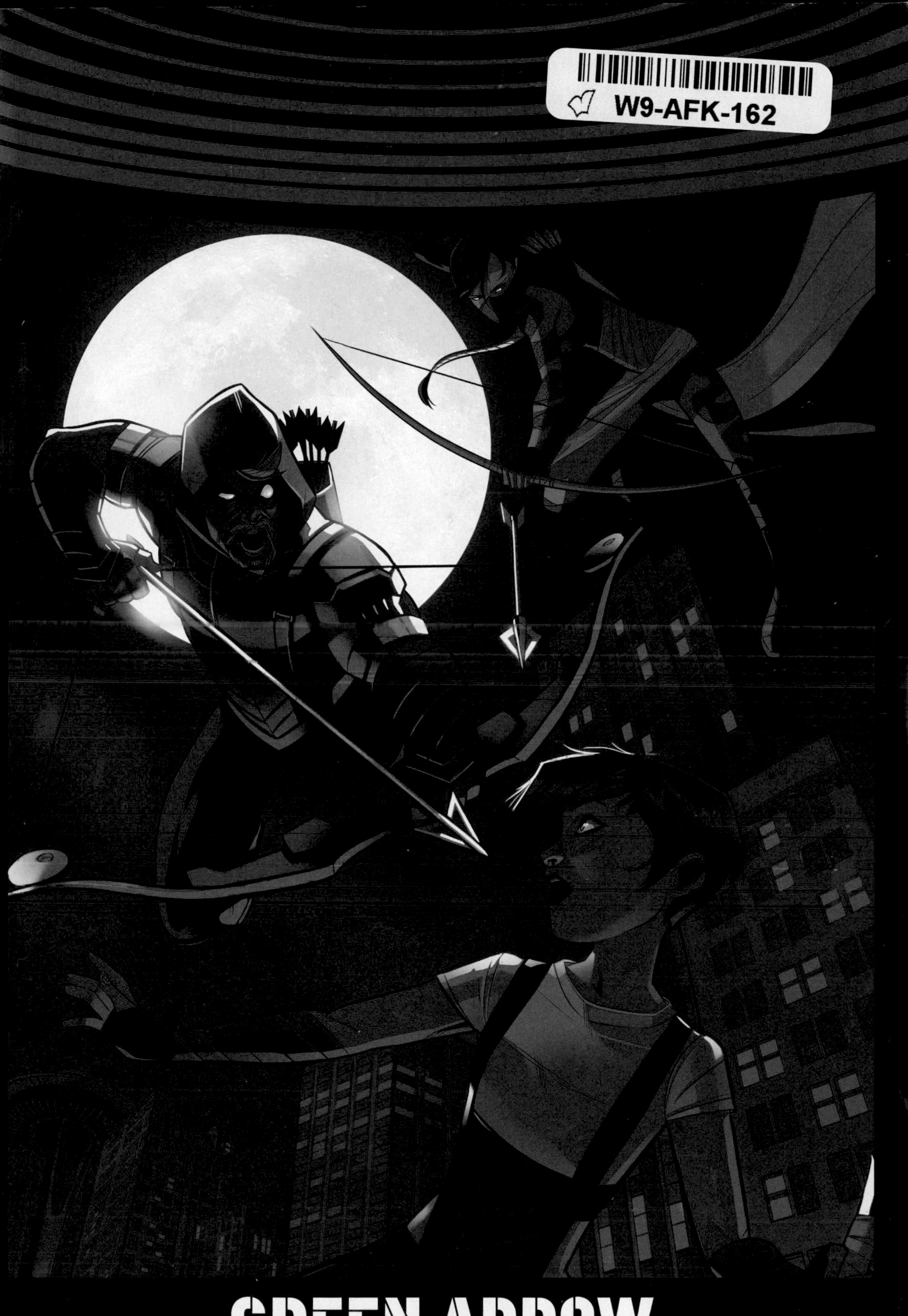

GREEN ARROW

VOL.2 ISLAND OF SCARS

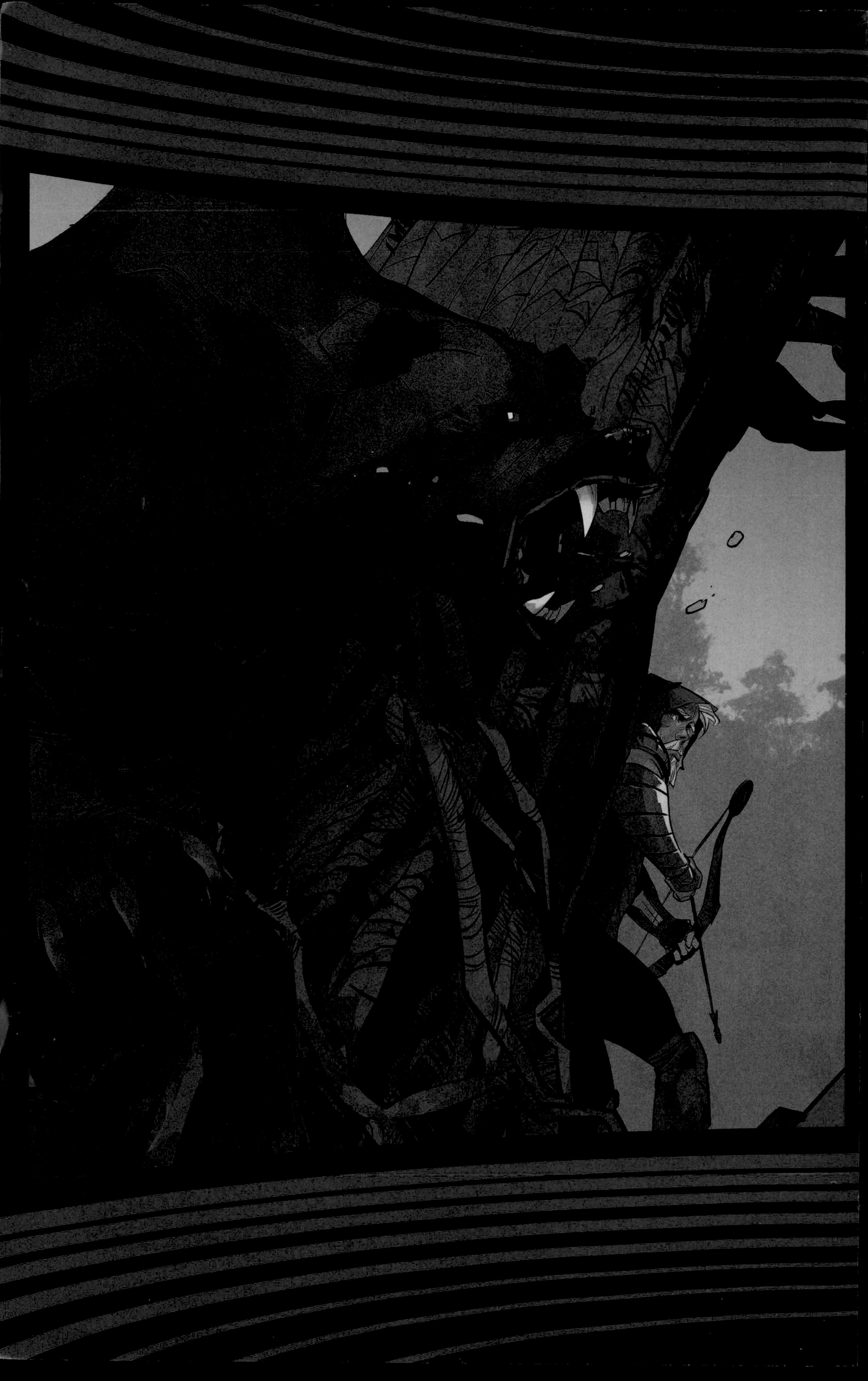

GREEN ARROW
VOL.2 ISLAND OF SCARS

BENJAMIN PERCY
writer

STEPHEN BYRNE * **OTTO SCHMIDT** * **JUAN FERREYRA**
artists and colorists

NATE PIEKOS OF BLAMBOT®
letterer

OTTO SCHMIDT
collection cover artist

ANDY KHOURI Editor - Original Series   **HARVEY RICHARDS** Associate Editor - Original Series
JEB WOODARD Group Editor - Collected Editions   **STEVE COOK** Design Director - Books   **MONIQUE GRUSPE** Publication Design

BOB HARRAS Senior VP - Editor-in-Chief, DC Comics

DIANE NELSON President   **DAN DiDIO** Publisher   **JIM LEE** Publisher   **GEOFF JOHNS** President & Chief Creative Officer
AMIT DESAI Executive VP - Business & Marketing Strategy, Direct to Consumer & Global Franchise Management   **SAM ADES** Senior VP - Direct to Consumer
BOBBIE CHASE VP - Talent Development   **MARK CHIARELLO** Senior VP - Art, Design & Collected Editions
JOHN CUNNINGHAM Senior VP - Sales & Trade Marketing   **ANNE DePIES** Senior VP - Business Strategy, Finance & Administration
DON FALLETTI VP - Manufacturing Operations   **LAWRENCE GANEM** VP - Editorial Administration & Talent Relations
ALISON GILL Senior VP - Manufacturing & Operations   **HANK KANALZ** Senior VP - Editorial Strategy & Administration
JAY KOGAN VP - Legal Affairs   **THOMAS LOFTUS** VP - Business Affairs
JACK MAHAN VP - Business Affairs   **NICK J. NAPOLITANO** VP - Manufacturing Administration
EDDIE SCANNELL VP - Consumer Marketing   **COURTNEY SIMMONS** Senior VP - Publicity & Communications
JIM (SKI) SOKOLOWSKI VP - Comic Book Specialty Sales & Trade Marketing   **NANCY SPEARS** VP - Mass, Book, Digital Sales & Trade Marketing

GREEN ARROW VOLUME 2: ISLAND OF SCARS

Published by DC Comics. Compilation and all new material Copyright © 2017 DC Comics. All Rights Reserved.
Originally published in single magazine form in GREEN ARROW 6-11. Copyright © 2016 DC Comics.
All Rights Reserved. All characters, their distinctive likenesses and related elements featured in this publication are trademarks of DC Comics.
The stories, characters and incidents featured in this publication are entirely fictional.
DC Comics does not read or accept unsolicited submissions of ideas, stories or artwork.

DC Comics, 2900 West Alameda Ave., Burbank, CA 91505. Printed by LSC Communications, Salem, VA, USA. 3/3/17.
First Printing. ISBN: 978-1-4012-7040-7

Library of Congress Cataloging-in-Publication Data is available.

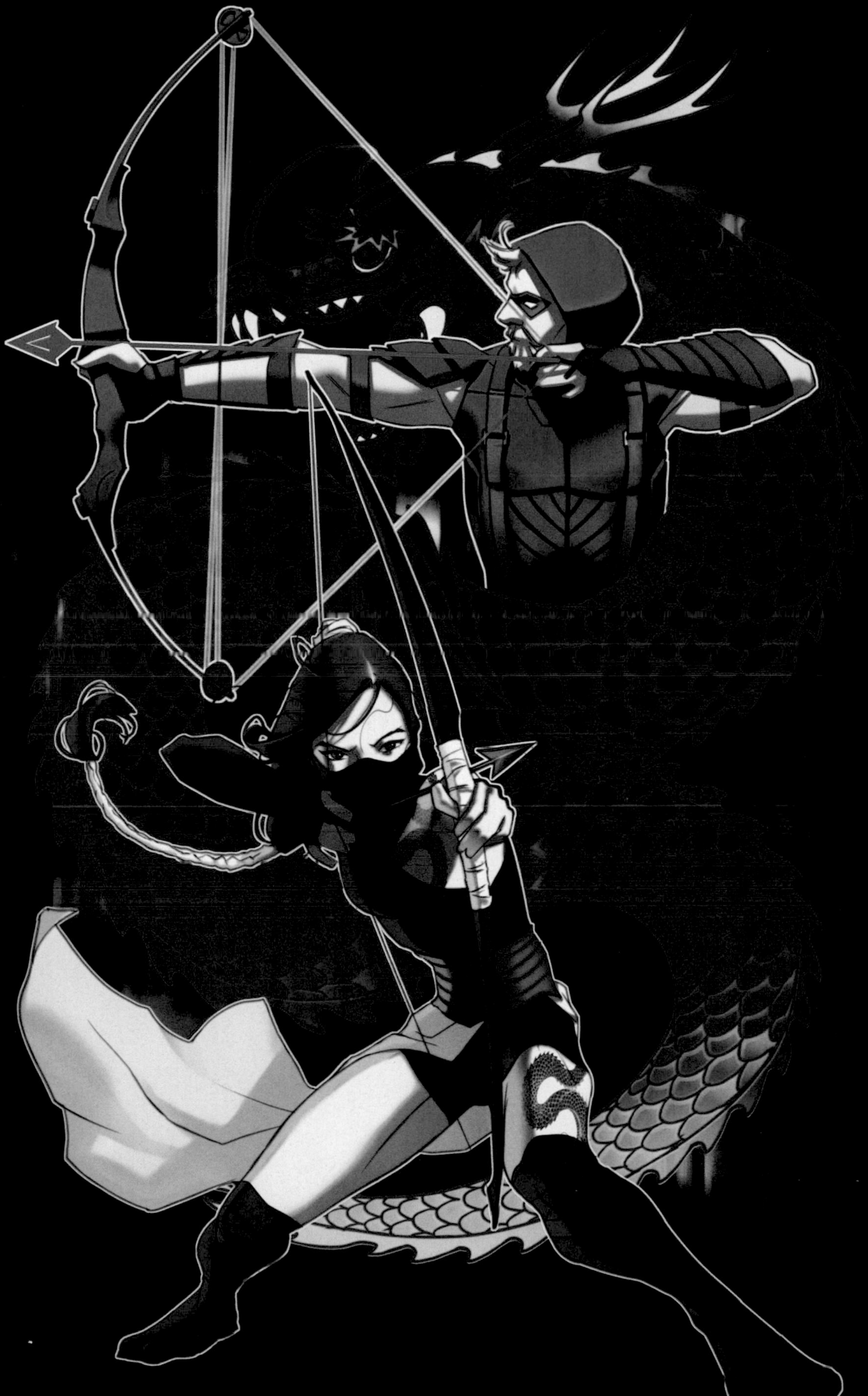

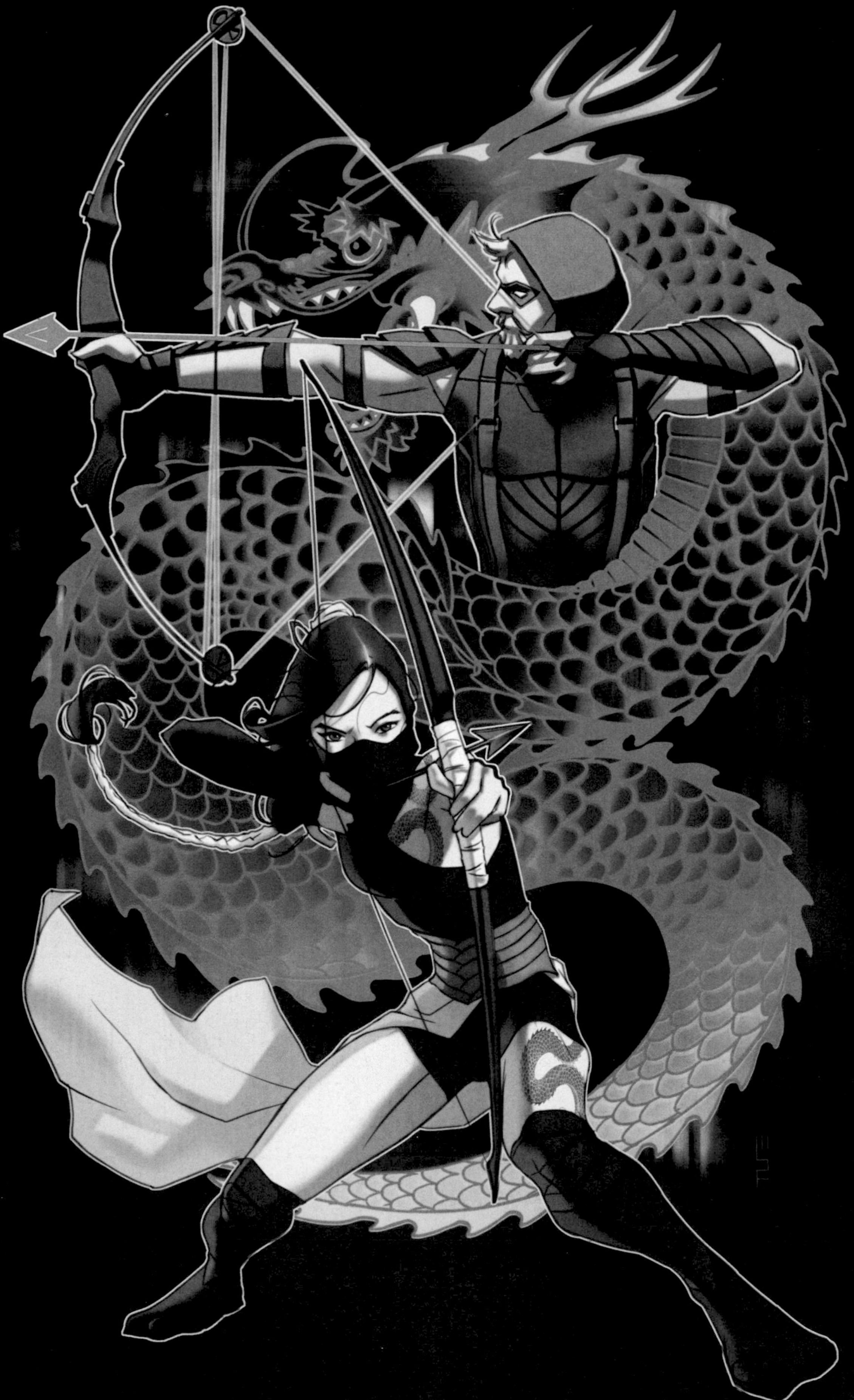

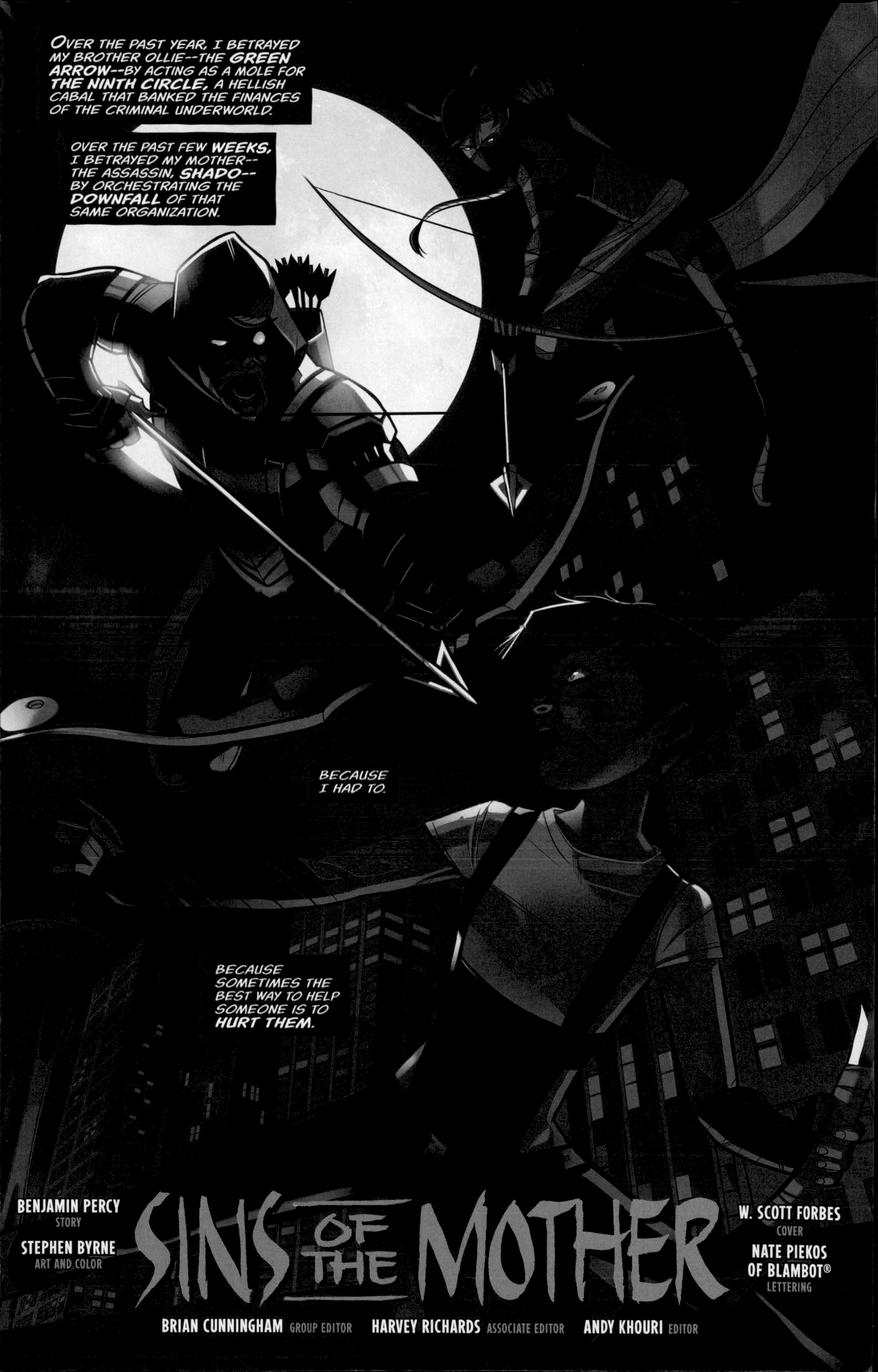
OVER THE PAST YEAR, I BETRAYED MY BROTHER OLLIE--THE GREEN ARROW--BY ACTING AS A MOLE FOR THE NINTH CIRCLE, A HELLISH CABAL THAT BANKED THE FINANCES OF THE CRIMINAL UNDERWORLD.
OVER THE PAST FEW WEEKS, I BETRAYED MY MOTHER-- THE ASSASSIN, SHADO-- BY ORCHESTRATING THE DOWNFALL OF THAT SAME ORGANIZATION.
BECAUSE I HAD TO.
BECAUSE SOMETIMES THE BEST WAY TO HELP SOMEONE IS TO HURT THEM.
BENJAMIN PERCY STORY
STEPHEN BYRNE ART AND COLOR
SINS OF THE MOTHER
W. SCOTT FORBES COVER
NATE PIEKOS OF BLAMBOT® LETTERING
BRIAN CUNNINGHAM GROUP EDITOR
HARVEY RICHARDS ASSOCIATE EDITOR
ANDY KHOURI EDITOR

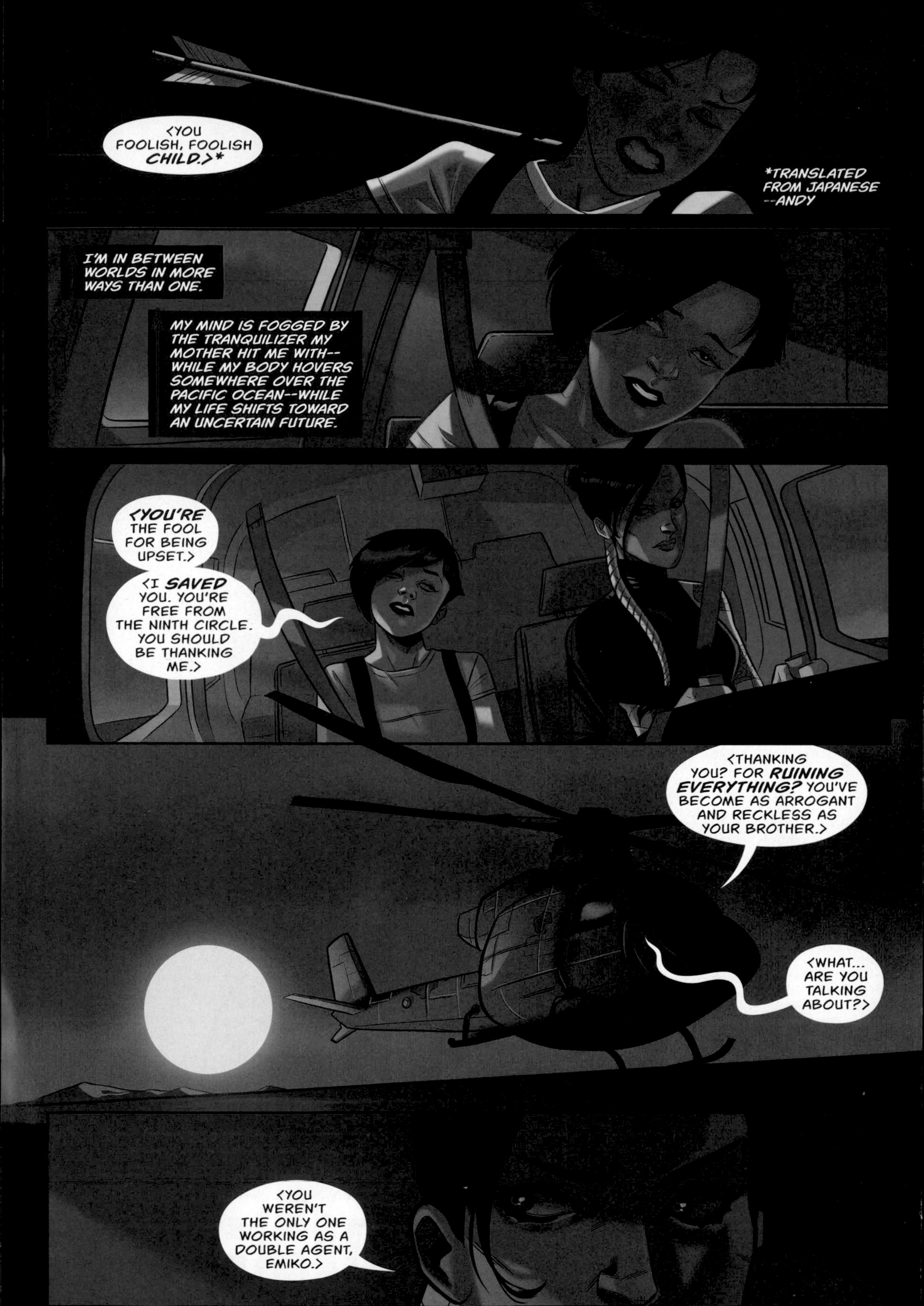
<YOU FOOLISH, FOOLISH CHILD.>*
*TRANSLATED FROM JAPANESE --ANDY
I'M IN BETWEEN WORLDS IN MORE WAYS THAN ONE.
MY MIND IS FOGGED BY THE TRANQUILIZER MY MOTHER HIT ME WITH-- WHILE MY BODY HOVERS SOMEWHERE OVER THE PACIFIC OCEAN--WHILE MY LIFE SHIFTS TOWARD AN UNCERTAIN FUTURE.
<YOU'RE THE FOOL FOR BEING UPSET.>
<I SAVED YOU. YOU'RE FREE FROM THE NINTH CIRCLE. YOU SHOULD BE THANKING ME.>
<THANKING YOU? FOR RUINING EVERYTHING? YOU'VE BECOME AS ARROGANT AND RECKLESS AS YOUR BROTHER.>
<WHAT... ARE YOU TALKING ABOUT?>
<YOU WEREN'T THE ONLY ONE WORKING AS A DOUBLE AGENT, EMIKO.>

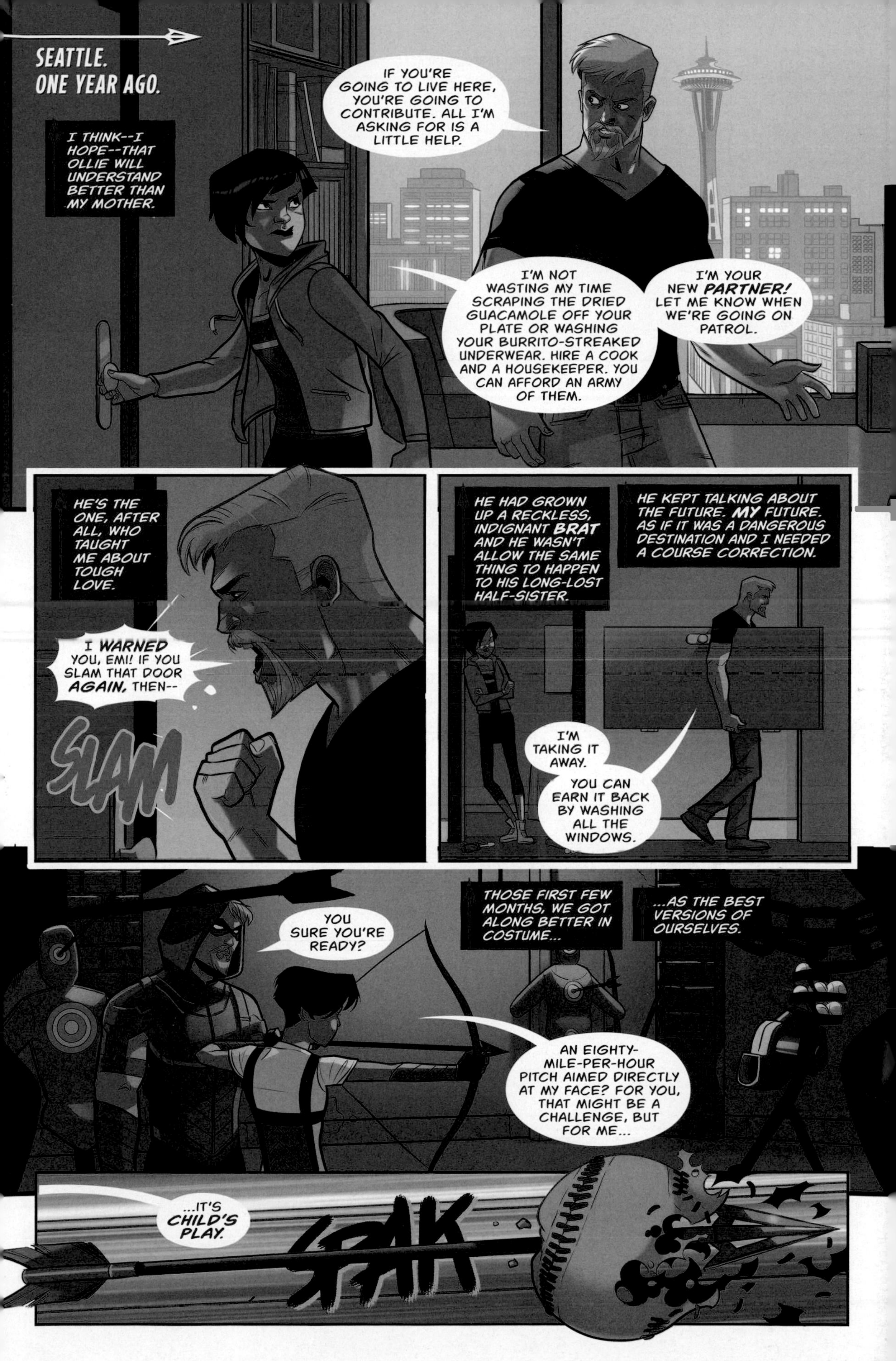
SEATTLE. ONE YEAR AGO.
I THINK--I HOPE--THAT OLLIE WILL UNDERSTAND BETTER THAN MY MOTHER.
IF YOU'RE GOING TO LIVE HERE, YOU'RE GOING TO CONTRIBUTE. ALL I'M ASKING FOR IS A LITTLE HELP.
I'M NOT WASTING MY TIME SCRAPING THE DRIED GUACAMOLE OFF YOUR PLATE OR WASHING YOUR BURRITO-STREAKED UNDERWEAR. HIRE A COOK AND A HOUSEKEEPER. YOU CAN AFFORD AN ARMY OF THEM.
I'M YOUR NEW PARTNER! LET ME KNOW WHEN WE'RE GOING ON PATROL.
HE'S THE ONE, AFTER ALL, WHO TAUGHT ME ABOUT TOUGH LOVE.
I WARNED YOU, EMI! IF YOU SLAM THAT DOOR AGAIN, THEN--
SLAM
HE HAD GROWN UP A RECKLESS, INDIGNANT BRAT AND HE WASN'T ALLOW THE SAME THING TO HAPPEN TO HIS LONG-LOST HALF-SISTER.
HE KEPT TALKING ABOUT THE FUTURE. MY FUTURE. AS IF IT WAS A DANGEROUS DESTINATION AND I NEEDED A COURSE CORRECTION.
I'M TAKING IT AWAY.
YOU CAN EARN IT BACK BY WASHING ALL THE WINDOWS.
THOSE FIRST FEW MONTHS, WE GOT ALONG BETTER IN COSTUME...
...AS THE BEST VERSIONS OF OURSELVES.
YOU SURE YOU'RE READY?
AN EIGHTY-MILE-PER-HOUR PITCH AIMED DIRECTLY AT MY FACE? FOR YOU, THAT MIGHT BE A CHALLENGE, BUT FOR ME...
...IT'S CHILD'S PLAY.
SPAK

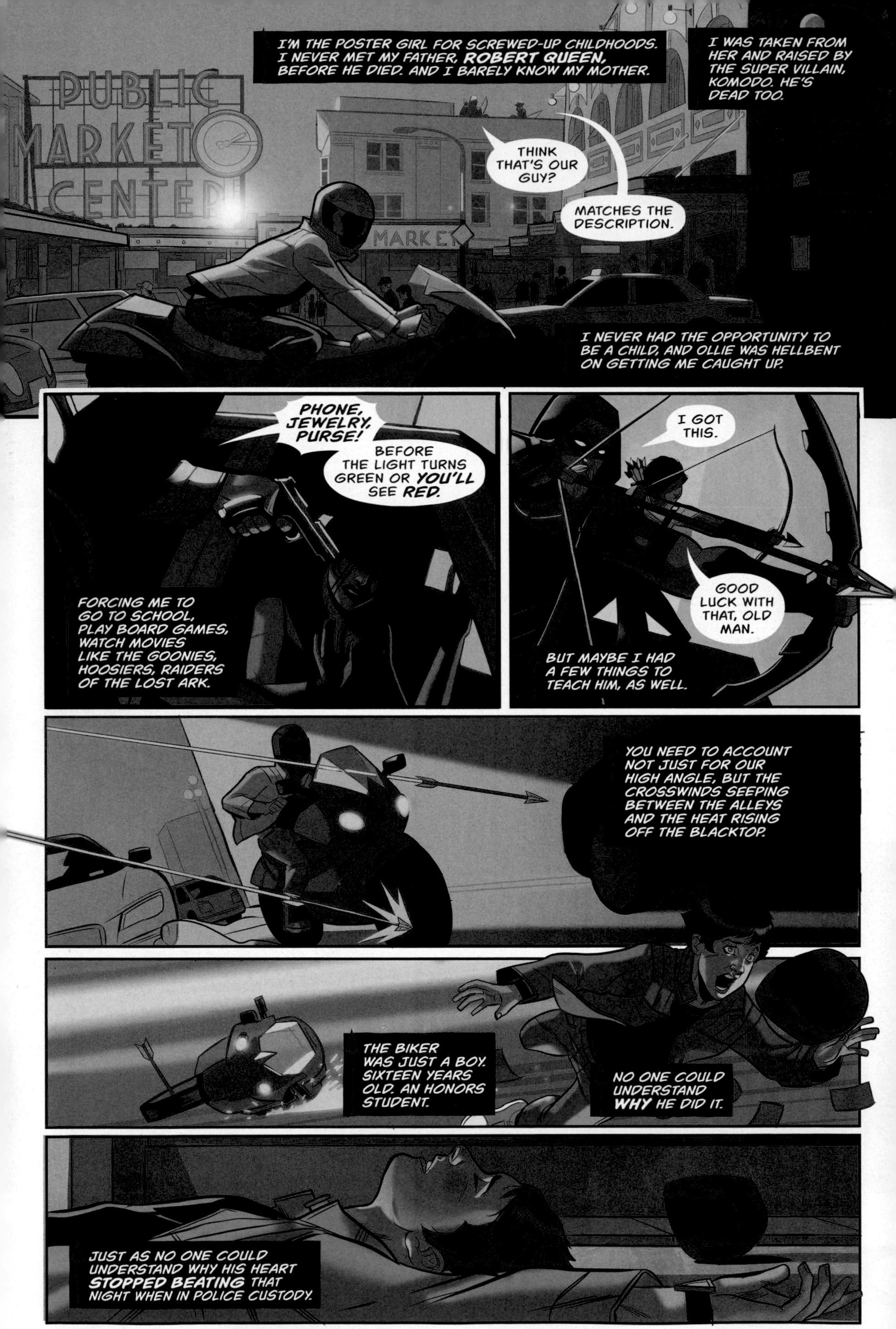

I'M THE POSTER GIRL FOR SCREWED-UP CHILDHOODS. I NEVER MET MY FATHER, ROBERT QUEEN, BEFORE HE DIED. AND I BARELY KNOW MY MOTHER.
I WAS TAKEN FROM HER AND RAISED BY THE SUPER VILLAIN, KOMODO. HE'S DEAD TOO.
PUBLIC MARKET CENTER
THINK THAT'S OUR GUY?
MATCHES THE DESCRIPTION.
I NEVER HAD THE OPPORTUNITY TO BE A CHILD, AND OLLIE WAS HELLBENT ON GETTING ME CAUGHT UP.
PHONE, JEWELRY, PURSE!
BEFORE THE LIGHT TURNS GREEN OR YOU'LL SEE RED.
FORCING ME TO GO TO SCHOOL, PLAY BOARD GAMES, WATCH MOVIES LIKE THE GOONIES, HOOSIERS, RAIDERS OF THE LOST ARK.
I GOT THIS.
GOOD LUCK WITH THAT, OLD MAN.
BUT MAYBE I HAD A FEW THINGS TO TEACH HIM, AS WELL.
YOU NEED TO ACCOUNT NOT JUST FOR OUR HIGH ANGLE, BUT THE CROSSWINDS SEEPING BETWEEN THE ALLEYS AND THE HEAT RISING OFF THE BLACKTOP.
THE BIKER WAS JUST A BOY. SIXTEEN YEARS OLD. AN HONORS STUDENT.
NO ONE COULD UNDERSTAND WHY HE DID IT.
JUST AS NO ONE COULD UNDERSTAND WHY HIS HEART STOPPED BEATING THAT NIGHT WHEN IN POLICE CUSTODY.

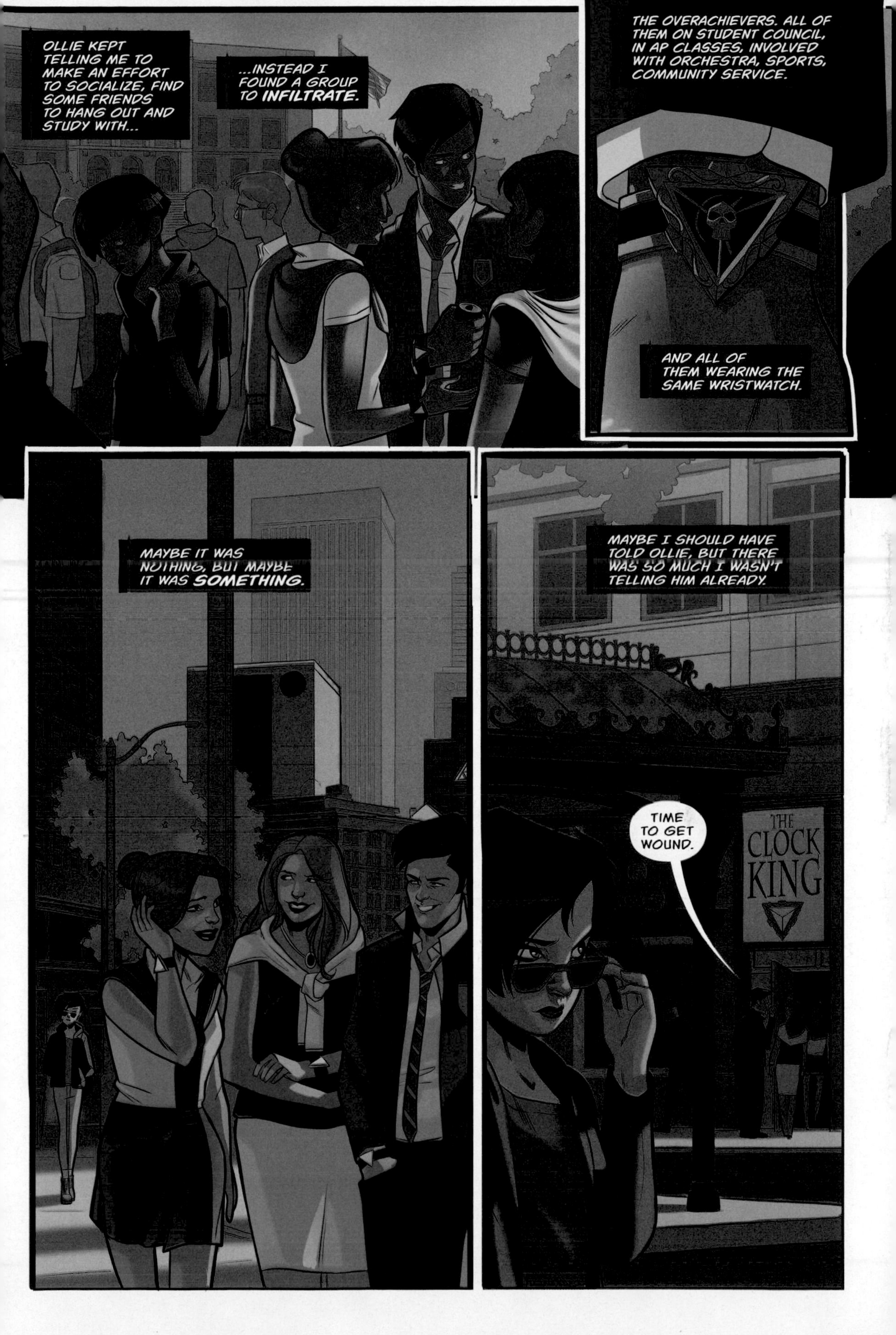
OLLIE KEPT TELLING ME TO MAKE AN EFFORT TO SOCIALIZE, FIND SOME FRIENDS TO HANG OUT AND STUDY WITH...
...INSTEAD I FOUND A GROUP TO INFILTRATE.
THE OVERACHIEVERS. ALL OF THEM ON STUDENT COUNCIL, IN AP CLASSES, INVOLVED WITH ORCHESTRA, SPORTS, COMMUNITY SERVICE.
AND ALL OF THEM WEARING THE SAME WRISTWATCH.
MAYBE IT WAS NOTHING, BUT MAYBE IT WAS SOMETHING.
MAYBE I SHOULD HAVE TOLD OLLIE, BUT THERE WAS SO MUCH I WASN'T TELLING HIM ALREADY.
THE CLOCK KING
TIME TO GET WOUND.

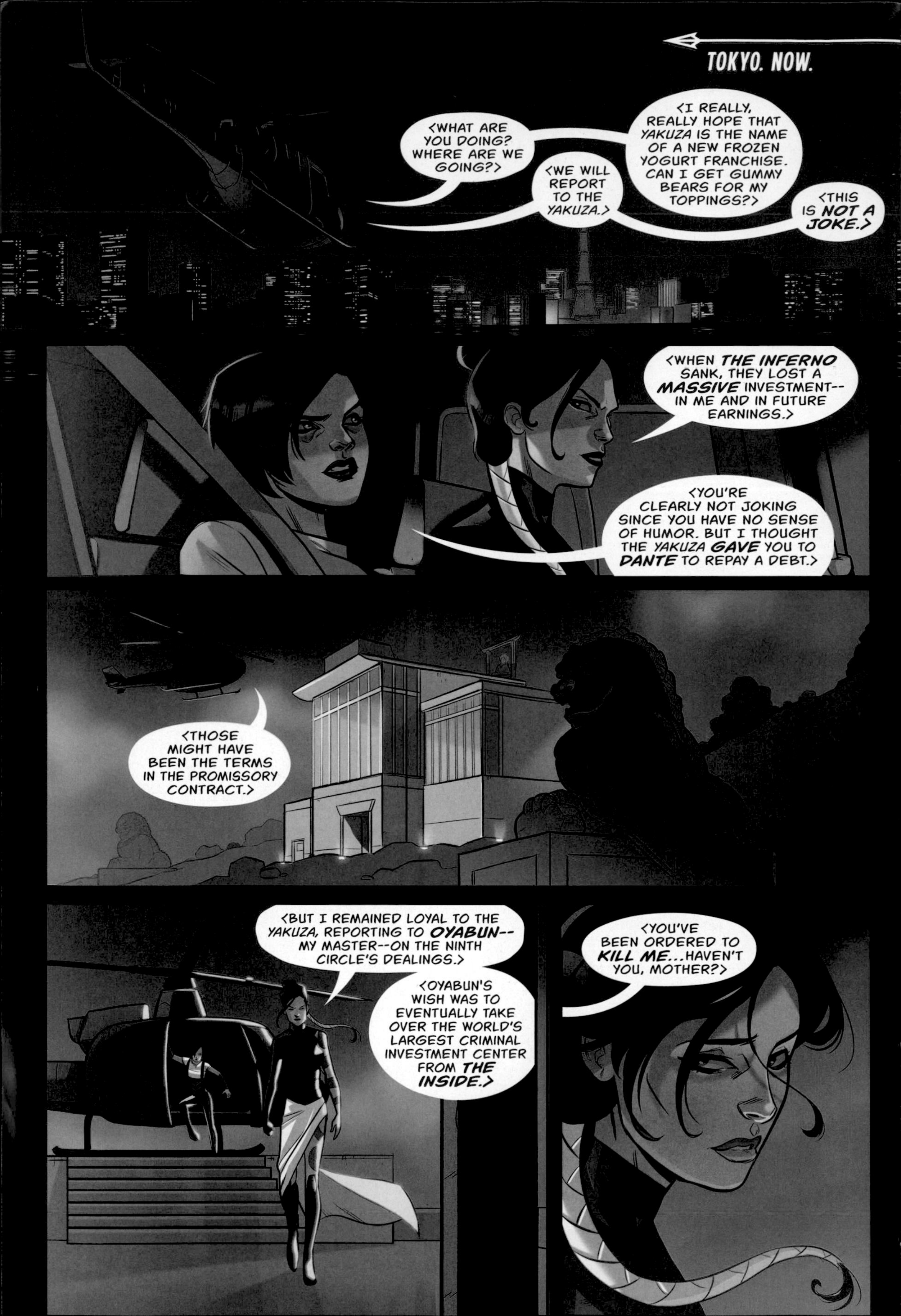

TOKYO. NOW.
<WHAT ARE YOU DOING? WHERE ARE WE GOING?>
<WE WILL REPORT TO THE YAKUZA.>
<I REALLY, REALLY HOPE THAT YAKUZA IS THE NAME OF A NEW FROZEN YOGURT FRANCHISE. CAN I GET GUMMY BEARS FOR MY TOPPINGS?>
<THIS IS NOT A JOKE.>
<WHEN THE INFERNO SANK, THEY LOST A MASSIVE INVESTMENT-- IN ME AND IN FUTURE EARNINGS.>
<YOU'RE CLEARLY NOT JOKING SINCE YOU HAVE NO SENSE OF HUMOR. BUT I THOUGHT THE YAKUZA GAVE YOU TO DANTE TO REPAY A DEBT.>
<THOSE MIGHT HAVE BEEN THE TERMS IN THE PROMISSORY CONTRACT.>
<BUT I REMAINED LOYAL TO THE YAKUZA, REPORTING TO OYABUN-- MY MASTER--ON THE NINTH CIRCLE'S DEALINGS.>
<OYABUN'S WISH WAS TO EVENTUALLY TAKE OVER THE WORLD'S LARGEST CRIMINAL INVESTMENT CENTER FROM THE INSIDE.>
<YOU'VE BEEN ORDERED TO KILL ME...HAVEN'T YOU, MOTHER?>

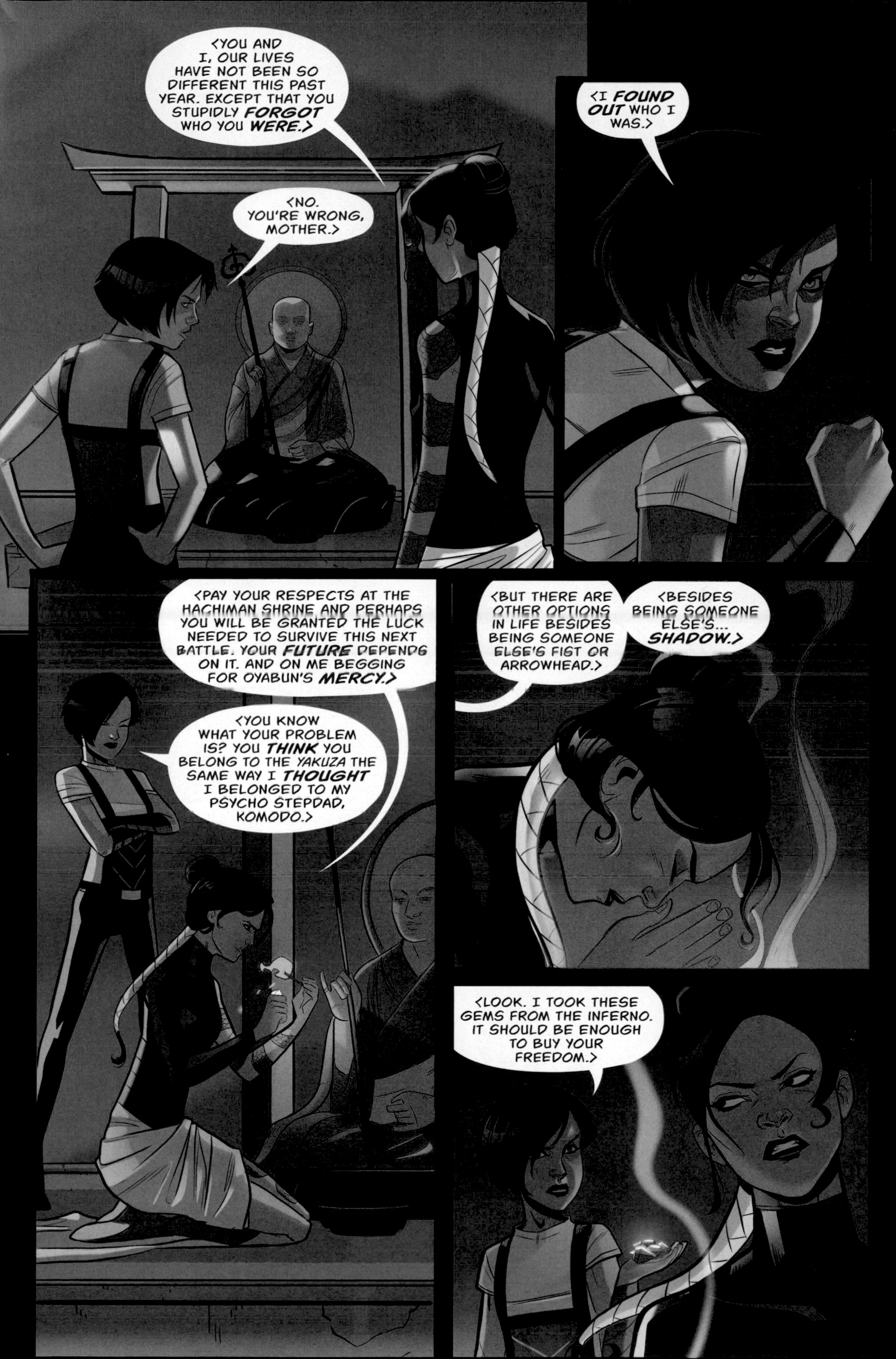
<YOU AND I, OUR LIVES HAVE NOT BEEN SO DIFFERENT THIS PAST YEAR. EXCEPT THAT YOU STUPIDLY FORGOT WHO YOU WERE.>
<NO. YOU'RE WRONG, MOTHER.>
<I FOUND OUT WHO I WAS.>
<PAY YOUR RESPECTS AT THE HACHIMAN SHRINE AND PERHAPS YOU WILL BE GRANTED THE LUCK NEEDED TO SURVIVE THIS NEXT BATTLE. YOUR FUTURE DEPENDS ON IT. AND ON ME BEGGING FOR OYABUN'S MERCY.>
<YOU KNOW WHAT YOUR PROBLEM IS? YOU THINK YOU BELONG TO THE YAKUZA THE SAME WAY I THOUGHT I BELONGED TO MY PSYCHO STEPDAD, KOMODO.>
<BUT THERE ARE OTHER OPTIONS IN LIFE BESIDES BEING SOMEONE ELSE'S FIST OR ARROWHEAD.>
<BESIDES BEING SOMEONE ELSE'S... SHADOW.>
<LOOK. I TOOK THESE GEMS FROM THE INFERNO. IT SHOULD BE ENOUGH TO BUY YOUR FREEDOM.>

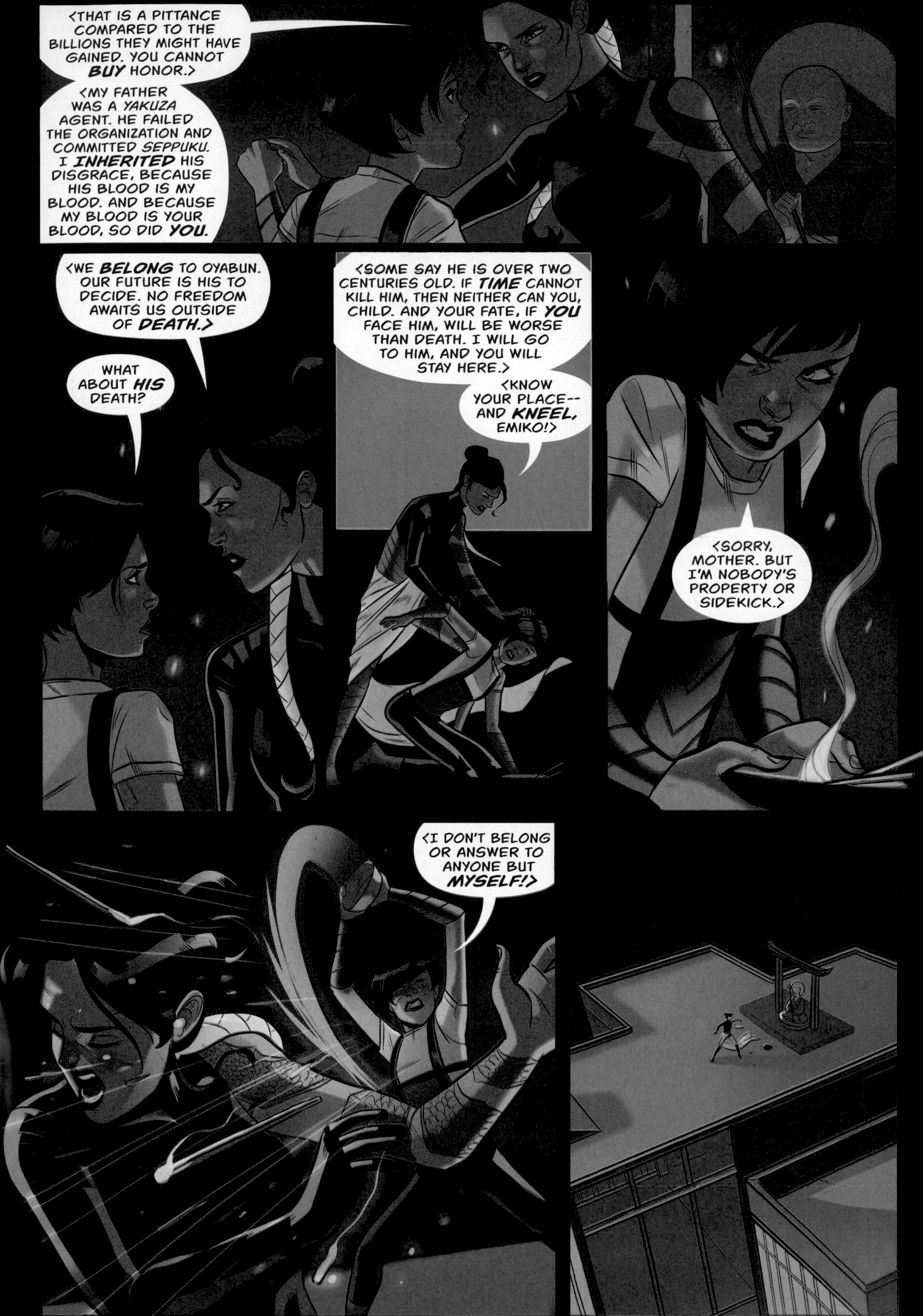
<THAT IS A PITTANCE COMPARED TO THE BILLIONS THEY MIGHT HAVE GAINED. YOU CANNOT BUY HONOR.>
<MY FATHER WAS A YAKUZA AGENT. HE FAILED THE ORGANIZATION AND COMMITTED SEPPUKU. I INHERITED HIS DISGRACE, BECAUSE HIS BLOOD IS MY BLOOD. AND BECAUSE MY BLOOD IS YOUR BLOOD, SO DID YOU.
<WE BELONG TO OYABUN. OUR FUTURE IS HIS TO DECIDE. NO FREEDOM AWAITS US OUTSIDE OF DEATH.>
WHAT ABOUT HIS DEATH?
<SOME SAY HE IS OVER TWO CENTURIES OLD. IF TIME CANNOT KILL HIM, THEN NEITHER CAN YOU, CHILD. AND YOUR FATE, IF YOU FACE HIM, WILL BE WORSE THAN DEATH. I WILL GO TO HIM, AND YOU WILL STAY HERE.>
<KNOW YOUR PLACE-- AND KNEEL, EMIKO!>
<SORRY, MOTHER. BUT I'M NOBODY'S PROPERTY OR SIDEKICK.>
<I DON'T BELONG OR ANSWER TO ANYONE BUT MYSELF!>

SEATTLE. THEN.

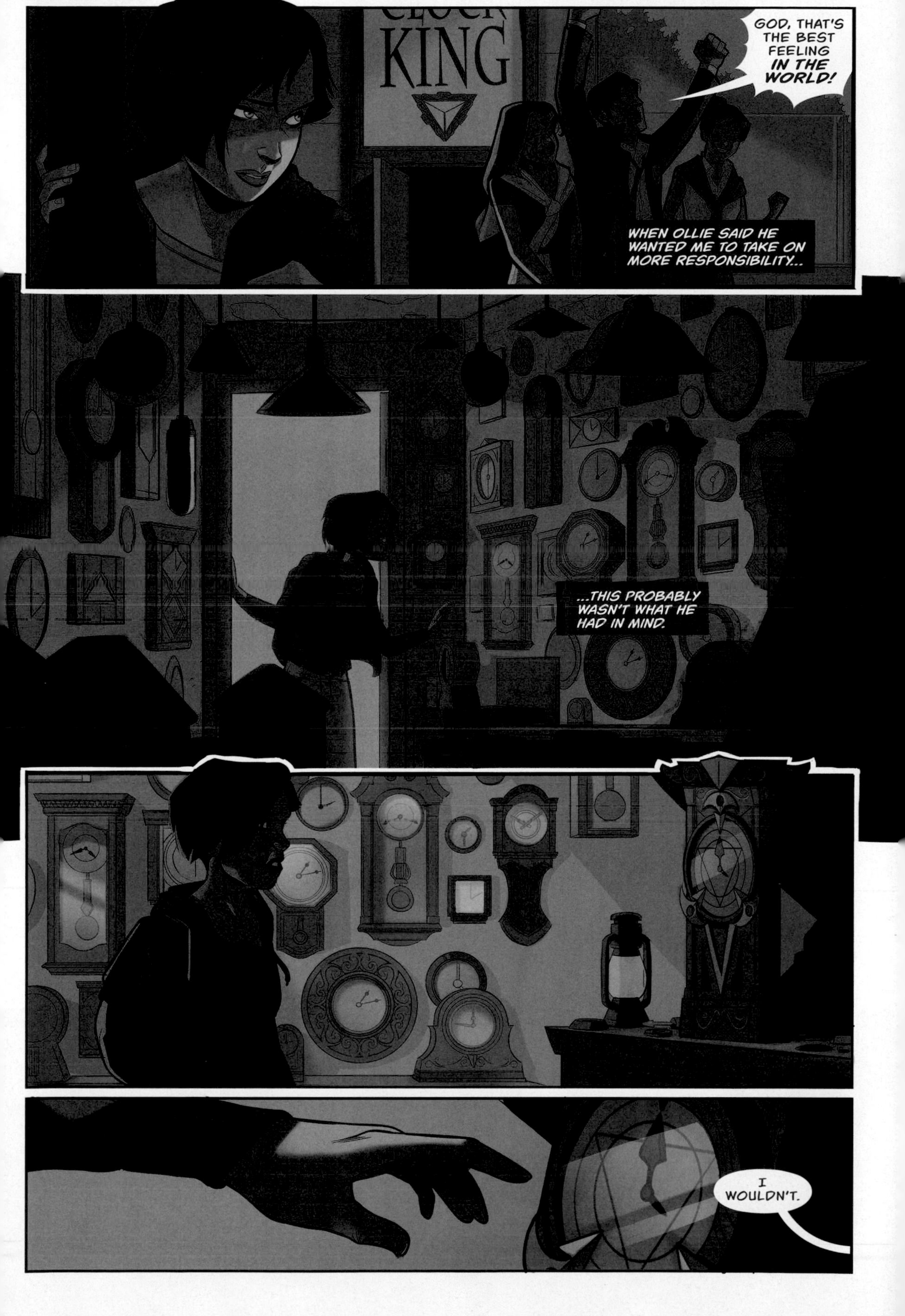
KING
GOD, THAT'S THE BEST FEELING IN THE WORLD!
WHEN OLLIE SAID HE WANTED ME TO TAKE ON MORE RESPONSIBILITY...
...THIS PROBABLY WASN'T WHAT HE HAD IN MIND.
I WOULDN'T.

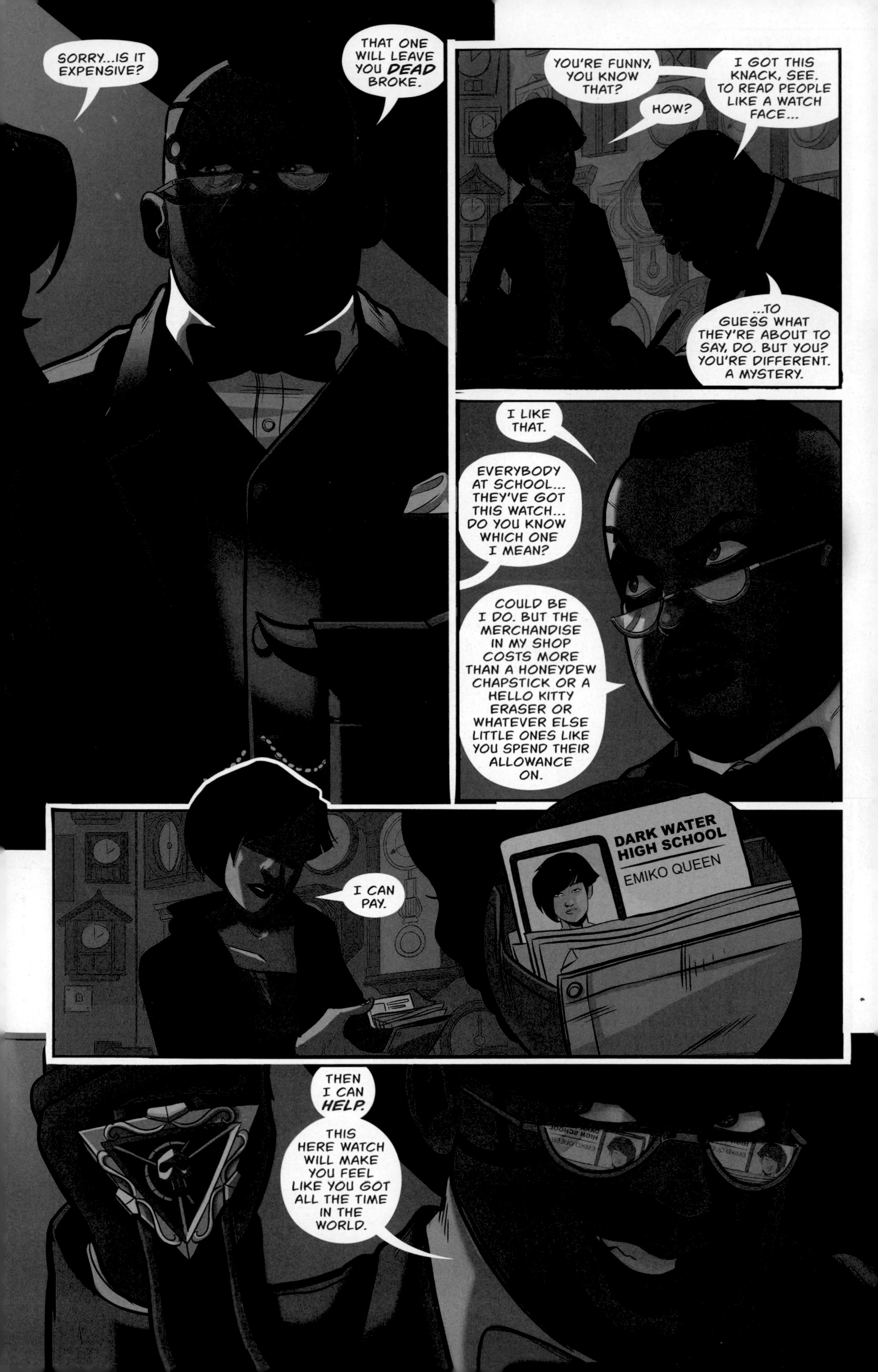
SORRY...IS IT EXPENSIVE?
THAT ONE WILL LEAVE YOU *DEAD* BROKE.
YOU'RE FUNNY, YOU KNOW THAT?
HOW?
I GOT THIS KNACK, SEE. TO READ PEOPLE LIKE A WATCH FACE...
...TO GUESS WHAT THEY'RE ABOUT TO SAY, DO. BUT YOU? YOU'RE DIFFERENT. A MYSTERY.
I LIKE THAT.
EVERYBODY AT SCHOOL... THEY'VE GOT THIS WATCH... DO YOU KNOW WHICH ONE I MEAN?
COULD BE I DO. BUT THE MERCHANDISE IN MY SHOP COSTS MORE THAN A HONEYDEW CHAPSTICK OR A HELLO KITTY ERASER OR WHATEVER ELSE LITTLE ONES LIKE YOU SPEND THEIR ALLOWANCE ON.
I CAN PAY.
DARK WATER HIGH SCHOOL
EMIKO QUEEN
THEN I CAN *HELP.*
THIS HERE WATCH WILL MAKE YOU FEEL LIKE YOU GOT ALL THE TIME IN THE WORLD.

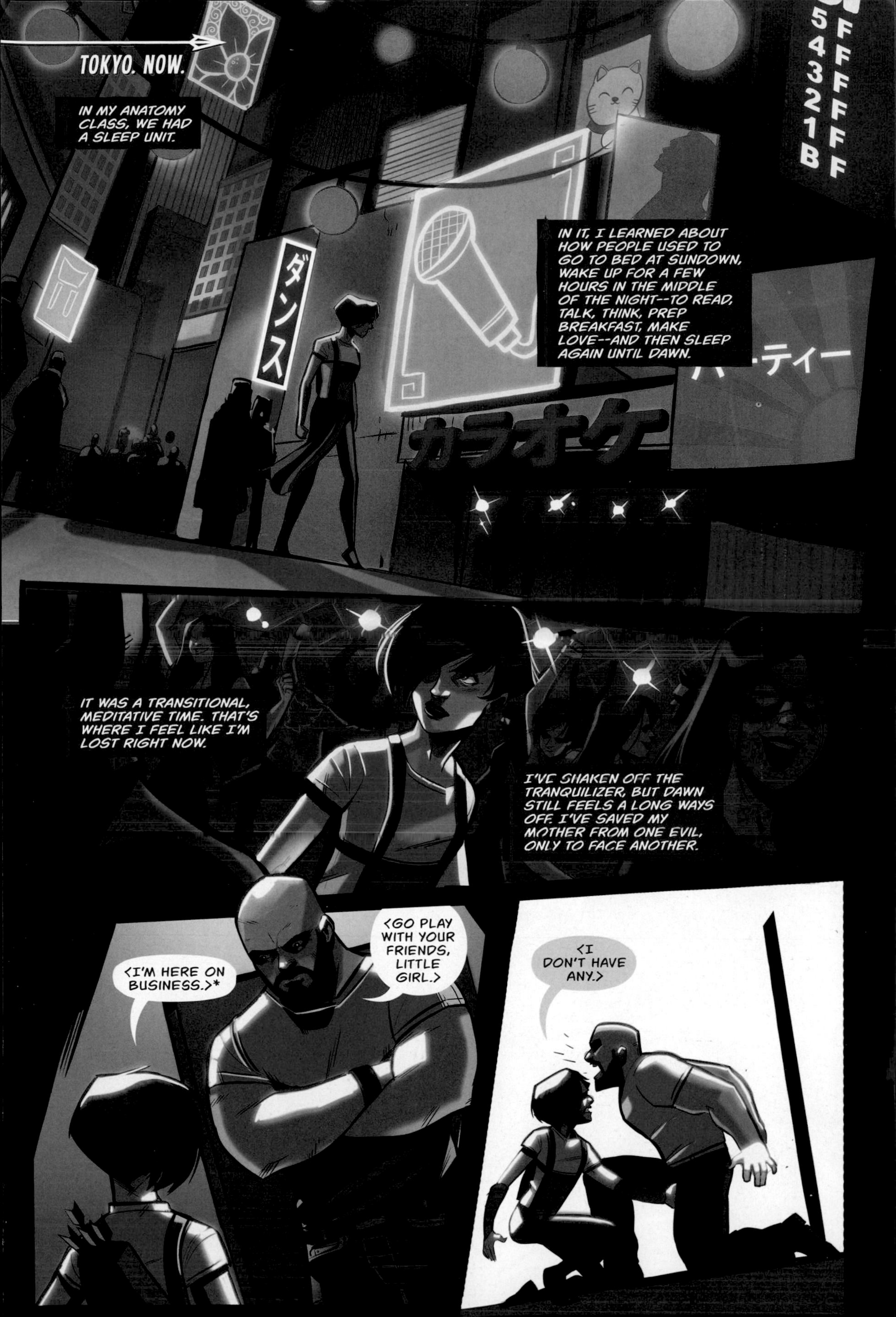
TOKYO. NOW.
IN MY ANATOMY CLASS, WE HAD A SLEEP UNIT.
IN IT, I LEARNED ABOUT HOW PEOPLE USED TO GO TO BED AT SUNDOWN, WAKE UP FOR A FEW HOURS IN THE MIDDLE OF THE NIGHT--TO READ, TALK, THINK, PREP BREAKFAST, MAKE LOVE--AND THEN SLEEP AGAIN UNTIL DAWN.
5F
4F
3F
2F
1F
BF
ダンス
カラオケ
IT WAS A TRANSITIONAL, MEDITATIVE TIME. THAT'S WHERE I FEEL LIKE I'M LOST RIGHT NOW.
I'VE SHAKEN OFF THE TRANQUILIZER, BUT DAWN STILL FEELS A LONG WAYS OFF. I'VE SAVED MY MOTHER FROM ONE EVIL, ONLY TO FACE ANOTHER.
<I'M HERE ON BUSINESS.>*
<GO PLAY WITH YOUR FRIENDS, LITTLE GIRL.>
<I DON'T HAVE ANY.>

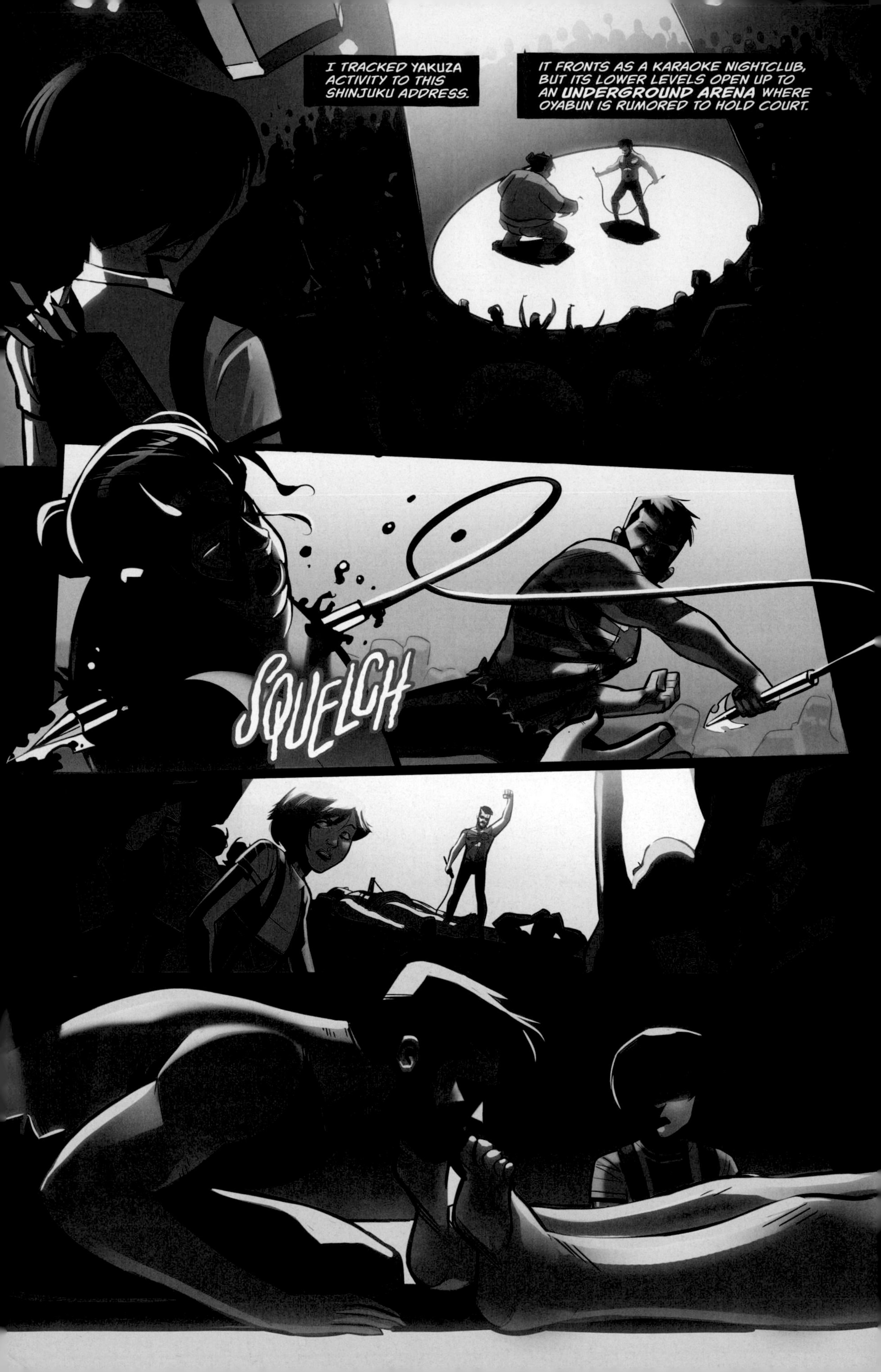
I TRACKED YAKUZA ACTIVITY TO THIS SHINJUKU ADDRESS.
IT FRONTS AS A KARAOKE NIGHTCLUB, BUT ITS LOWER LEVELS OPEN UP TO AN UNDERGROUND ARENA WHERE OYABUN IS RUMORED TO HOLD COURT.
SQUELCH

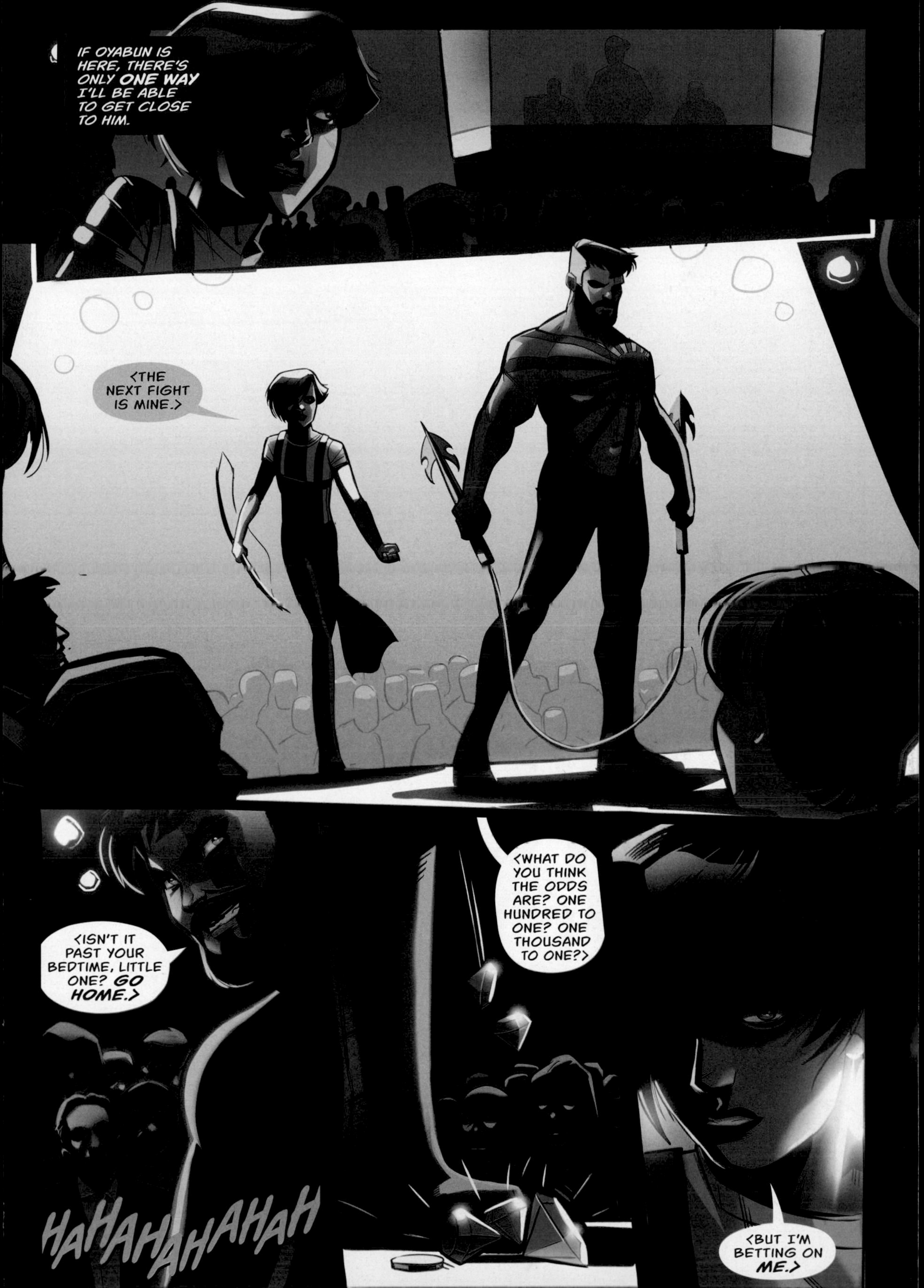
IF OYABUN IS HERE, THERE'S ONLY ONE WAY I'LL BE ABLE TO GET CLOSE TO HIM.
<THE NEXT FIGHT IS MINE.>
<ISN'T IT PAST YOUR BEDTIME, LITTLE ONE? GO HOME.>
HAHAHAHAHAHAH
<WHAT DO YOU THINK THE ODDS ARE? ONE HUNDRED TO ONE? ONE THOUSAND TO ONE?>
<BUT I'M BETTING ON ME.>

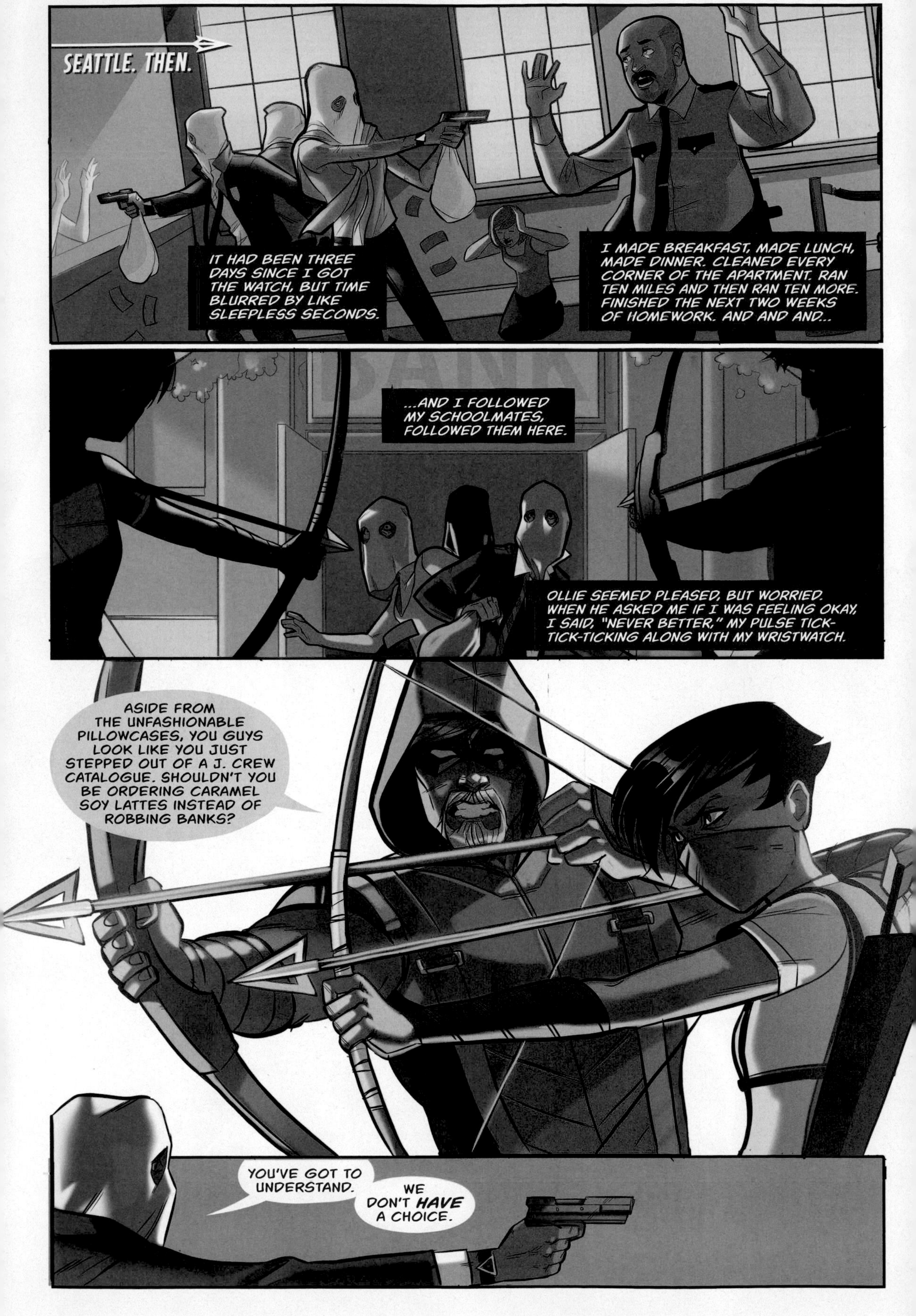
SEATTLE. THEN.
IT HAD BEEN THREE DAYS SINCE I GOT THE WATCH, BUT TIME BLURRED BY LIKE SLEEPLESS SECONDS.
I MADE BREAKFAST, MADE LUNCH, MADE DINNER. CLEANED EVERY CORNER OF THE APARTMENT. RAN TEN MILES AND THEN RAN TEN MORE. FINISHED THE NEXT TWO WEEKS OF HOMEWORK. AND AND AND...
...AND I FOLLOWED MY SCHOOLMATES, FOLLOWED THEM HERE.
OLLIE SEEMED PLEASED, BUT WORRIED. WHEN HE ASKED ME IF I WAS FEELING OKAY, I SAID, "NEVER BETTER," MY PULSE TICK-TICK-TICKING ALONG WITH MY WRISTWATCH.
ASIDE FROM THE UNFASHIONABLE PILLOWCASES, YOU GUYS LOOK LIKE YOU JUST STEPPED OUT OF A J. CREW CATALOGUE. SHOULDN'T YOU BE ORDERING CARAMEL SOY LATTES INSTEAD OF ROBBING BANKS?
YOU'VE GOT TO UNDERSTAND.
WE DON'T HAVE A CHOICE.

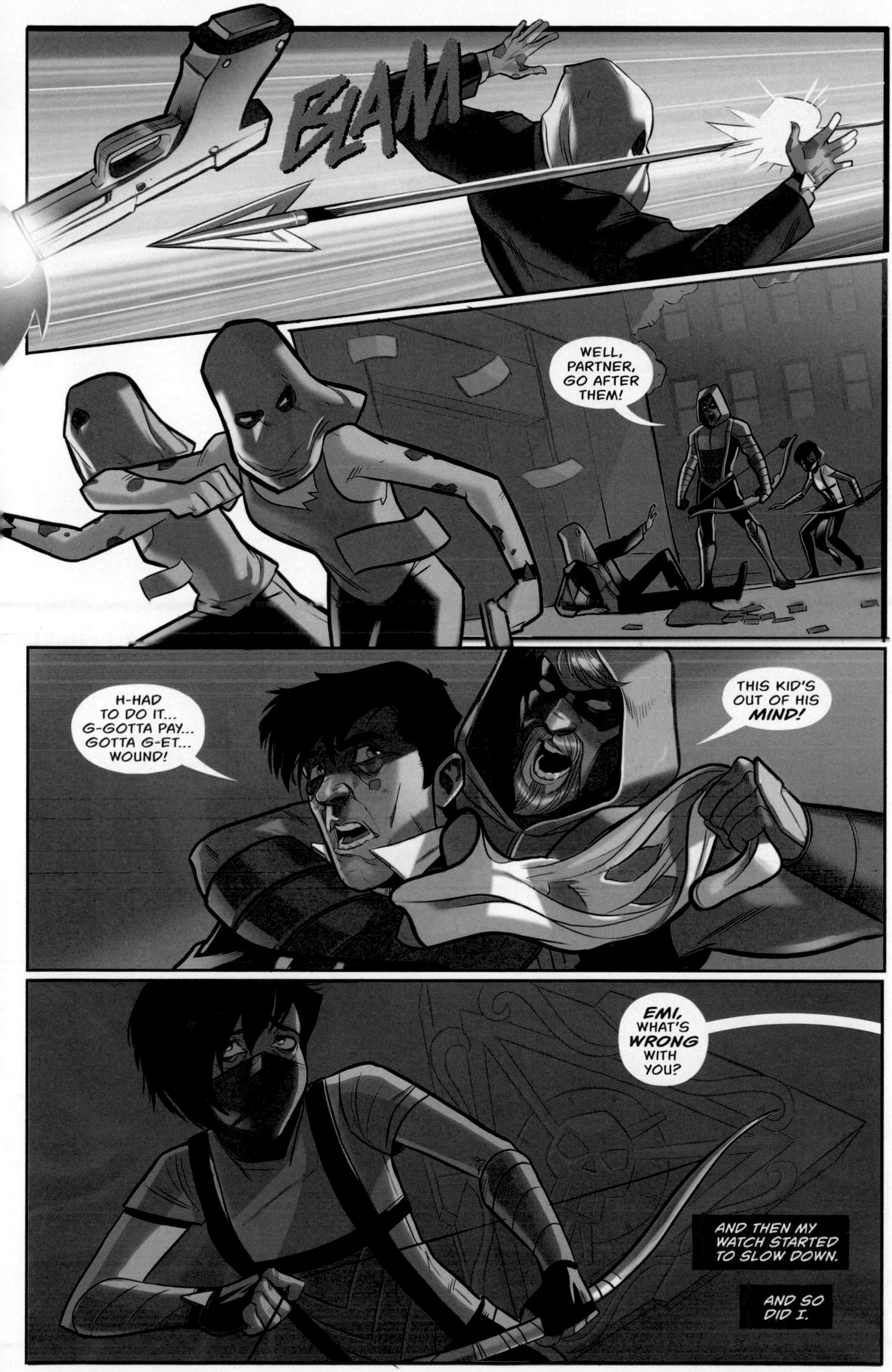
BLAM
WELL, PARTNER, GO AFTER THEM!
H-HAD TO DO IT... G-GOTTA PAY... GOTTA G-ET... WOUND!
THIS KID'S OUT OF HIS MIND!
EMI, WHAT'S WRONG WITH YOU?
AND THEN MY WATCH STARTED TO SLOW DOWN.
AND SO DID I.

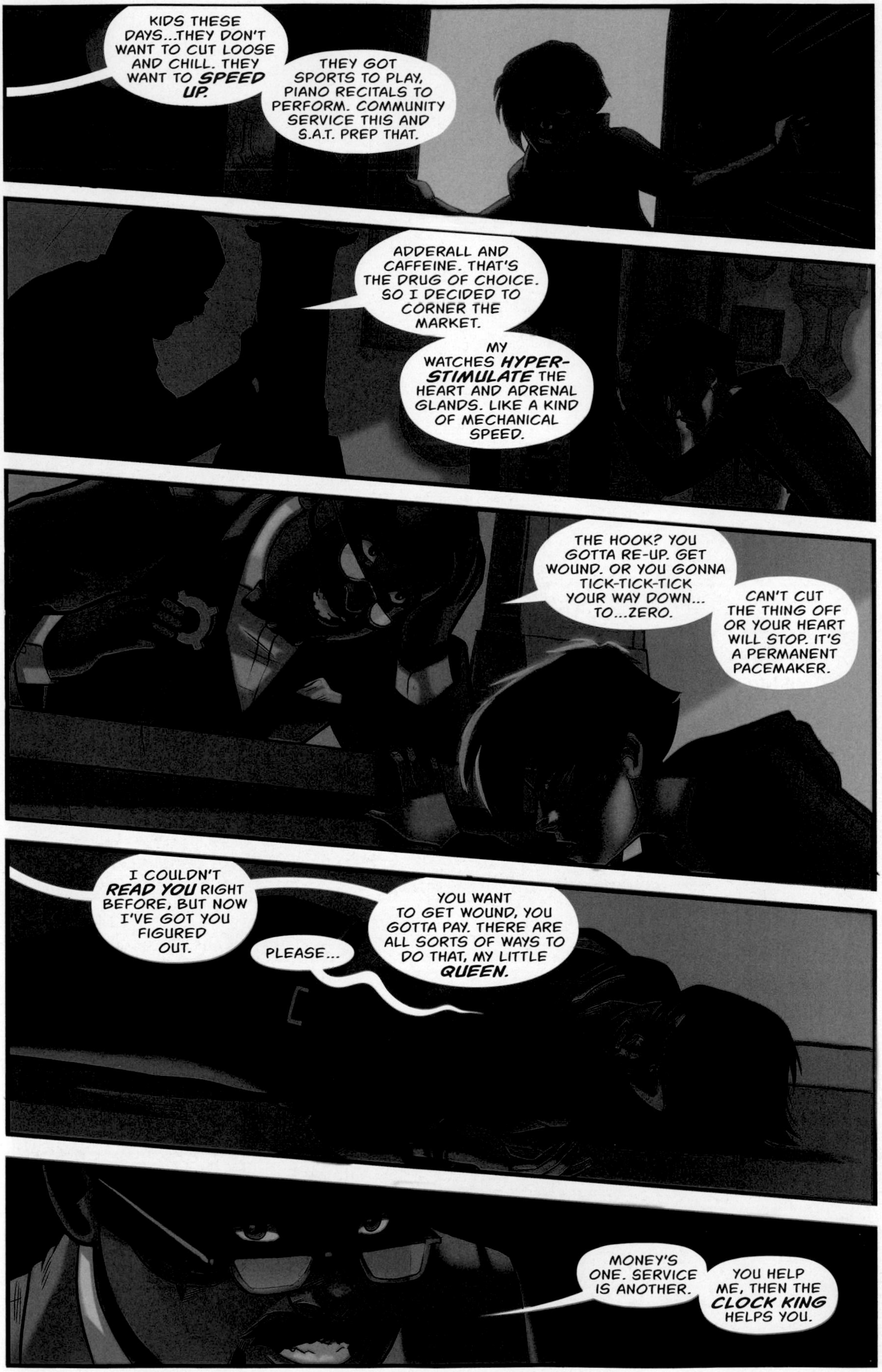
KIDS THESE DAYS...THEY DON'T WANT TO CUT LOOSE AND CHILL. THEY WANT TO SPEED UP.
THEY GOT SPORTS TO PLAY, PIANO RECITALS TO PERFORM. COMMUNITY SERVICE THIS AND S.A.T. PREP THAT.
ADDERALL AND CAFFEINE. THAT'S THE DRUG OF CHOICE. SO I DECIDED TO CORNER THE MARKET.
MY WATCHES HYPER-STIMULATE THE HEART AND ADRENAL GLANDS. LIKE A KIND OF MECHANICAL SPEED.
THE HOOK? YOU GOTTA RE-UP. GET WOUND. OR YOU GONNA TICK-TICK-TICK YOUR WAY DOWN... TO...ZERO.
CAN'T CUT THE THING OFF OR YOUR HEART WILL STOP. IT'S A PERMANENT PACEMAKER.
I COULDN'T READ YOU RIGHT BEFORE, BUT NOW I'VE GOT YOU FIGURED OUT.
PLEASE...
YOU WANT TO GET WOUND, YOU GOTTA PAY. THERE ARE ALL SORTS OF WAYS TO DO THAT, MY LITTLE QUEEN.
MONEY'S ONE. SERVICE IS ANOTHER.
YOU HELP ME, THEN THE CLOCK KING HELPS YOU.

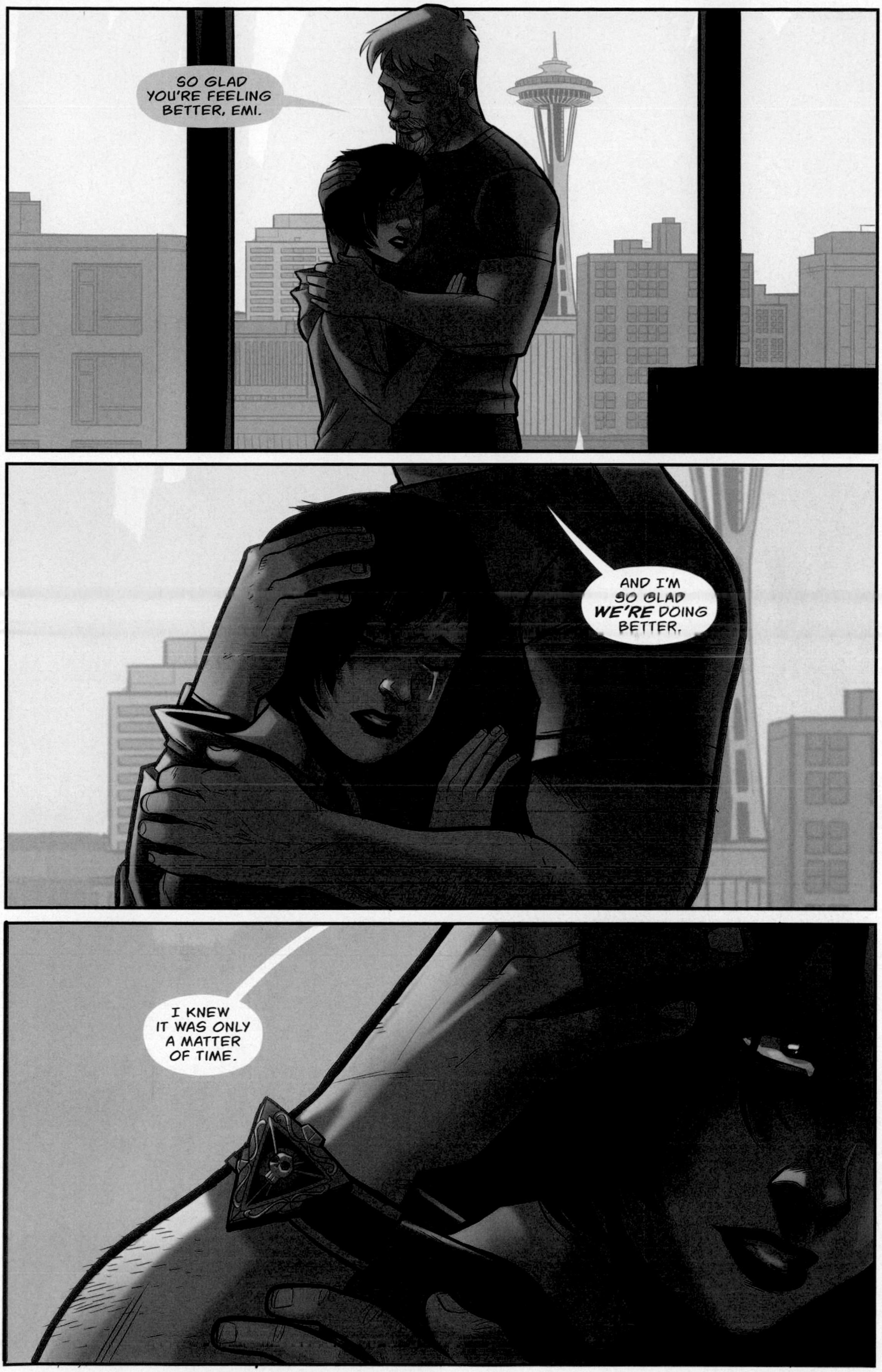
SO GLAD YOU'RE FEELING BETTER, EMI.
AND I'M SO GLAD *WE'RE* DOING BETTER.
I KNEW IT WAS ONLY A MATTER OF TIME.

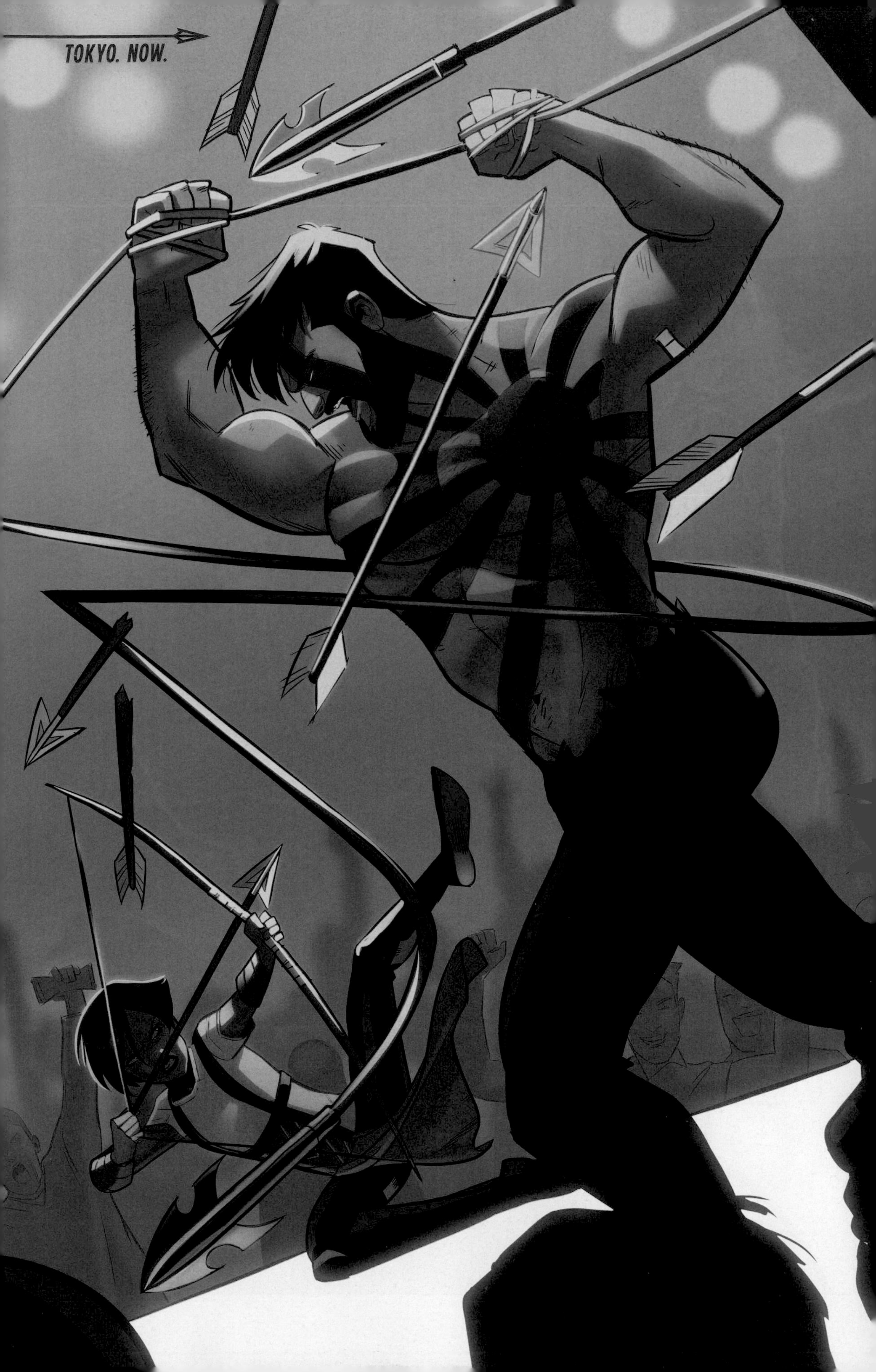
TOKYO. NOW.

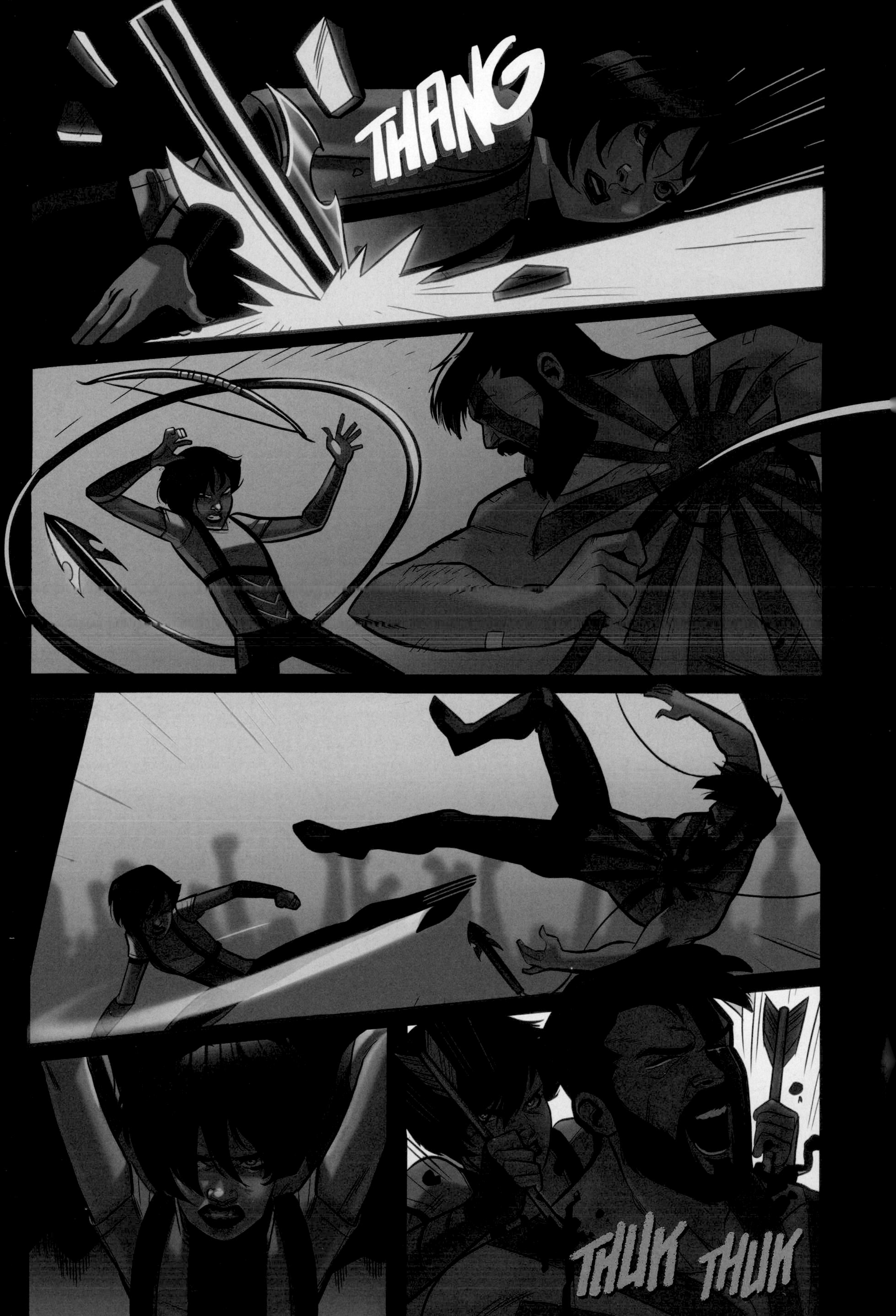
THANG
THUK THUK

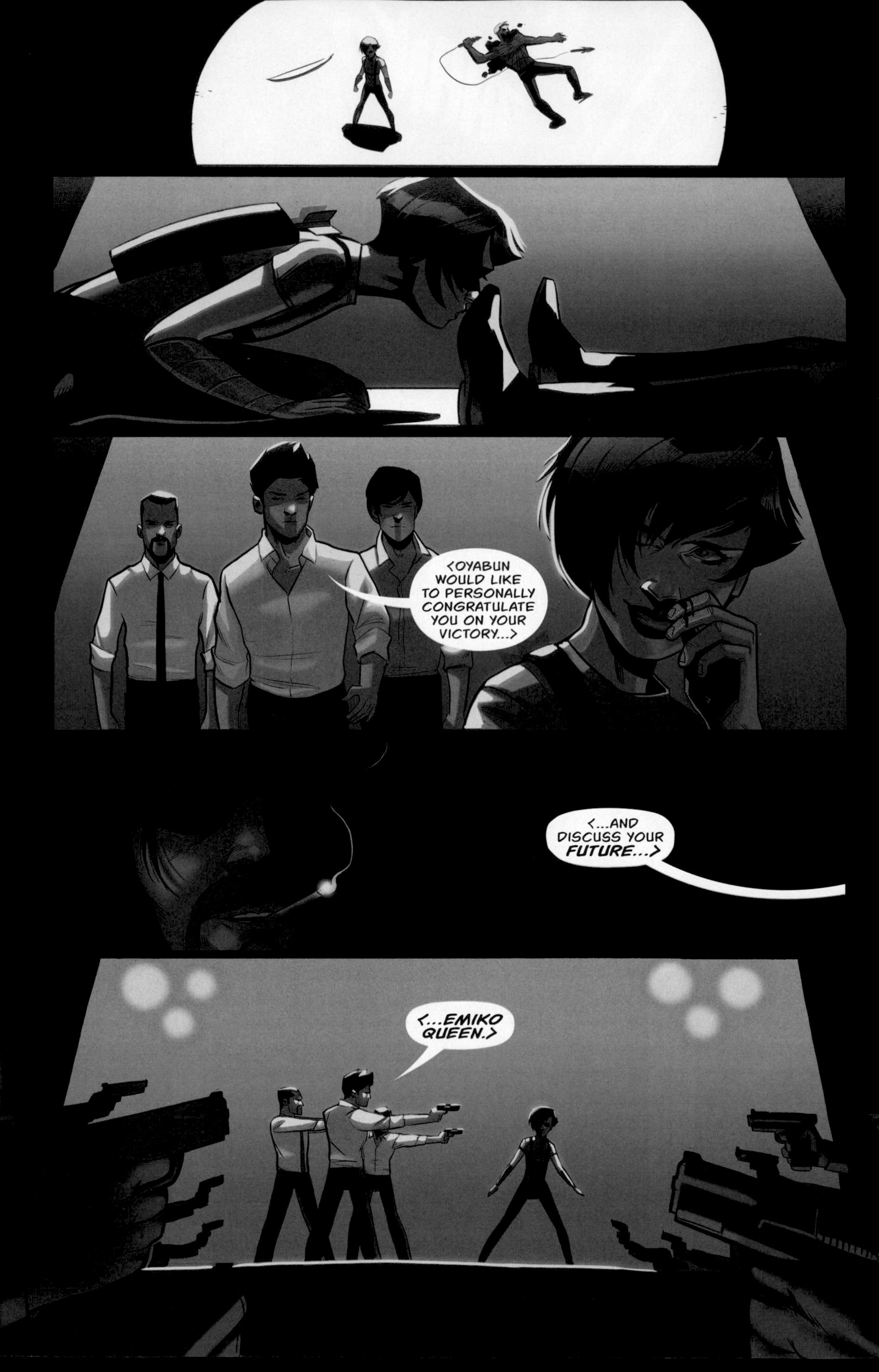
<OYABUN WOULD LIKE TO PERSONALLY CONGRATULATE YOU ON YOUR VICTORY...>
<...AND DISCUSS YOUR FUTURE...>
<...EMIKO QUEEN.>

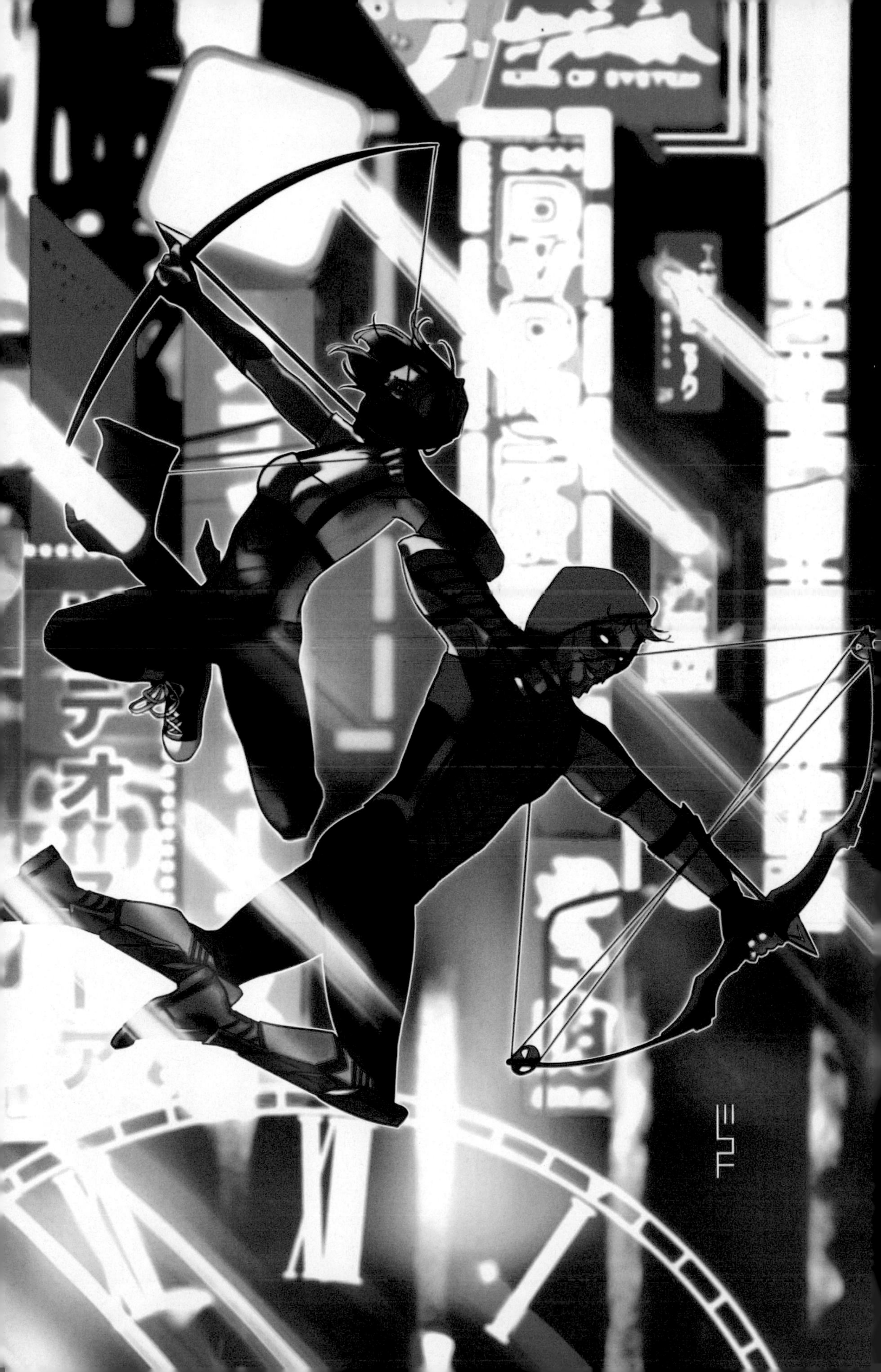

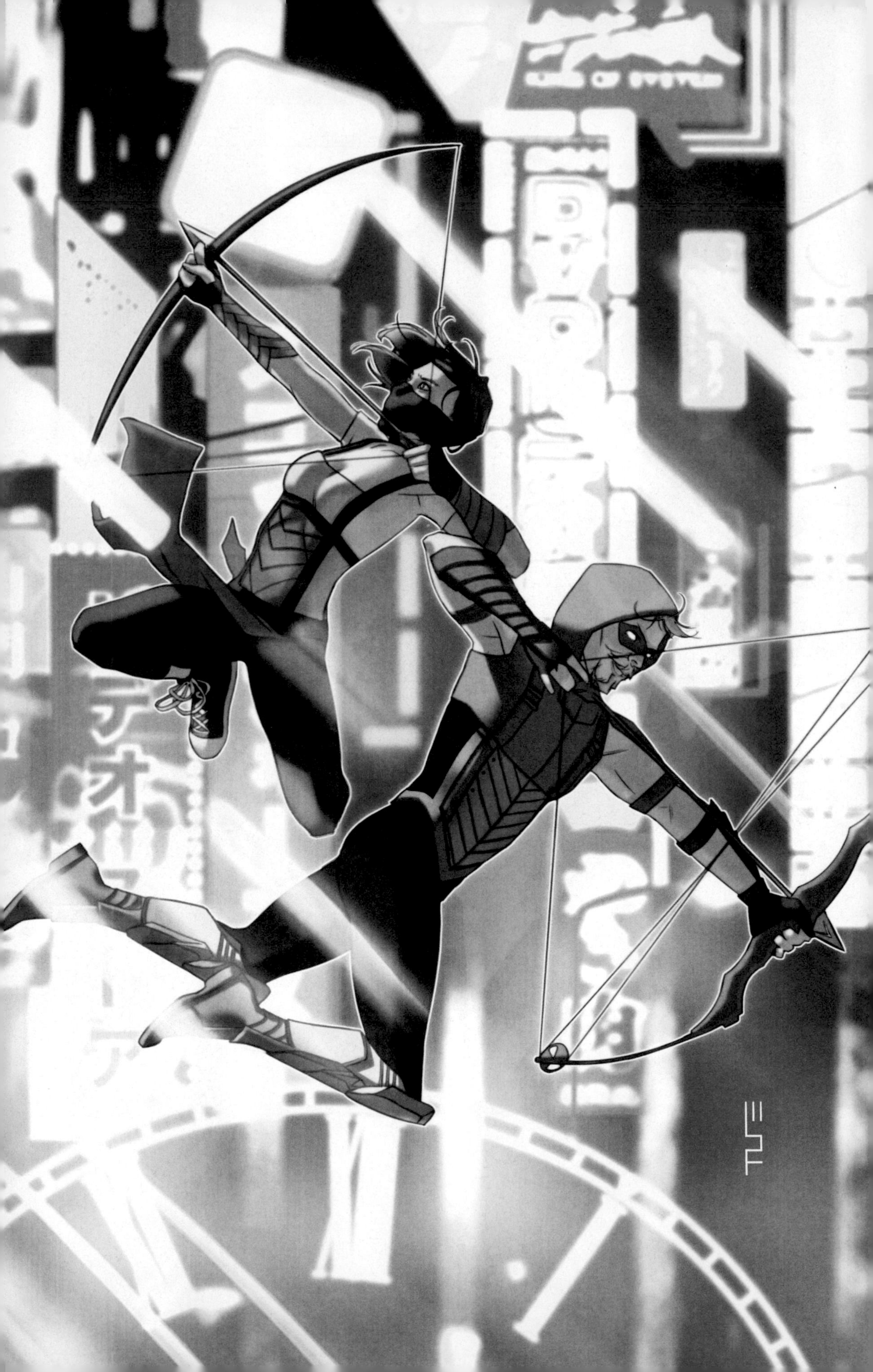

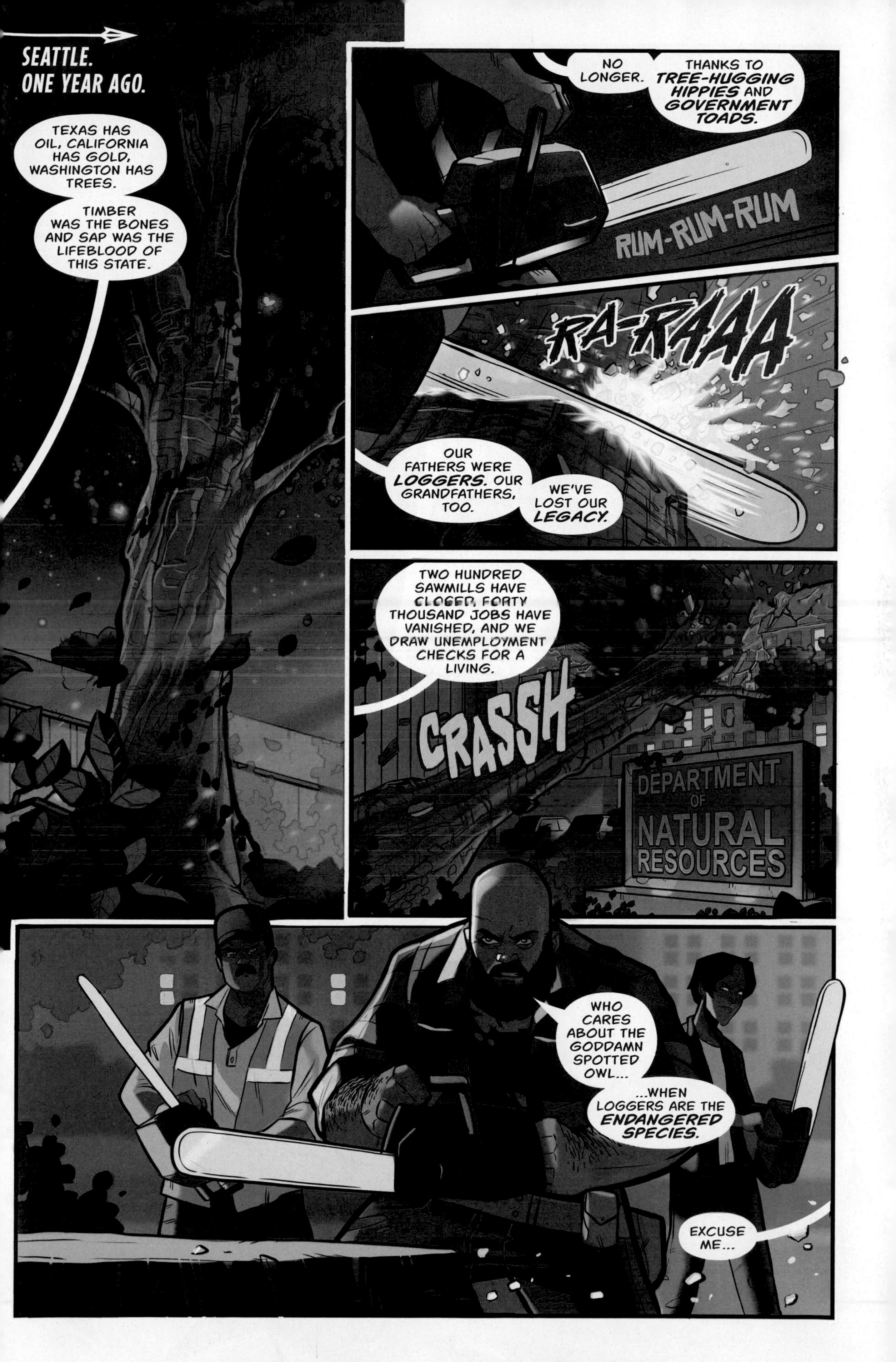
SEATTLE.
ONE YEAR AGO.
TEXAS HAS OIL, CALIFORNIA HAS GOLD, WASHINGTON HAS TREES.
TIMBER WAS THE BONES AND SAP WAS THE LIFEBLOOD OF THIS STATE.
NO LONGER.
THANKS TO TREE-HUGGING HIPPIES AND GOVERNMENT TOADS.
RUM-RUM-RUM
RA-RAAA
OUR FATHERS WERE LOGGERS. OUR GRANDFATHERS, TOO.
WE'VE LOST OUR LEGACY.
TWO HUNDRED SAWMILLS HAVE CLOSED, FORTY THOUSAND JOBS HAVE VANISHED, AND WE DRAW UNEMPLOYMENT CHECKS FOR A LIVING.
CRASSH
DEPARTMENT OF NATURAL RESOURCES
WHO CARES ABOUT THE GODDAMN SPOTTED OWL...
...WHEN LOGGERS ARE THE ENDANGERED SPECIES.
EXCUSE ME...

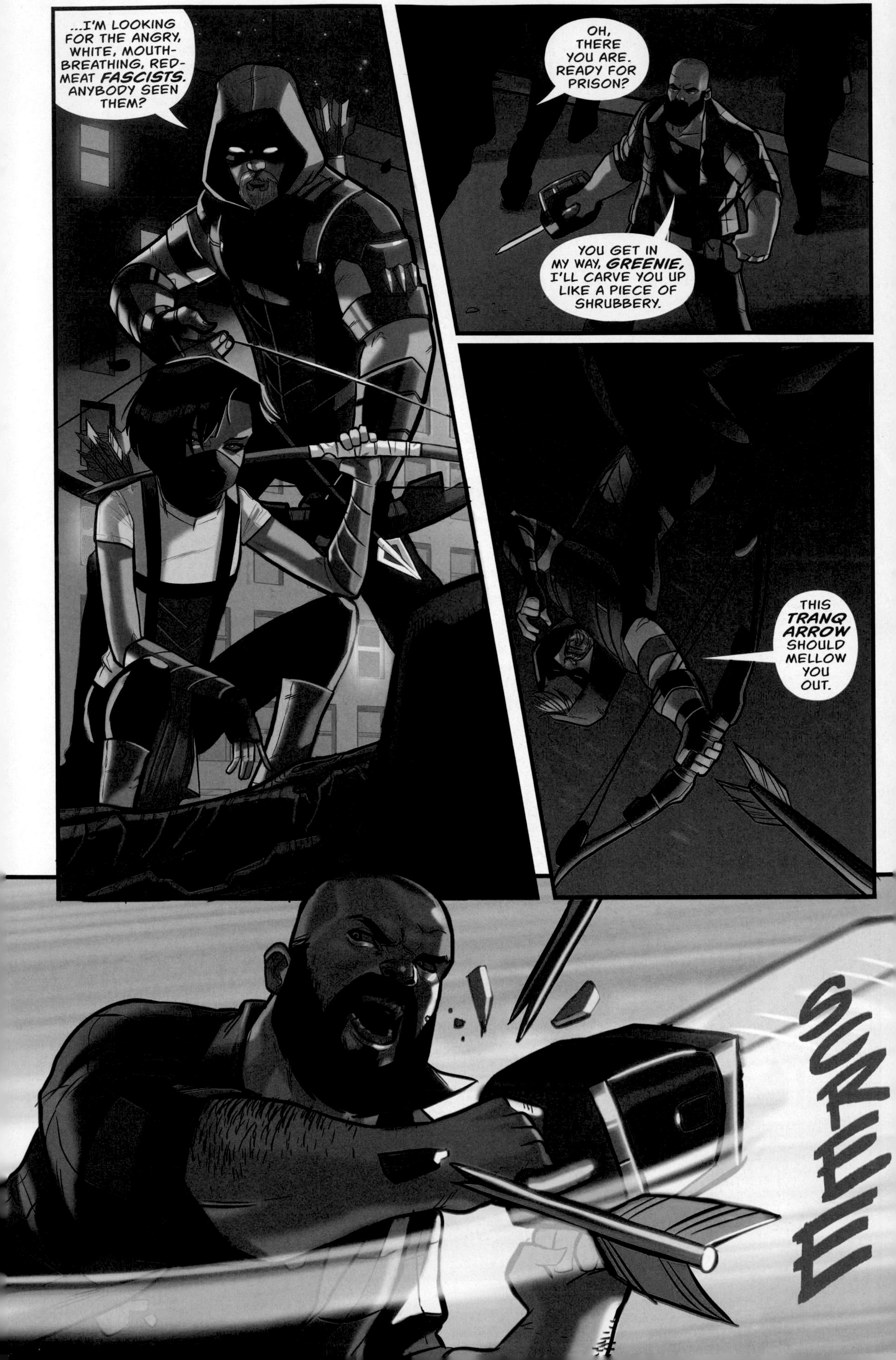
...I'M LOOKING FOR THE ANGRY, WHITE, MOUTH-BREATHING, RED-MEAT FASCISTS. ANYBODY SEEN THEM?
OH, THERE YOU ARE. READY FOR PRISON?
YOU GET IN MY WAY, GREENIE, I'LL CARVE YOU UP LIKE A PIECE OF SHRUBBERY.
THIS TRANQ ARROW SHOULD MELLOW YOU OUT.
SKREEE

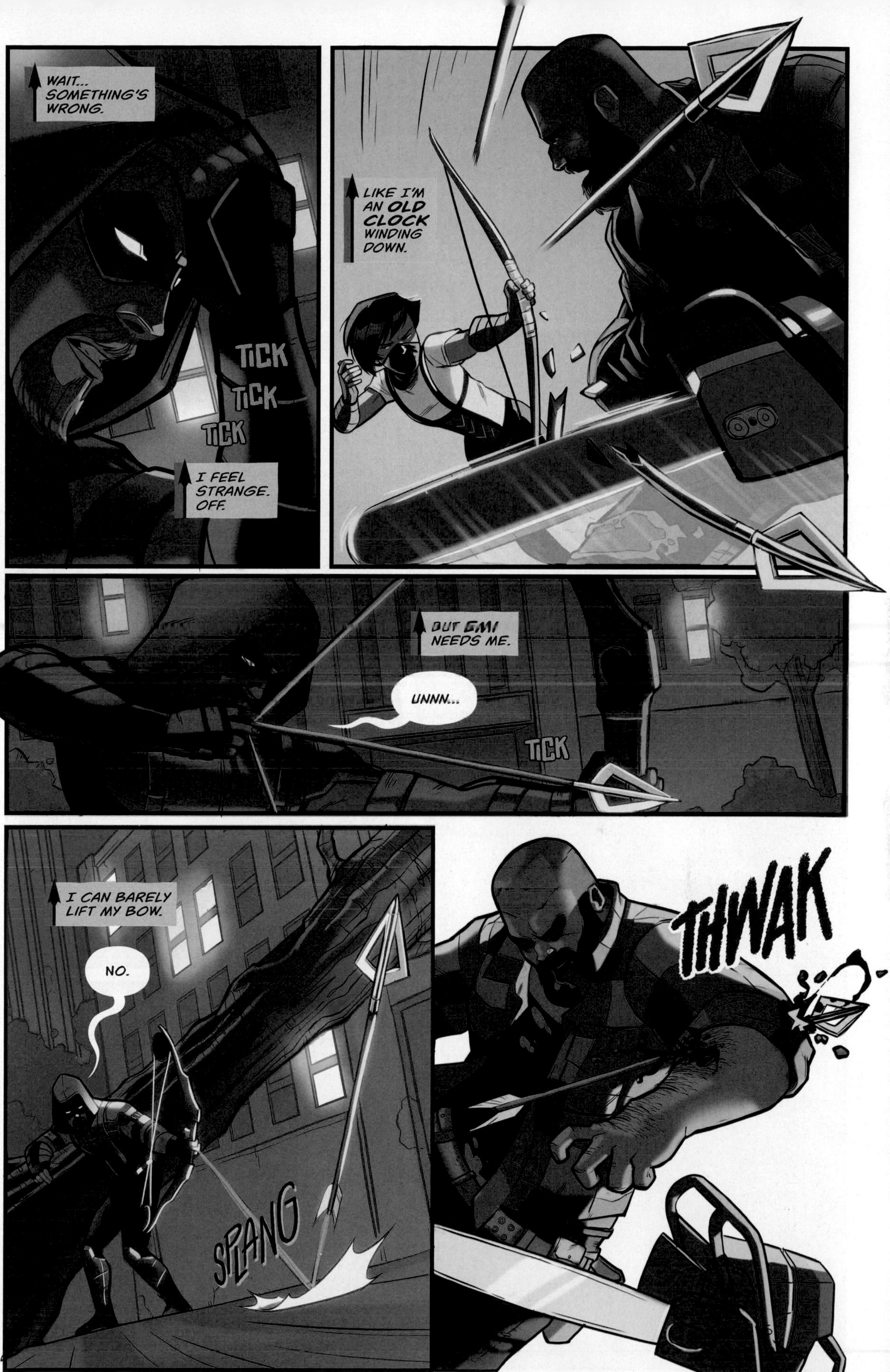

WAIT... SOMETHING'S WRONG.
TICK
TICK
TICK
I FEEL STRANGE. OFF.
LIKE I'M AN OLD CLOCK WINDING DOWN.
BUT EMI NEEDS ME.
UNNN...
TICK
I CAN BARELY LIFT MY BOW.
NO.
SPLANG
THWAK

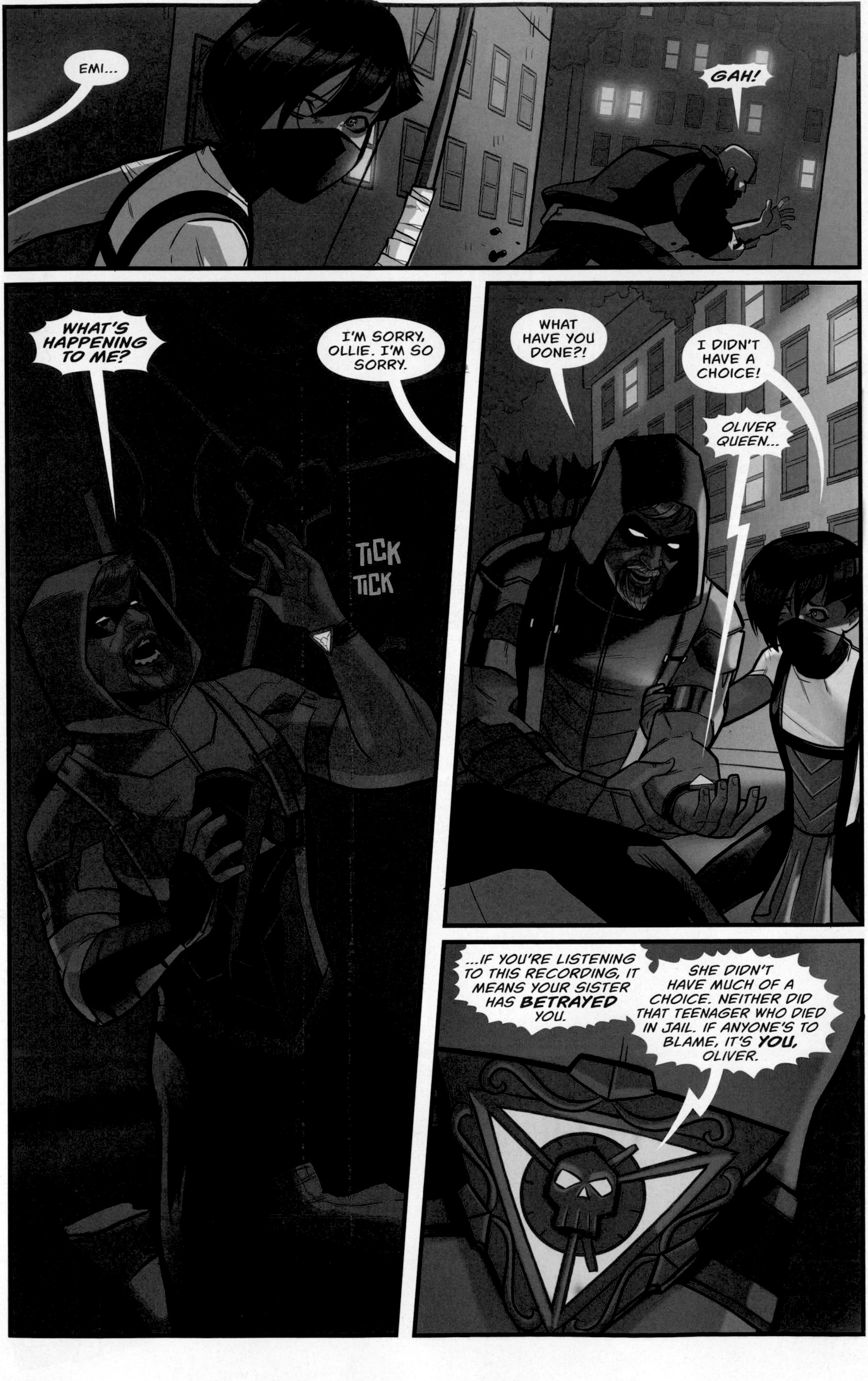
EMI...
GAH!
WHAT'S HAPPENING TO ME?
I'M SORRY, OLLIE. I'M SO SORRY.
TICK TICK
WHAT HAVE YOU DONE?!
I DIDN'T HAVE A CHOICE!
OLIVER QUEEN...
...IF YOU'RE LISTENING TO THIS RECORDING, IT MEANS YOUR SISTER HAS BETRAYED YOU.
SHE DIDN'T HAVE MUCH OF A CHOICE. NEITHER DID THAT TEENAGER WHO DIED IN JAIL. IF ANYONE'S TO BLAME, IT'S YOU, OLIVER.

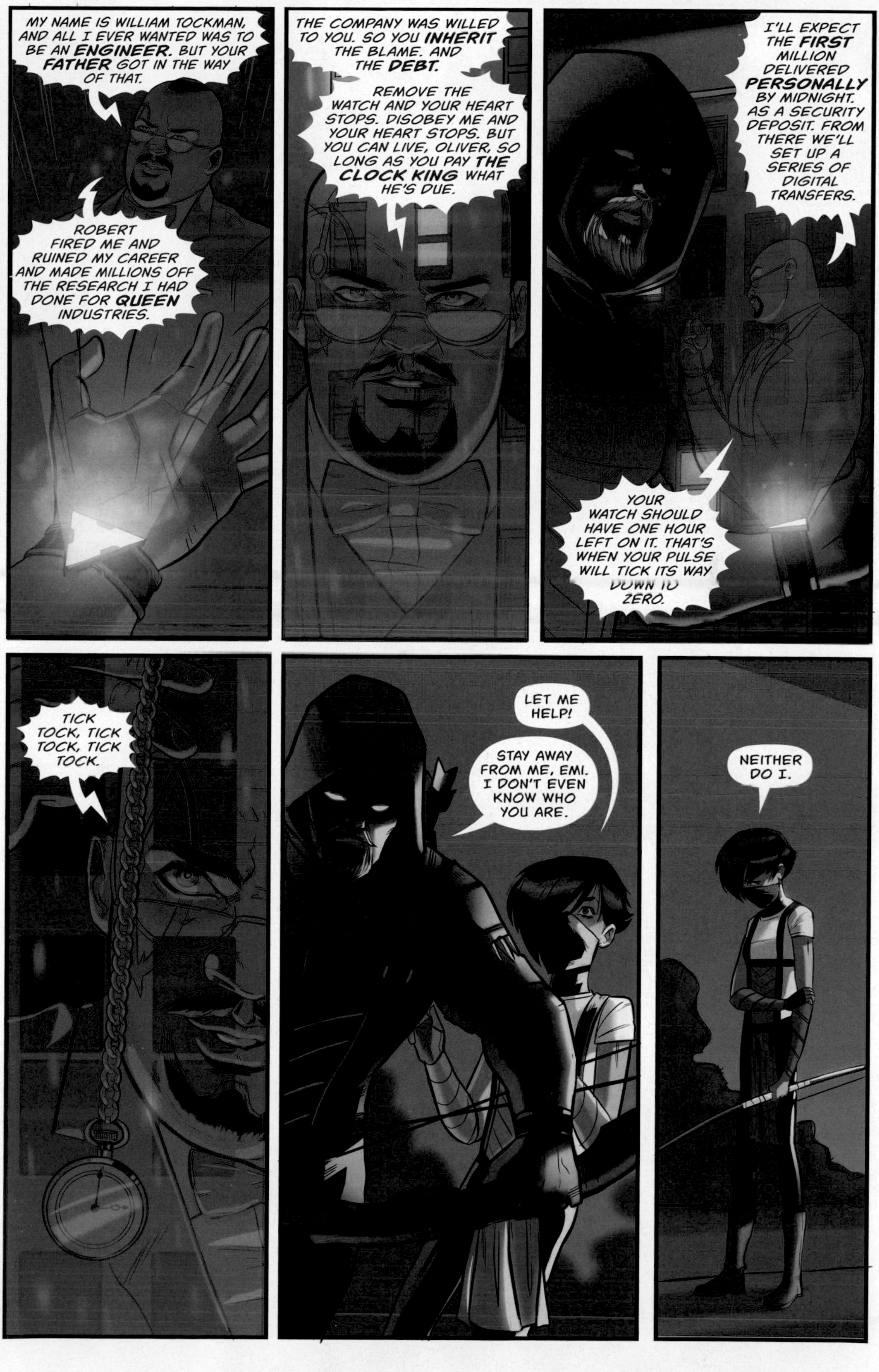
MY NAME IS WILLIAM TOCKMAN, AND ALL I EVER WANTED WAS TO BE AN ENGINEER. BUT YOUR FATHER GOT IN THE WAY OF THAT.
ROBERT FIRED ME AND RUINED MY CAREER AND MADE MILLIONS OFF THE RESEARCH I HAD DONE FOR QUEEN INDUSTRIES.
THE COMPANY WAS WILLED TO YOU. SO YOU INHERIT THE BLAME. AND THE DEBT.
REMOVE THE WATCH AND YOUR HEART STOPS. DISOBEY ME AND YOUR HEART STOPS. BUT YOU CAN LIVE, OLIVER, SO LONG AS YOU PAY THE CLOCK KING WHAT HE'S DUE.
I'LL EXPECT THE FIRST MILLION DELIVERED PERSONALLY BY MIDNIGHT. AS A SECURITY DEPOSIT. FROM THERE WE'LL SET UP A SERIES OF DIGITAL TRANSFERS.
YOUR WATCH SHOULD HAVE ONE HOUR LEFT ON IT. THAT'S WHEN YOUR PULSE WILL TICK ITS WAY DOWN TO ZERO.
TICK TOCK, TICK TOCK, TICK TOCK.
LET ME HELP!
STAY AWAY FROM ME, EMI. I DON'T EVEN KNOW WHO YOU ARE.
NEITHER DO I.

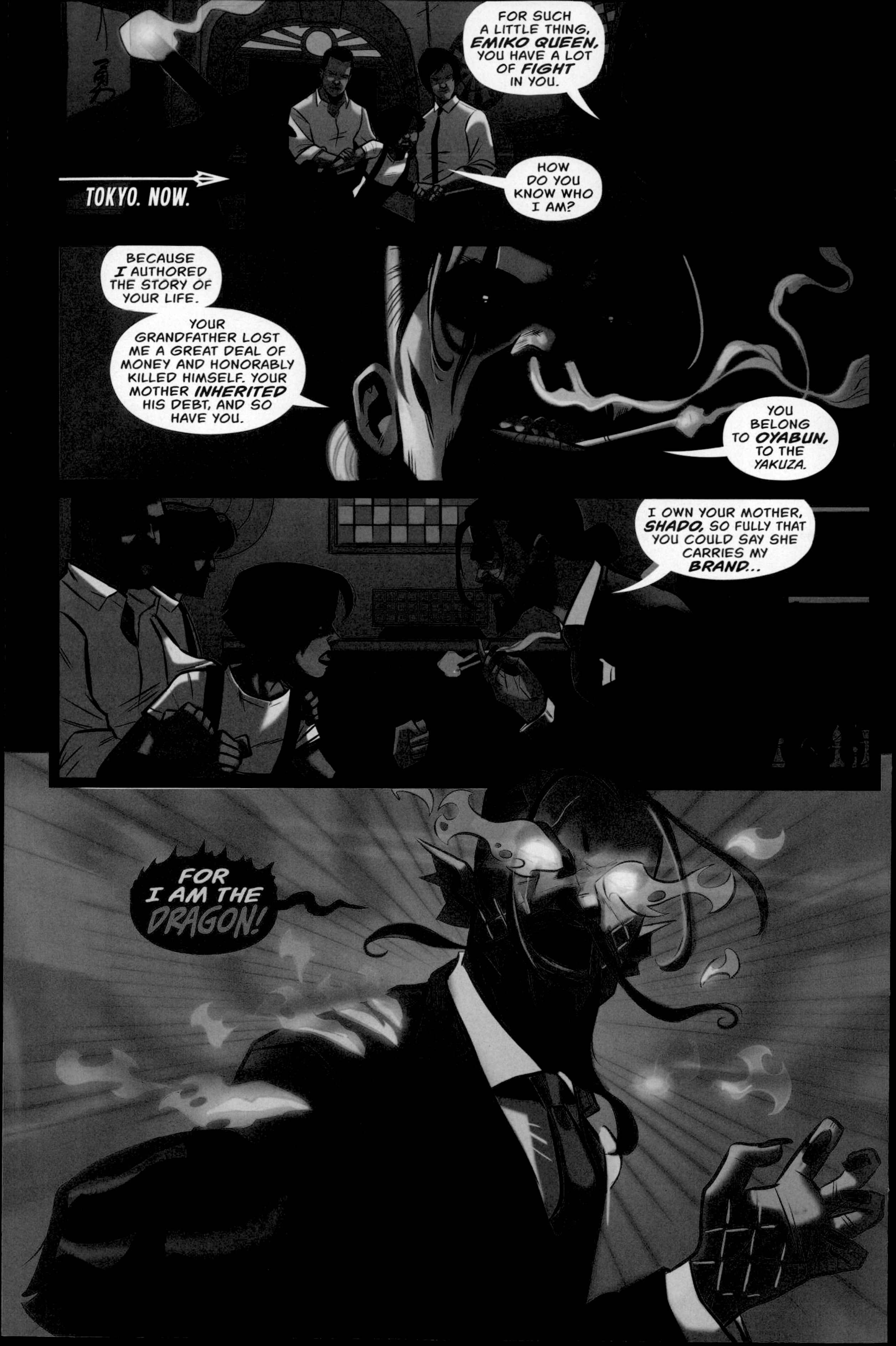
FOR SUCH A LITTLE THING, EMIKO QUEEN, YOU HAVE A LOT OF FIGHT IN YOU.
TOKYO. NOW.
HOW DO YOU KNOW WHO I AM?
BECAUSE I AUTHORED THE STORY OF YOUR LIFE.
YOUR GRANDFATHER LOST ME A GREAT DEAL OF MONEY AND HONORABLY KILLED HIMSELF. YOUR MOTHER INHERITED HIS DEBT, AND SO HAVE YOU.
YOU BELONG TO OYABUN, TO THE YAKUZA.
I OWN YOUR MOTHER, SHADO, SO FULLY THAT YOU COULD SAY SHE CARRIES MY BRAND...
FOR I AM THE DRAGON!

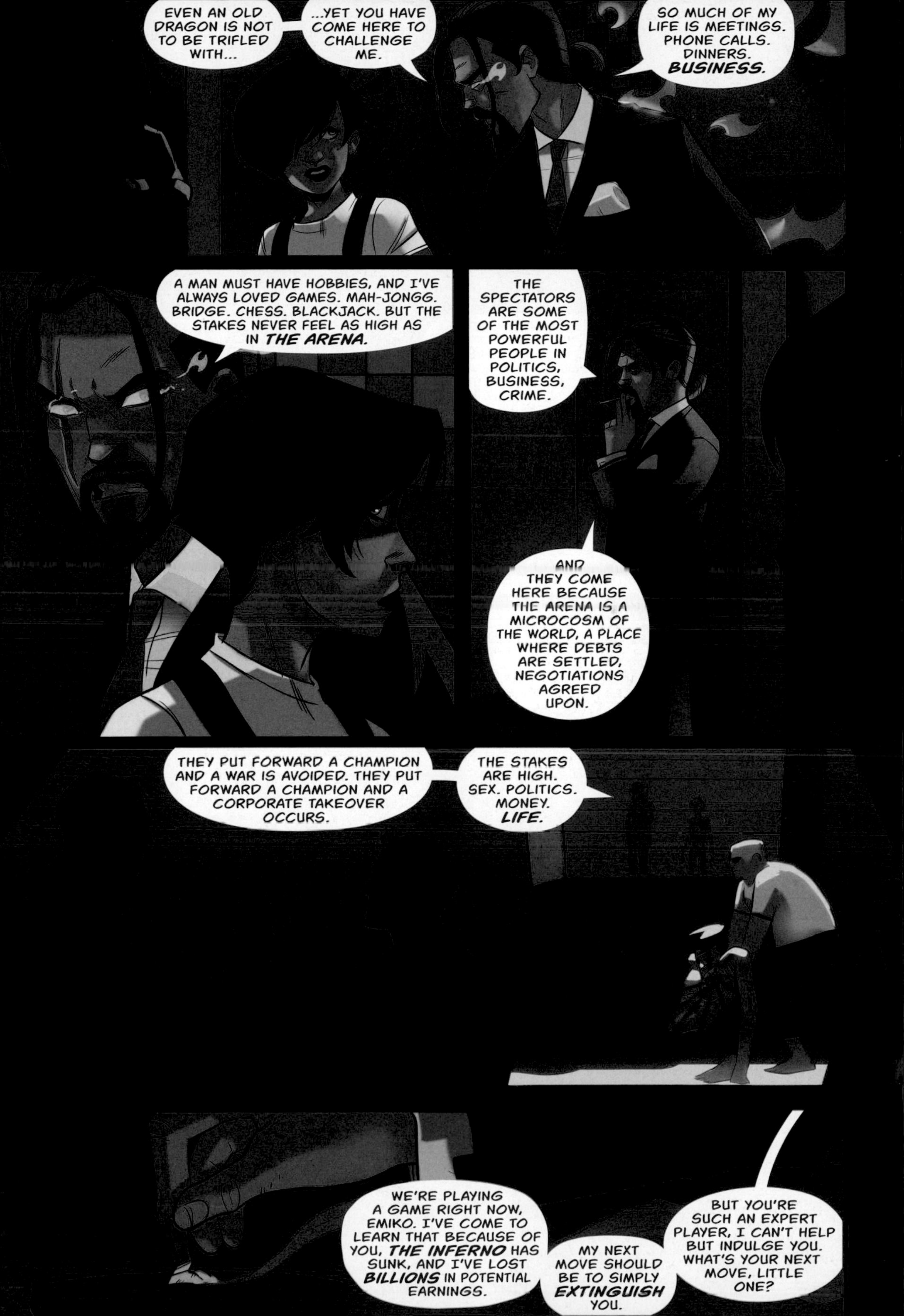
EVEN AN OLD DRAGON IS NOT TO BE TRIFLED WITH...
...YET YOU HAVE COME HERE TO CHALLENGE ME.
SO MUCH OF MY LIFE IS MEETINGS. PHONE CALLS. DINNERS. ***BUSINESS.***
A MAN MUST HAVE HOBBIES, AND I'VE ALWAYS LOVED GAMES. MAH-JONGG. BRIDGE. CHESS. BLACKJACK. BUT THE STAKES NEVER FEEL AS HIGH AS IN ***THE ARENA.***
THE SPECTATORS ARE SOME OF THE MOST POWERFUL PEOPLE IN POLITICS, BUSINESS, CRIME.
AND THEY COME HERE BECAUSE THE ARENA IS A MICROCOSM OF THE WORLD, A PLACE WHERE DEBTS ARE SETTLED, NEGOTIATIONS AGREED UPON.
THEY PUT FORWARD A CHAMPION AND A WAR IS AVOIDED. THEY PUT FORWARD A CHAMPION AND A CORPORATE TAKEOVER OCCURS.
THE STAKES ARE HIGH. SEX. POLITICS. MONEY. ***LIFE.***
WE'RE PLAYING A GAME RIGHT NOW, EMIKO. I'VE COME TO LEARN THAT BECAUSE OF YOU, ***THE INFERNO*** HAS SUNK, AND I'VE LOST ***BILLIONS*** IN POTENTIAL EARNINGS.
MY NEXT MOVE SHOULD BE TO SIMPLY ***EXTINGUISH*** YOU.
BUT YOU'RE SUCH AN EXPERT PLAYER, I CAN'T HELP BUT INDULGE YOU. WHAT'S YOUR NEXT MOVE, LITTLE ONE?

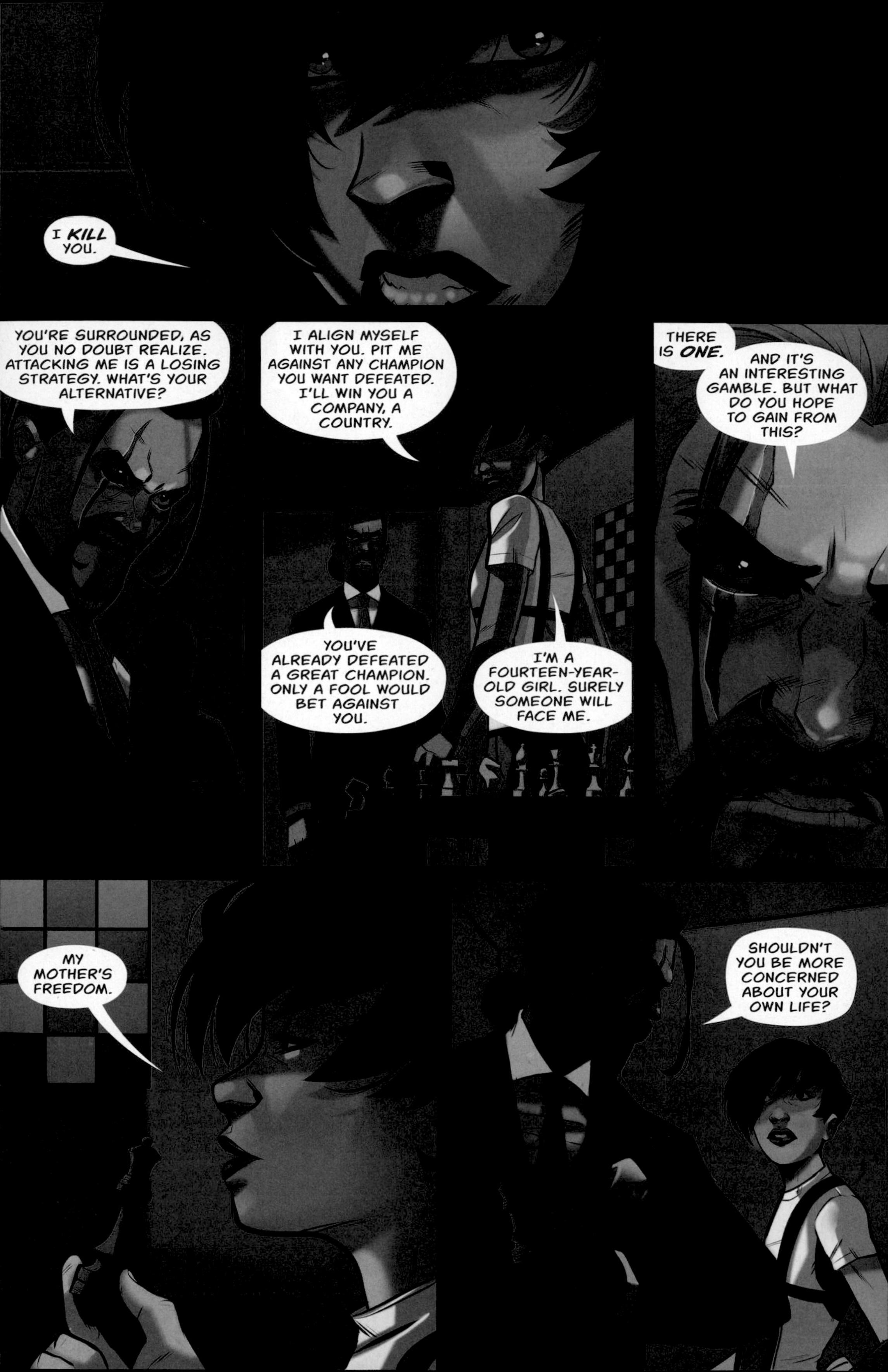
I KILL YOU.
YOU'RE SURROUNDED, AS YOU NO DOUBT REALIZE. ATTACKING ME IS A LOSING STRATEGY. WHAT'S YOUR ALTERNATIVE?
I ALIGN MYSELF WITH YOU. PIT ME AGAINST ANY CHAMPION YOU WANT DEFEATED. I'LL WIN YOU A COMPANY, A COUNTRY.
YOU'VE ALREADY DEFEATED A GREAT CHAMPION. ONLY A FOOL WOULD BET AGAINST YOU.
I'M A FOURTEEN-YEAR-OLD GIRL. SURELY SOMEONE WILL FACE ME.
THERE IS ONE.
AND IT'S AN INTERESTING GAMBLE. BUT WHAT DO YOU HOPE TO GAIN FROM THIS?
MY MOTHER'S FREEDOM.
SHOULDN'T YOU BE MORE CONCERNED ABOUT YOUR OWN LIFE?

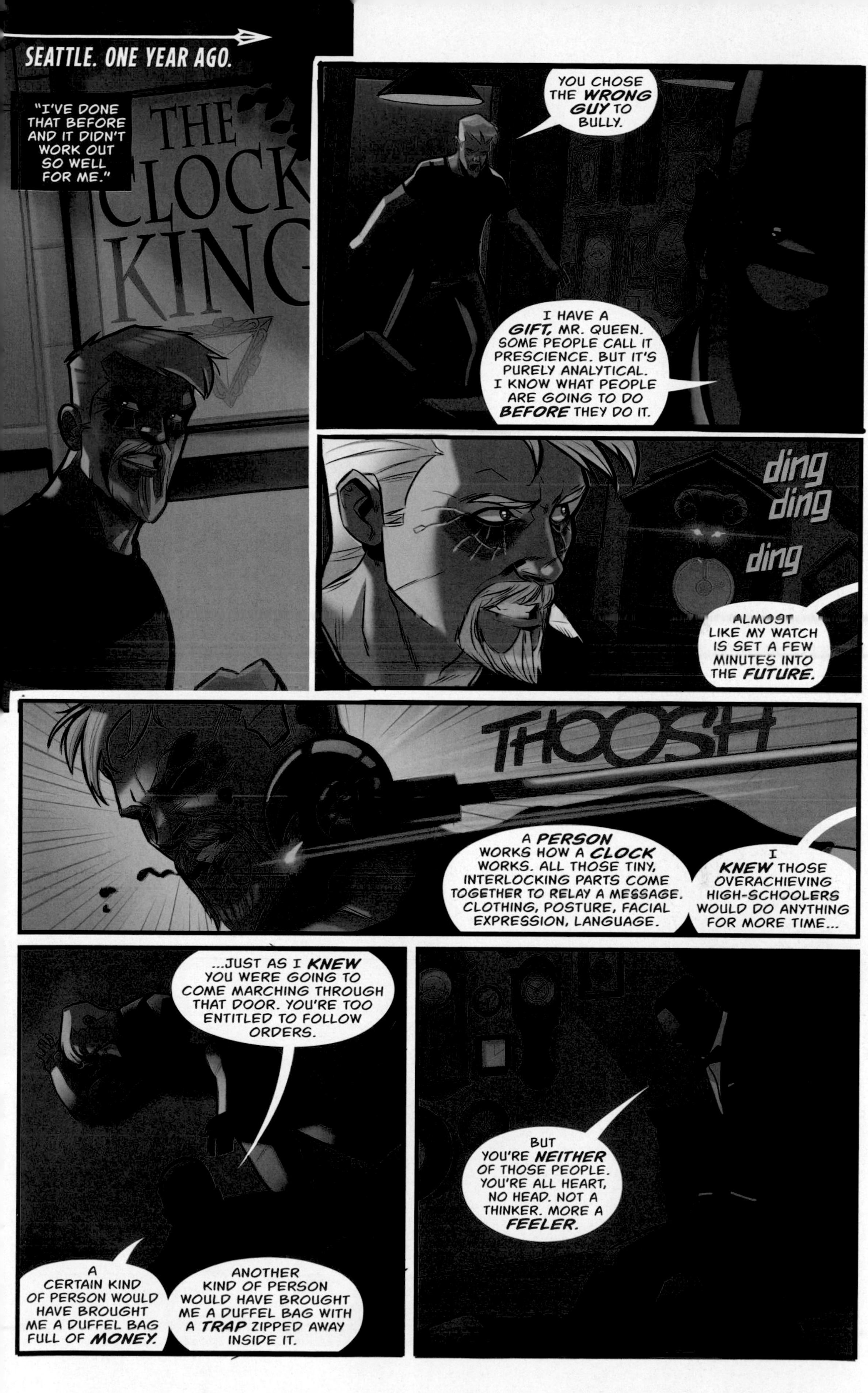
SEATTLE. ONE YEAR AGO.
"I'VE DONE THAT BEFORE AND IT DIDN'T WORK OUT SO WELL FOR ME."
THE CLOCK KING
YOU CHOSE THE WRONG GUY TO BULLY.
I HAVE A GIFT, MR. QUEEN. SOME PEOPLE CALL IT PRESCIENCE. BUT IT'S PURELY ANALYTICAL. I KNOW WHAT PEOPLE ARE GOING TO DO BEFORE THEY DO IT.
ding ding ding
ALMOST LIKE MY WATCH IS SET A FEW MINUTES INTO THE FUTURE.
THOOSH
A PERSON WORKS HOW A CLOCK WORKS. ALL THOSE TINY, INTERLOCKING PARTS COME TOGETHER TO RELAY A MESSAGE. CLOTHING, POSTURE, FACIAL EXPRESSION, LANGUAGE.
I KNEW THOSE OVERACHIEVING HIGH-SCHOOLERS WOULD DO ANYTHING FOR MORE TIME...
...JUST AS I KNEW YOU WERE GOING TO COME MARCHING THROUGH THAT DOOR. YOU'RE TOO ENTITLED TO FOLLOW ORDERS.
A CERTAIN KIND OF PERSON WOULD HAVE BROUGHT ME A DUFFEL BAG FULL OF MONEY.
ANOTHER KIND OF PERSON WOULD HAVE BROUGHT ME A DUFFEL BAG WITH A TRAP ZIPPED AWAY INSIDE IT.
BUT YOU'RE NEITHER OF THOSE PEOPLE. YOU'RE ALL HEART, NO HEAD. NOT A THINKER. MORE A FEELER.

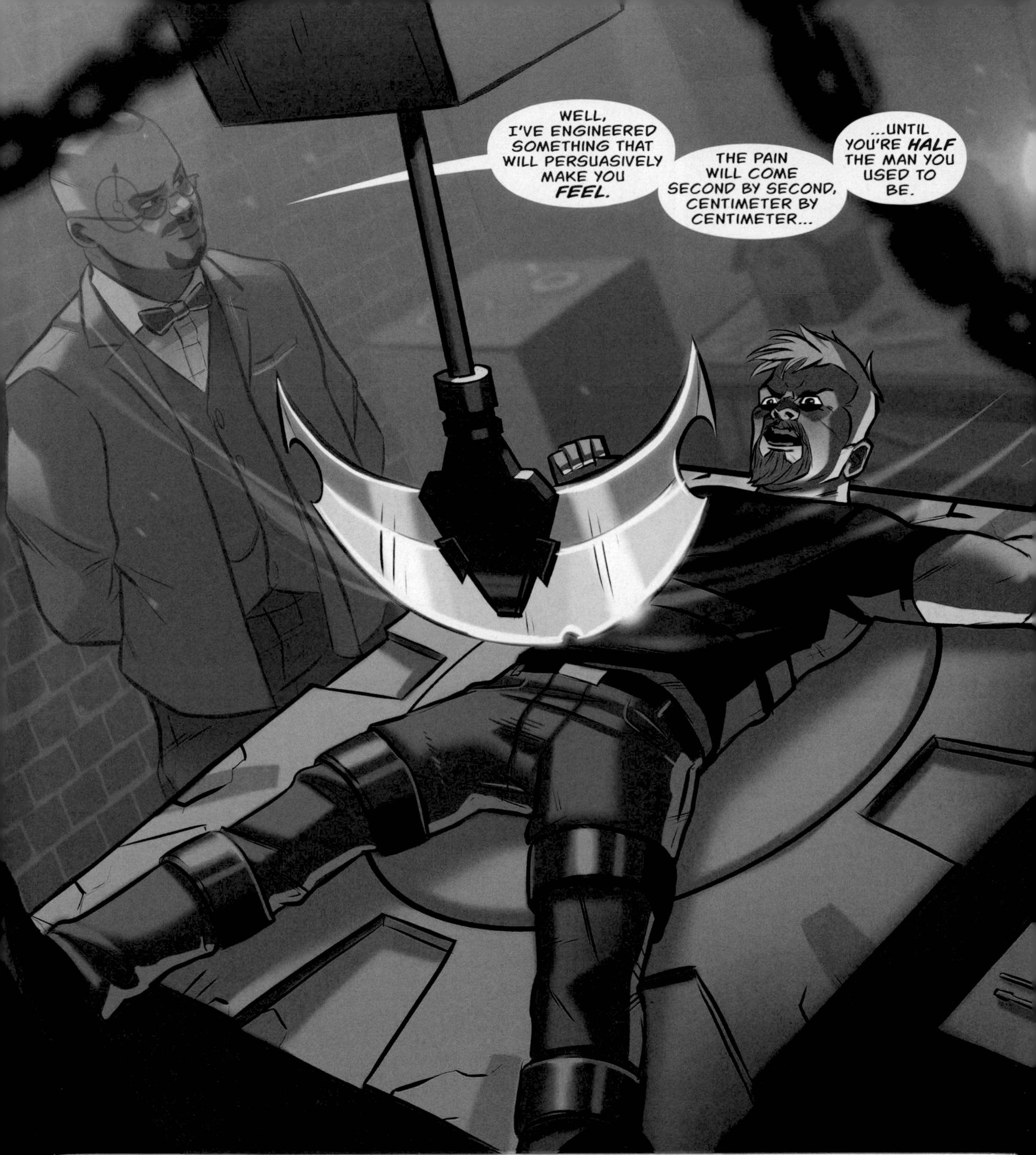
WELL, I'VE ENGINEERED SOMETHING THAT WILL PERSUASIVELY MAKE YOU FEEL.
THE PAIN WILL COME SECOND BY SECOND, CENTIMETER BY CENTIMETER...
...UNTIL YOU'RE HALF THE MAN YOU USED TO BE.

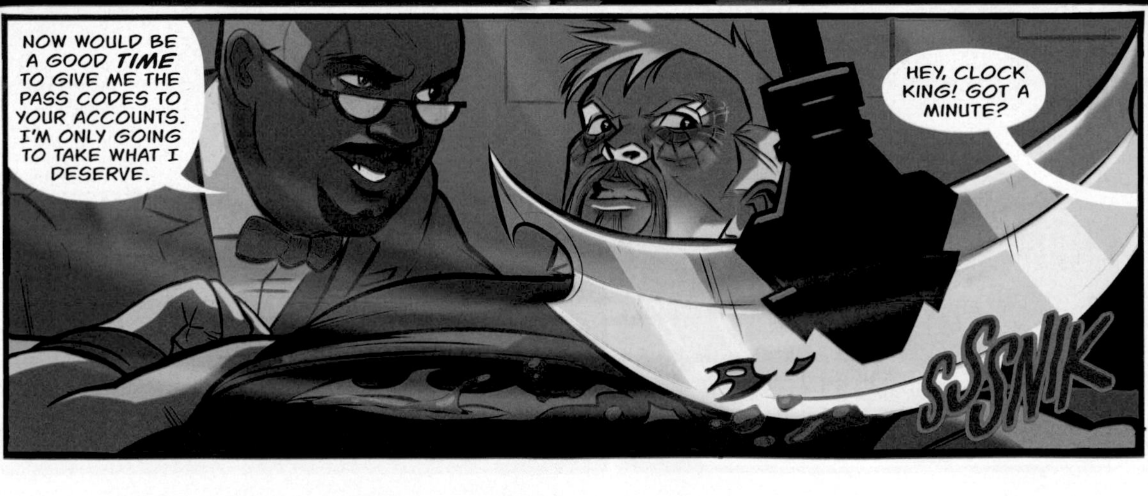
NOW WOULD BE A GOOD TIME TO GIVE ME THE PASS CODES TO YOUR ACCOUNTS. I'M ONLY GOING TO TAKE WHAT I DESERVE.
HEY, CLOCK KING! GOT A MINUTE?
SSSNIK

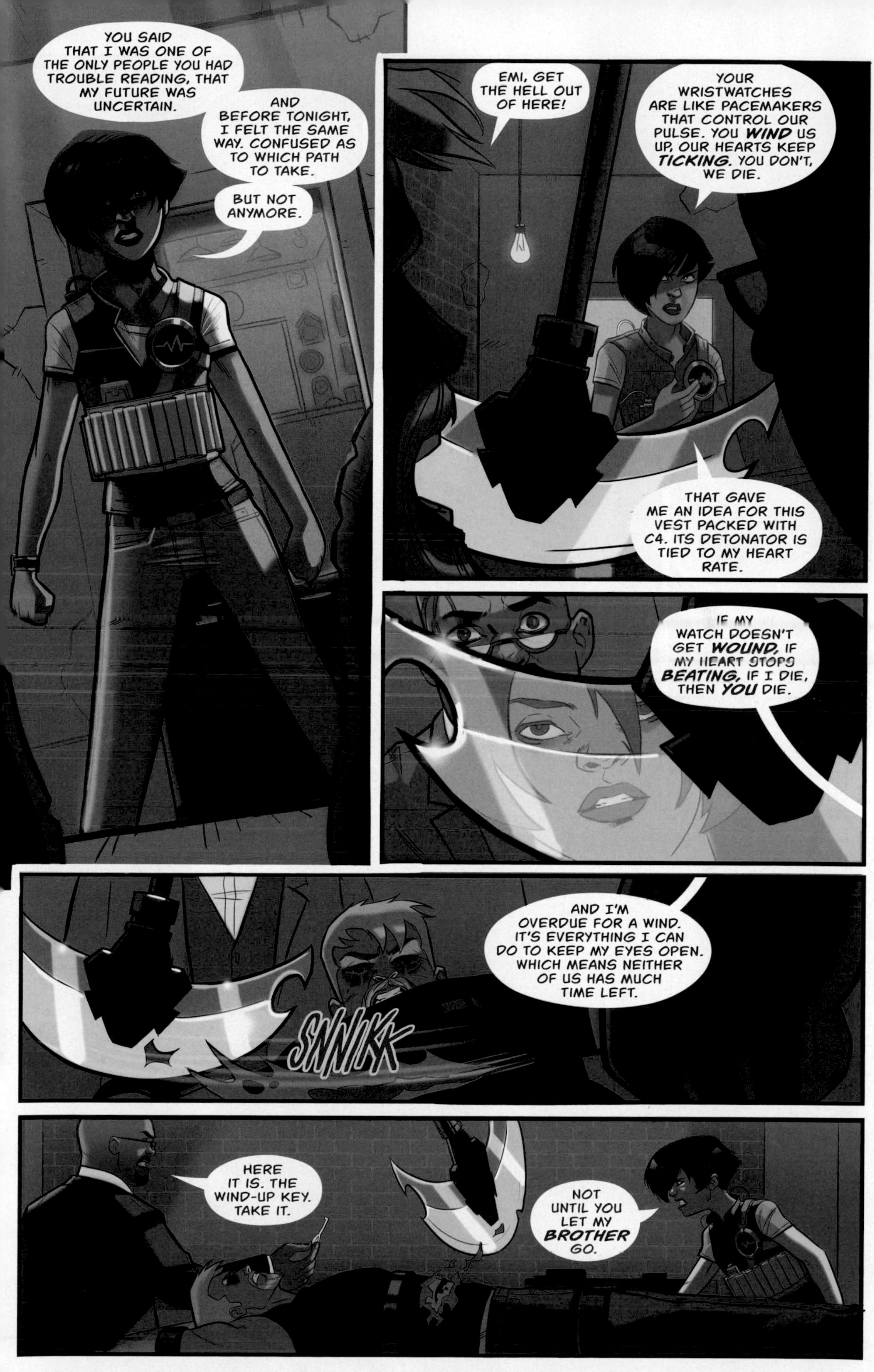
YOU SAID THAT I WAS ONE OF THE ONLY PEOPLE YOU HAD TROUBLE READING, THAT MY FUTURE WAS UNCERTAIN.
AND BEFORE TONIGHT, I FELT THE SAME WAY. CONFUSED AS TO WHICH PATH TO TAKE.
BUT NOT ANYMORE.
EMI, GET THE HELL OUT OF HERE!
YOUR WRISTWATCHES ARE LIKE PACEMAKERS THAT CONTROL OUR PULSE. YOU WIND US UP, OUR HEARTS KEEP TICKING. YOU DON'T, WE DIE.
THAT GAVE ME AN IDEA FOR THIS VEST PACKED WITH C4. ITS DETONATOR IS TIED TO MY HEART RATE.
IF MY WATCH DOESN'T GET WOUND, IF MY HEART STOPS BEATING, IF I DIE, THEN YOU DIE.
AND I'M OVERDUE FOR A WIND. IT'S EVERYTHING I CAN DO TO KEEP MY EYES OPEN. WHICH MEANS NEITHER OF US HAS MUCH TIME LEFT.
SNNIKK
HERE IT IS. THE WIND-UP KEY. TAKE IT.
NOT UNTIL YOU LET MY BROTHER GO.

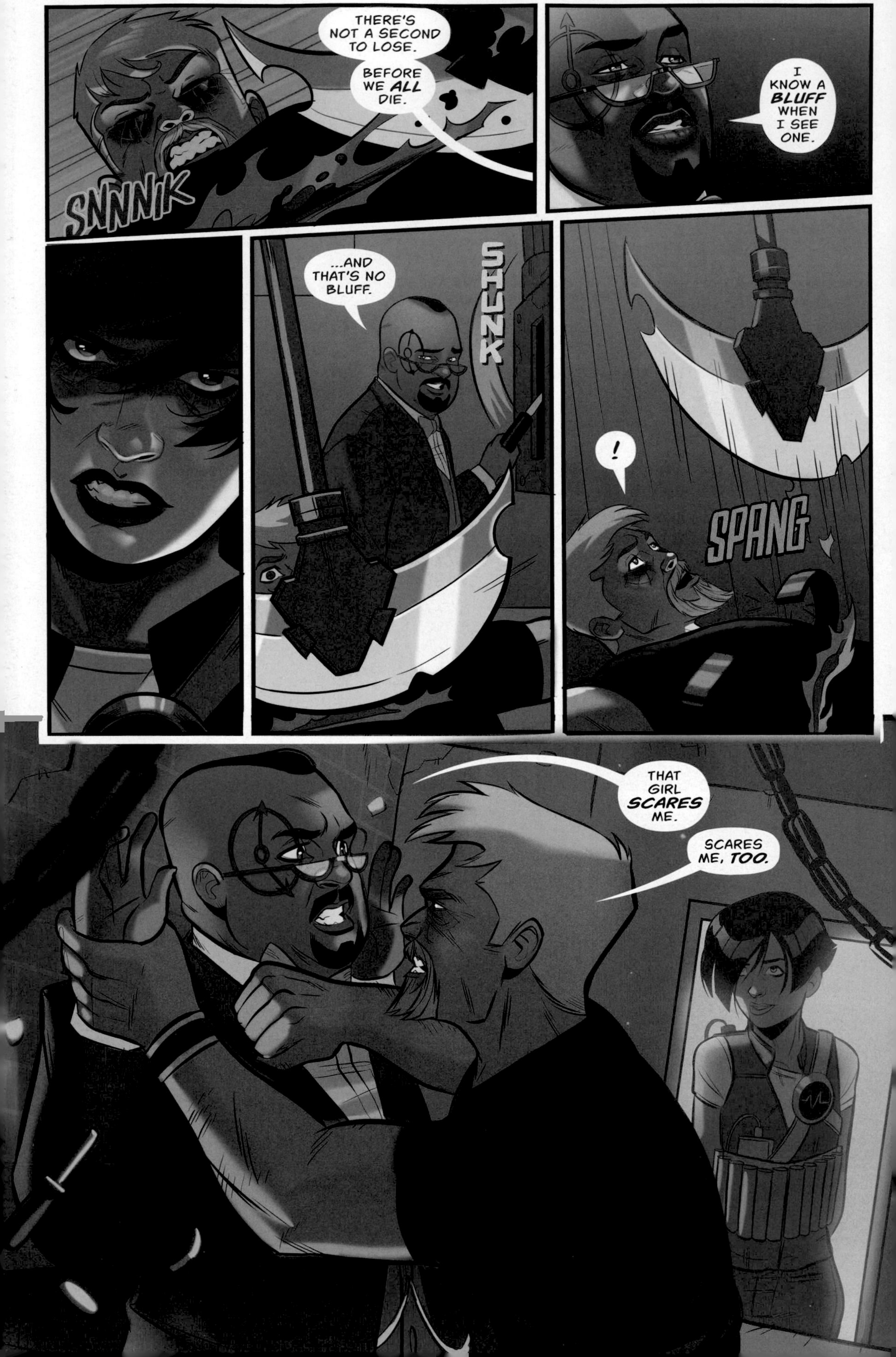
THERE'S NOT A SECOND TO LOSE.
BEFORE WE ALL DIE.
SNNNIK
I KNOW A BLUFF WHEN I SEE ONE.
...AND THAT'S NO BLUFF.
SHUNK
!
SPANG
THAT GIRL SCARES ME.
SCARES ME, TOO.

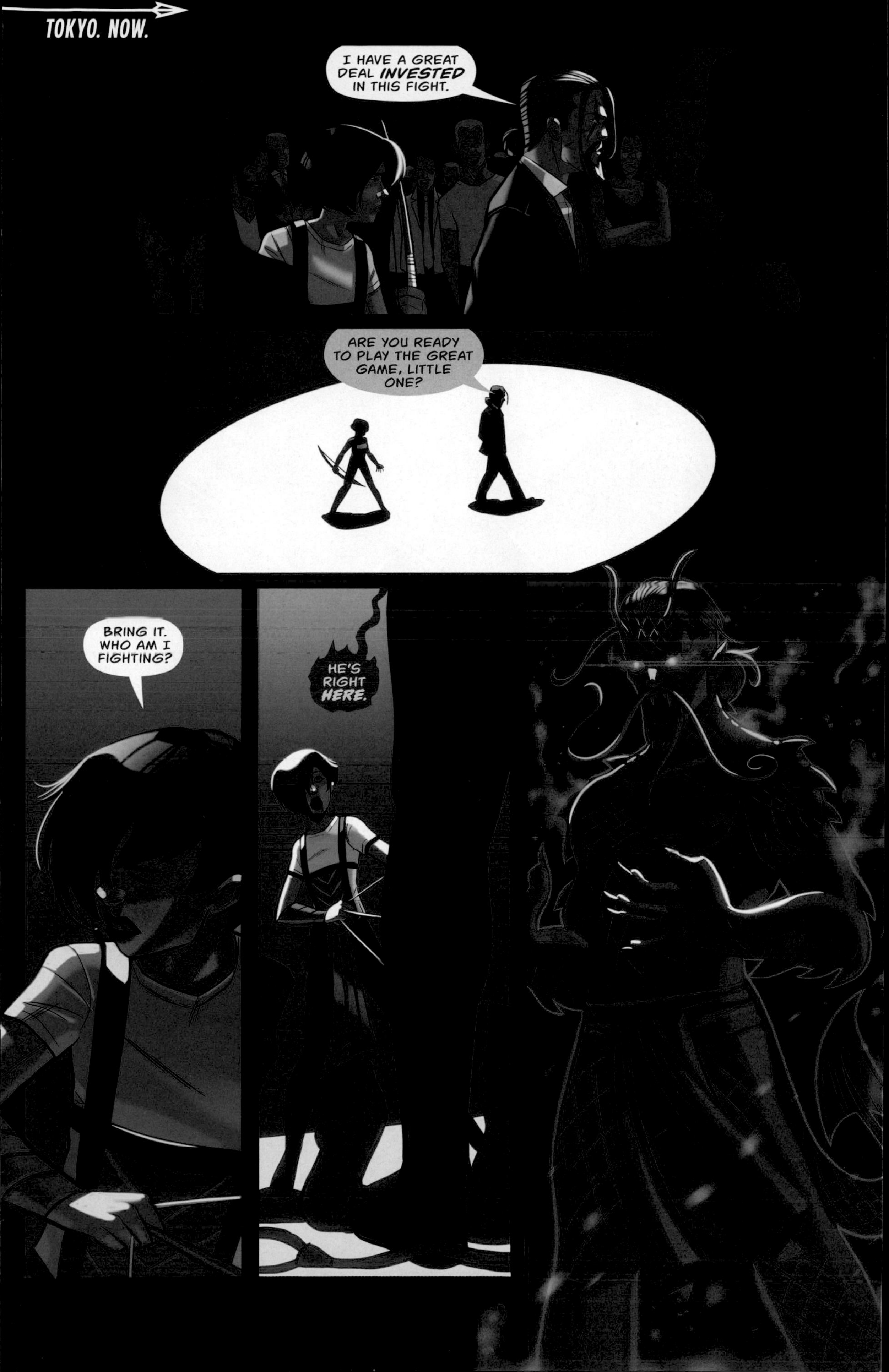
TOKYO. NOW.
I HAVE A GREAT DEAL INVESTED IN THIS FIGHT.
ARE YOU READY TO PLAY THE GREAT GAME, LITTLE ONE?
BRING IT. WHO AM I FIGHTING?
HE'S RIGHT HERE.

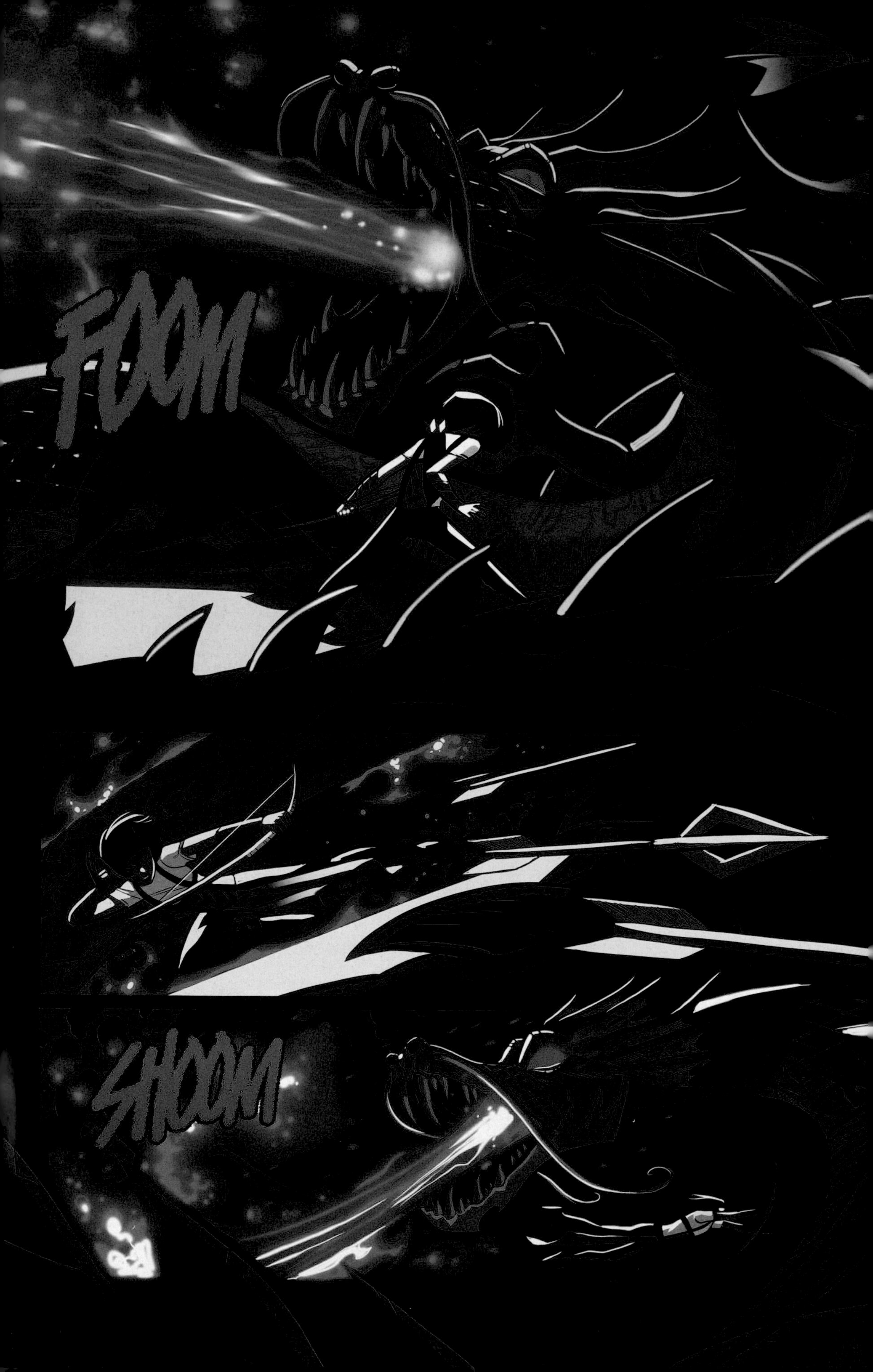
FOOM
SHOOM

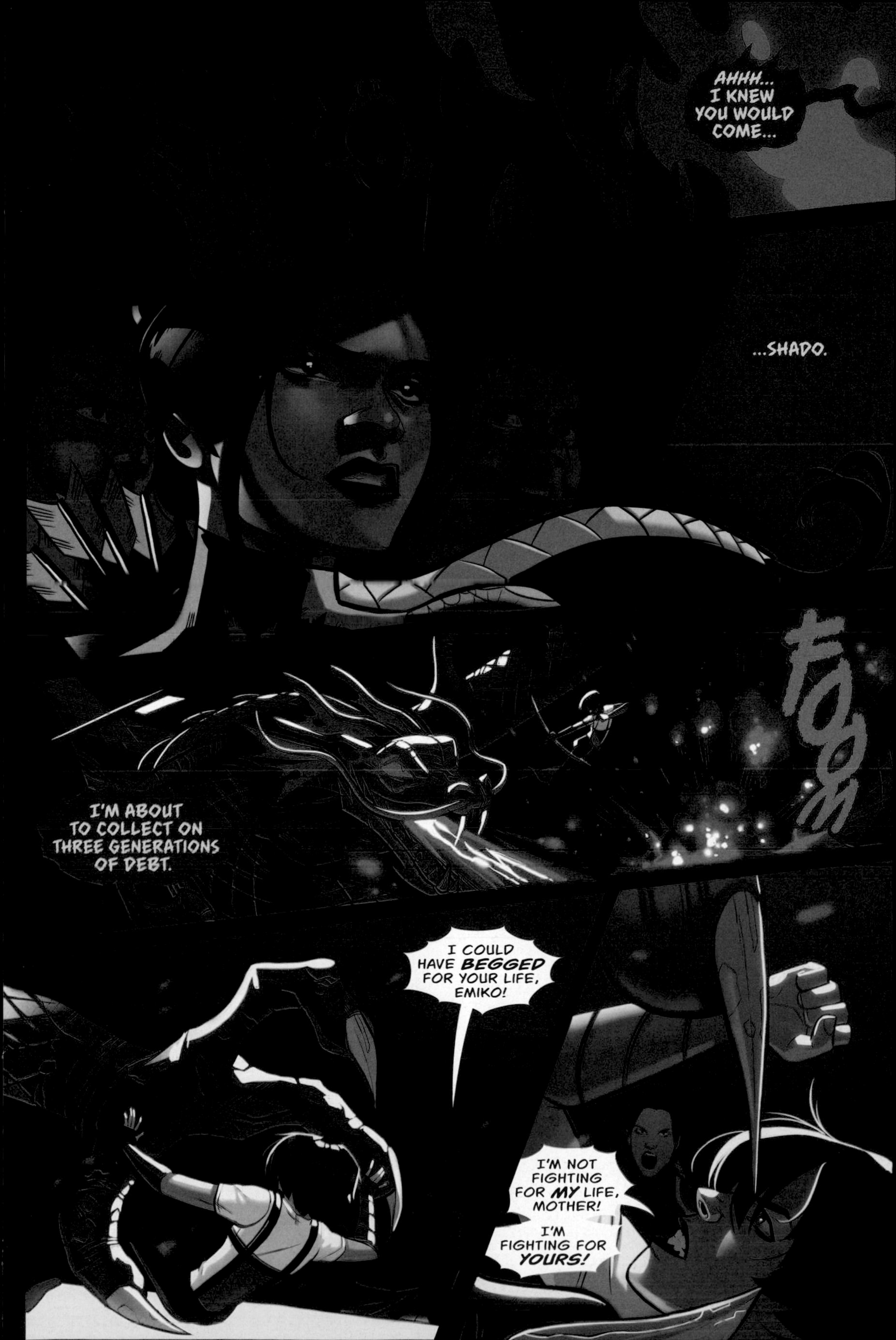
AHHH... I KNEW YOU WOULD COME...
...SHADO.
I'M ABOUT TO COLLECT ON THREE GENERATIONS OF DEBT.
I COULD HAVE BEGGED FOR YOUR LIFE, EMIKO!
I'M NOT FIGHTING FOR MY LIFE, MOTHER!
I'M FIGHTING FOR YOURS!

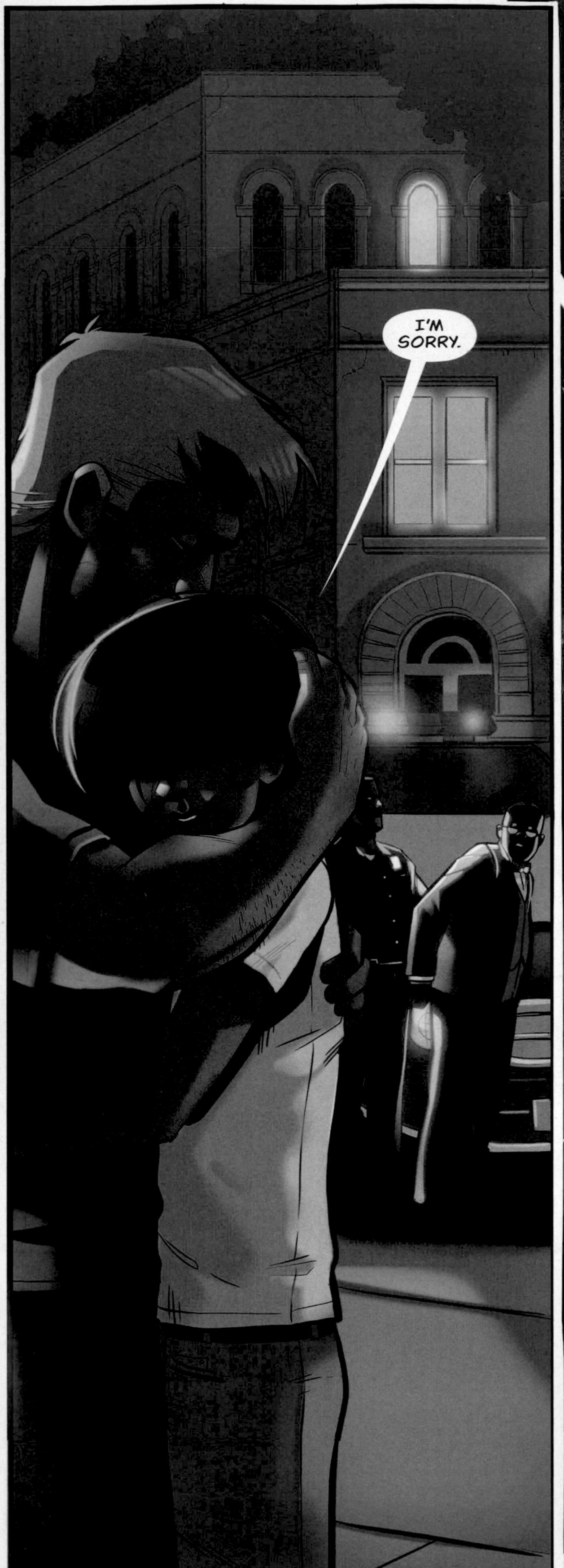
I'M SORRY.

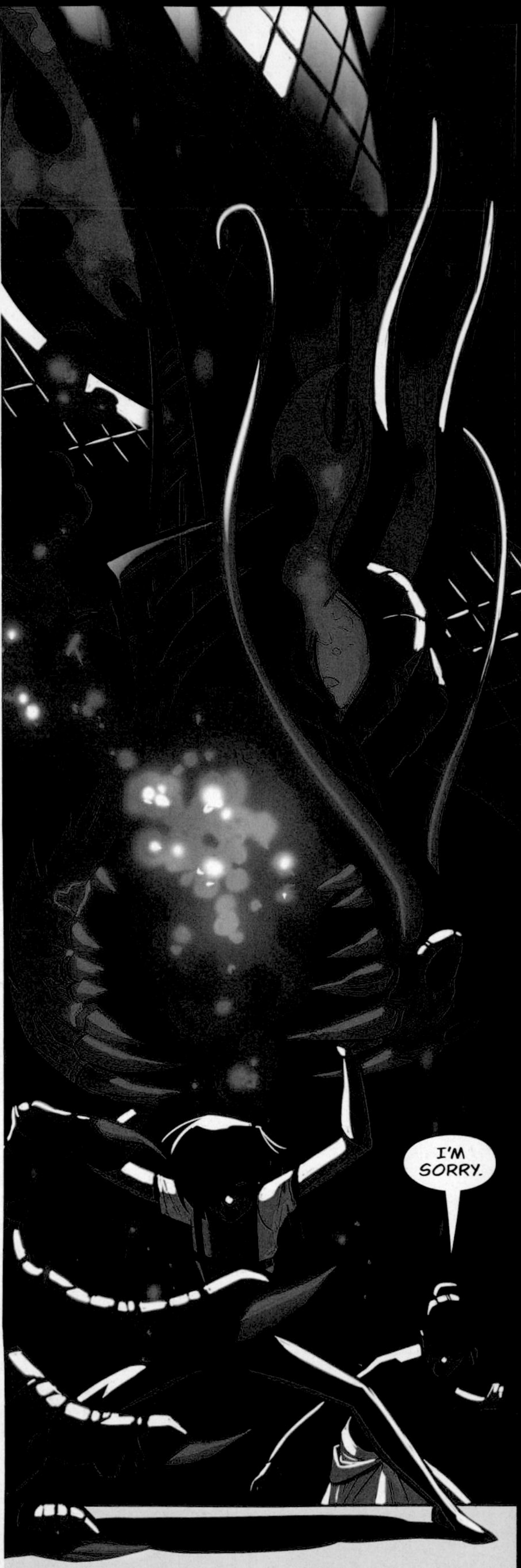
I'M SORRY.

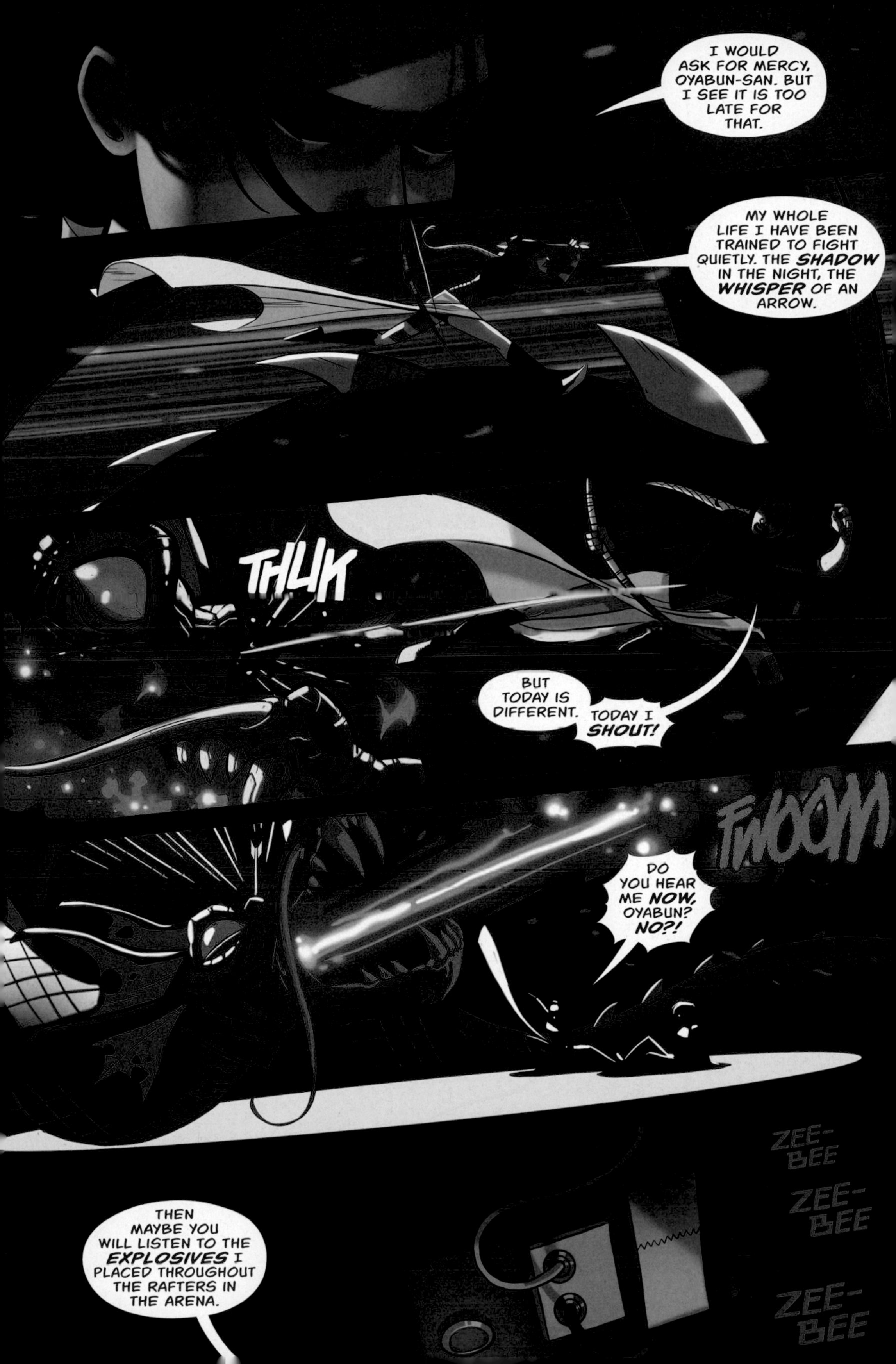
I WOULD ASK FOR MERCY, OYABUN-SAN. BUT I SEE IT IS TOO LATE FOR THAT.
MY WHOLE LIFE I HAVE BEEN TRAINED TO FIGHT QUIETLY. THE SHADOW IN THE NIGHT, THE WHISPER OF AN ARROW.
THUK
BUT TODAY IS DIFFERENT.
TODAY I SHOUT!
FWOOM
DO YOU HEAR ME NOW, OYABUN? NO?!
ZEE-BEE
ZEE-BEE
ZEE-BEE
THEN MAYBE YOU WILL LISTEN TO THE EXPLOSIVES I PLACED THROUGHOUT THE RAFTERS IN THE ARENA.

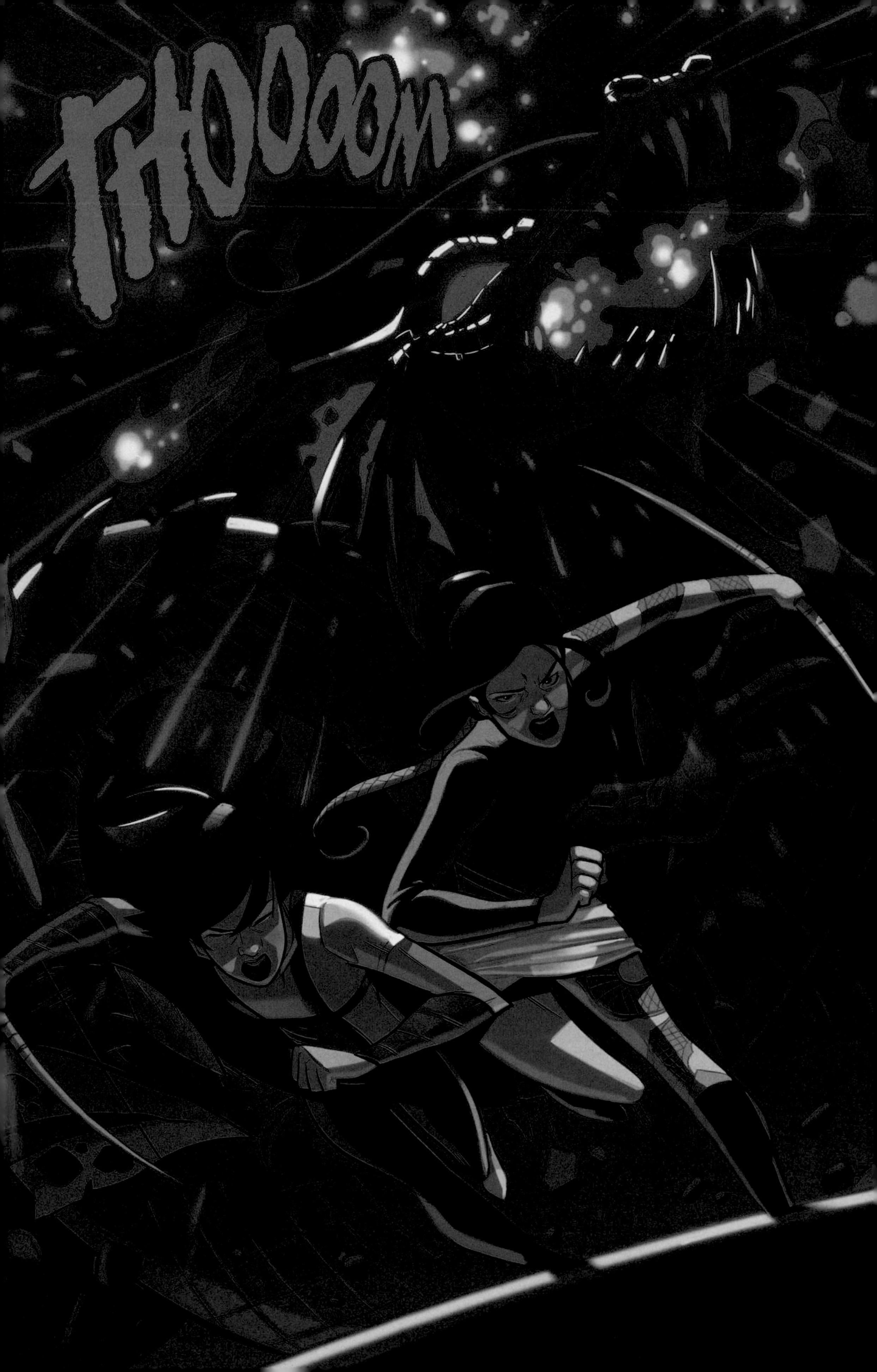
THOOOOM

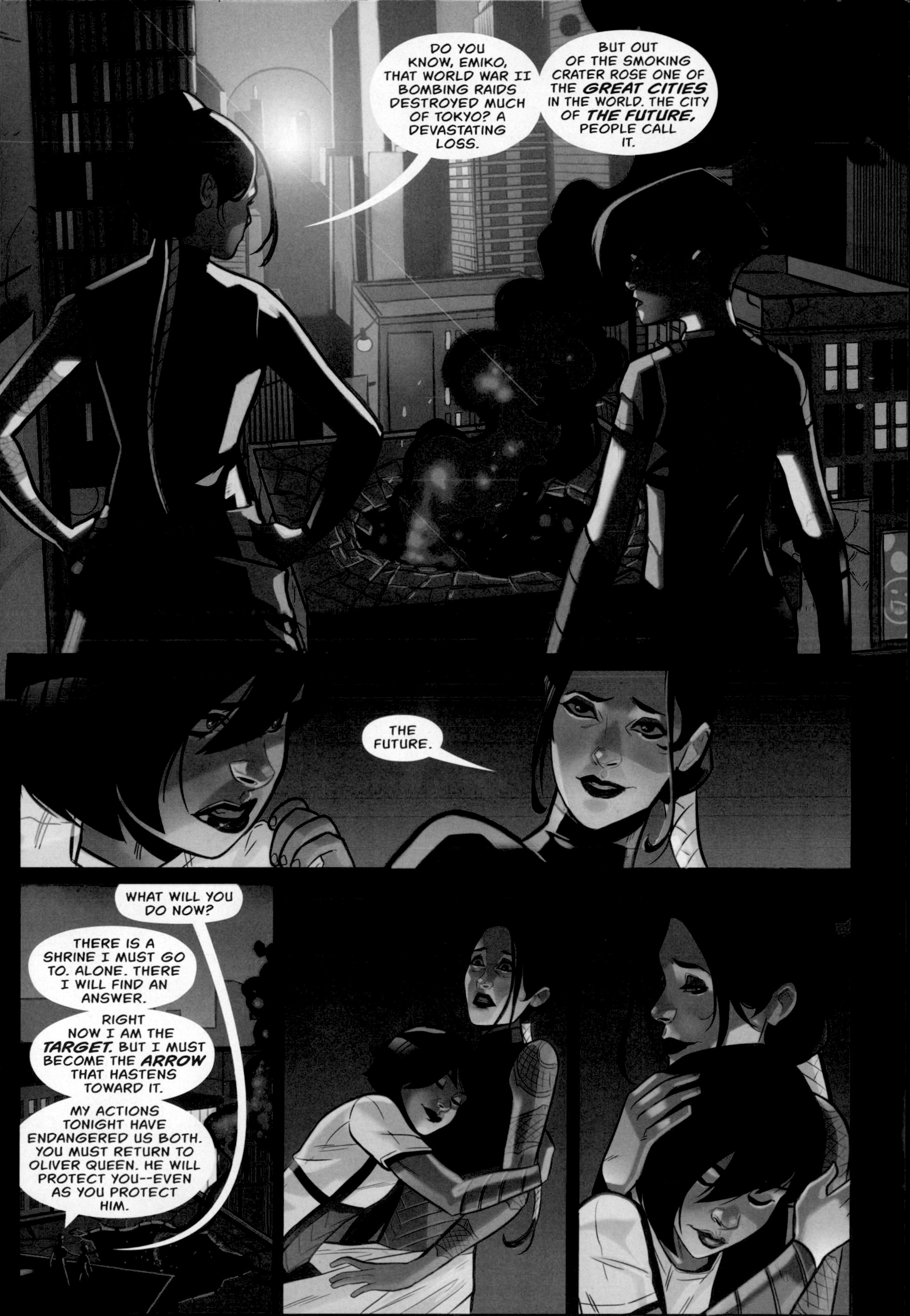
DO YOU KNOW, EMIKO, THAT WORLD WAR II BOMBING RAIDS DESTROYED MUCH OF TOKYO? A DEVASTATING LOSS.
BUT OUT OF THE SMOKING CRATER ROSE ONE OF THE GREAT CITIES IN THE WORLD. THE CITY OF THE FUTURE, PEOPLE CALL IT.
THE FUTURE.
WHAT WILL YOU DO NOW?
THERE IS A SHRINE I MUST GO TO. ALONE. THERE I WILL FIND AN ANSWER.
RIGHT NOW I AM THE TARGET. BUT I MUST BECOME THE ARROW THAT HASTENS TOWARD IT.
MY ACTIONS TONIGHT HAVE ENDANGERED US BOTH. YOU MUST RETURN TO OLIVER QUEEN. HE WILL PROTECT YOU--EVEN AS YOU PROTECT HIM.

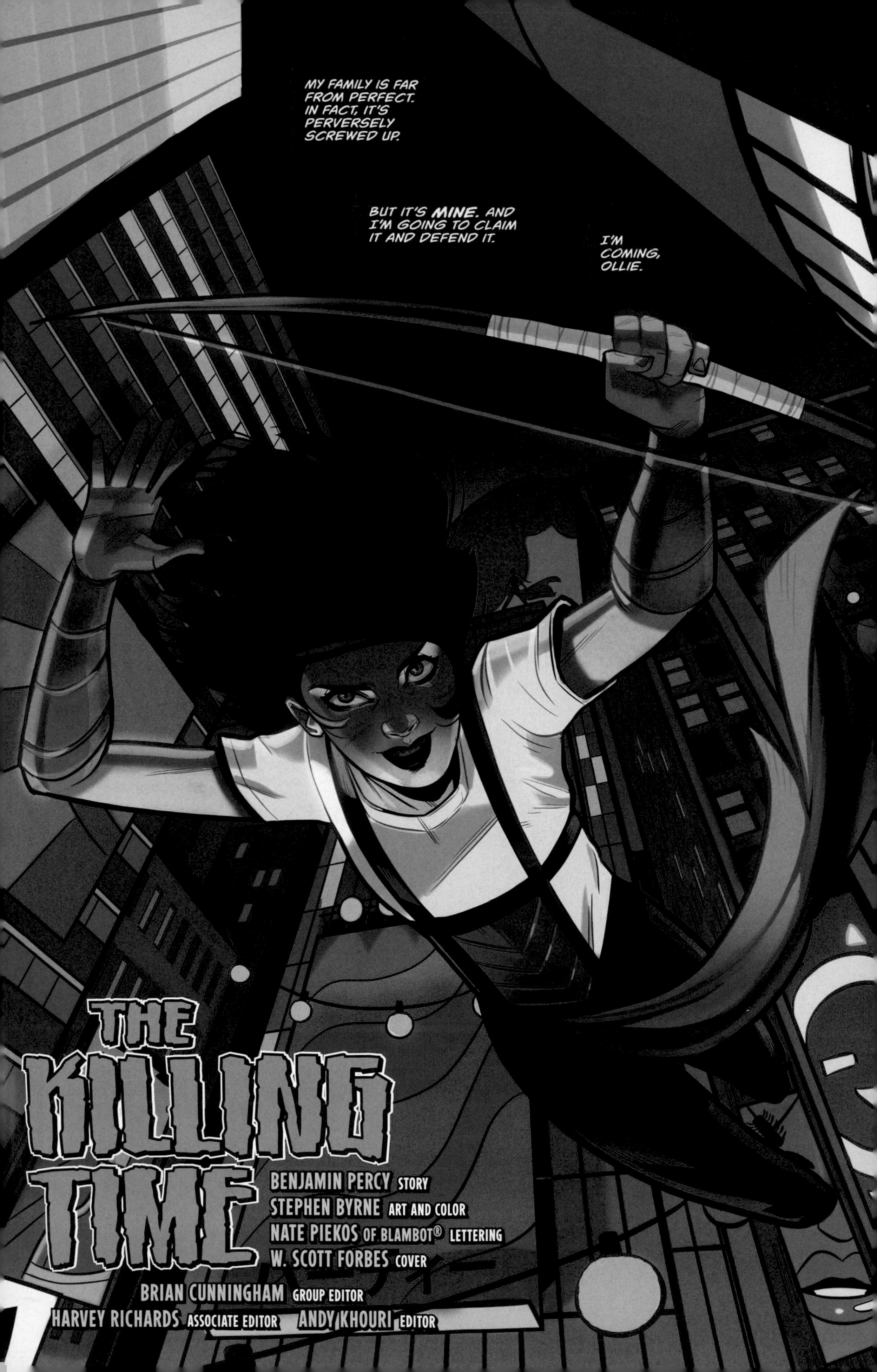
MY FAMILY IS FAR FROM PERFECT. IN FACT, IT'S PERVERSELY SCREWED UP.
BUT IT'S MINE. AND I'M GOING TO CLAIM IT AND DEFEND IT.
I'M COMING, OLLIE.
THE KILLING TIME
BENJAMIN PERCY STORY
STEPHEN BYRNE ART AND COLOR
NATE PIEKOS OF BLAMBOT® LETTERING
W. SCOTT FORBES COVER
BRIAN CUNNINGHAM GROUP EDITOR
HARVEY RICHARDS ASSOCIATE EDITOR ANDY KHOURI EDITOR

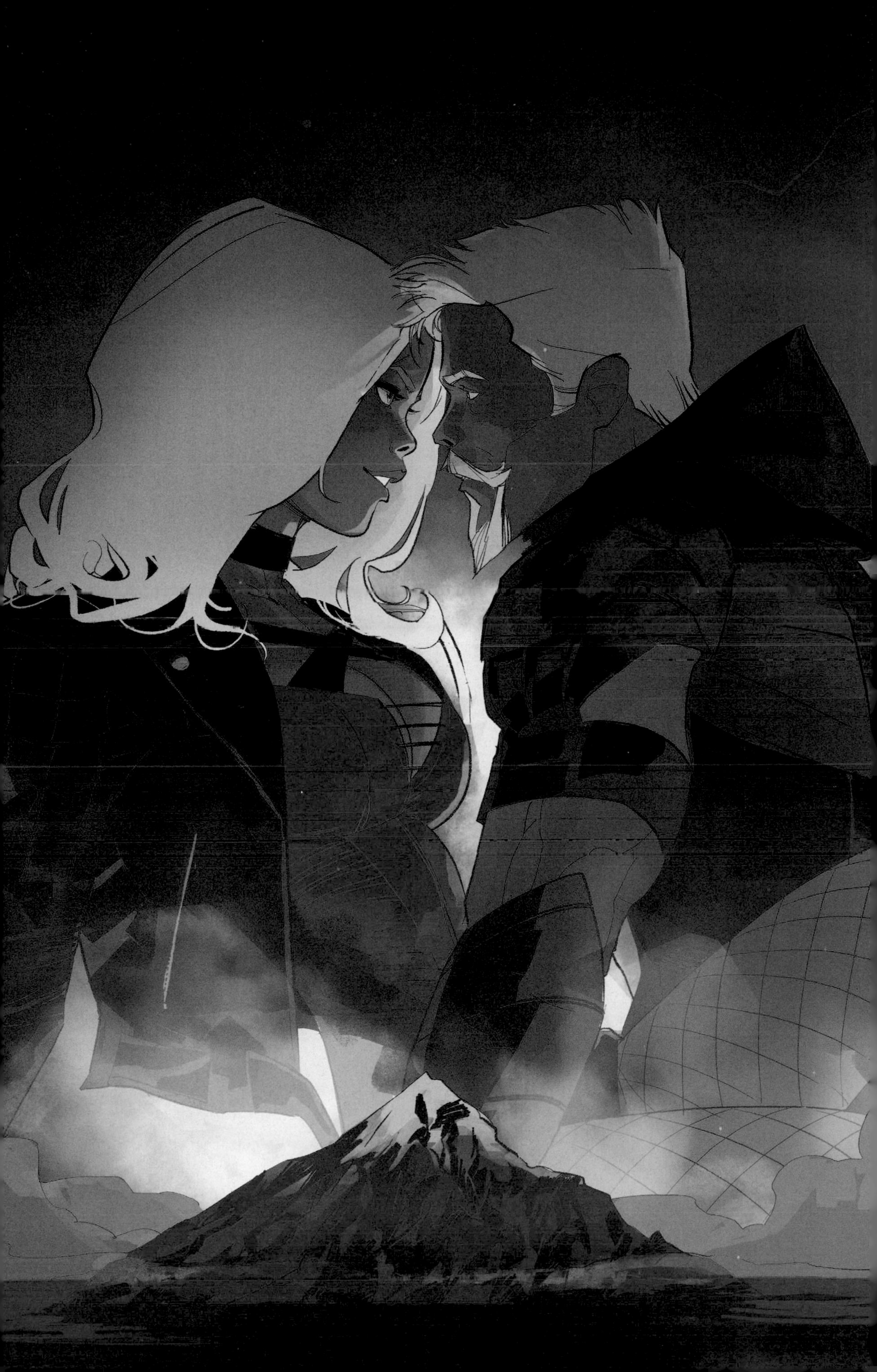

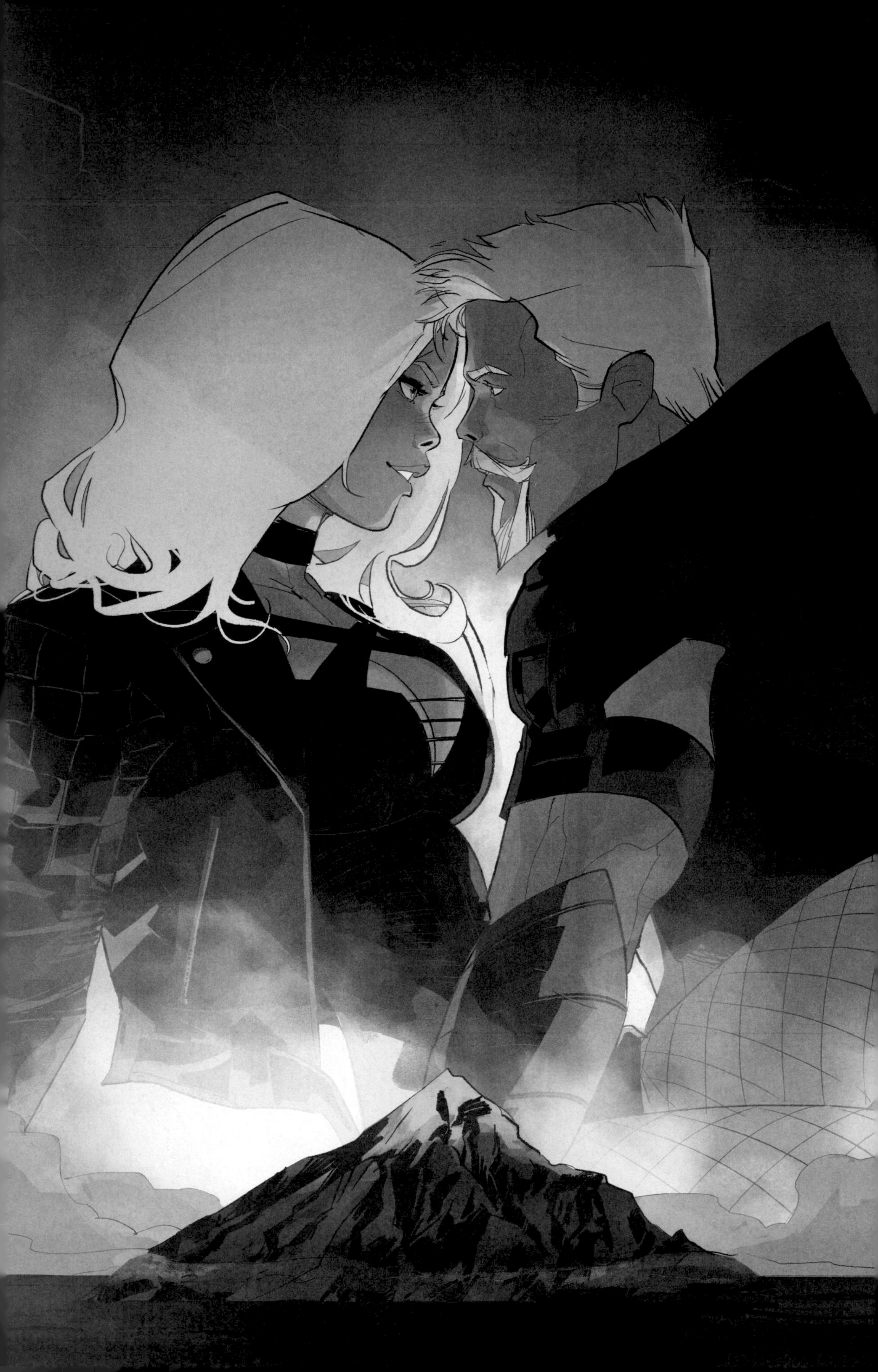

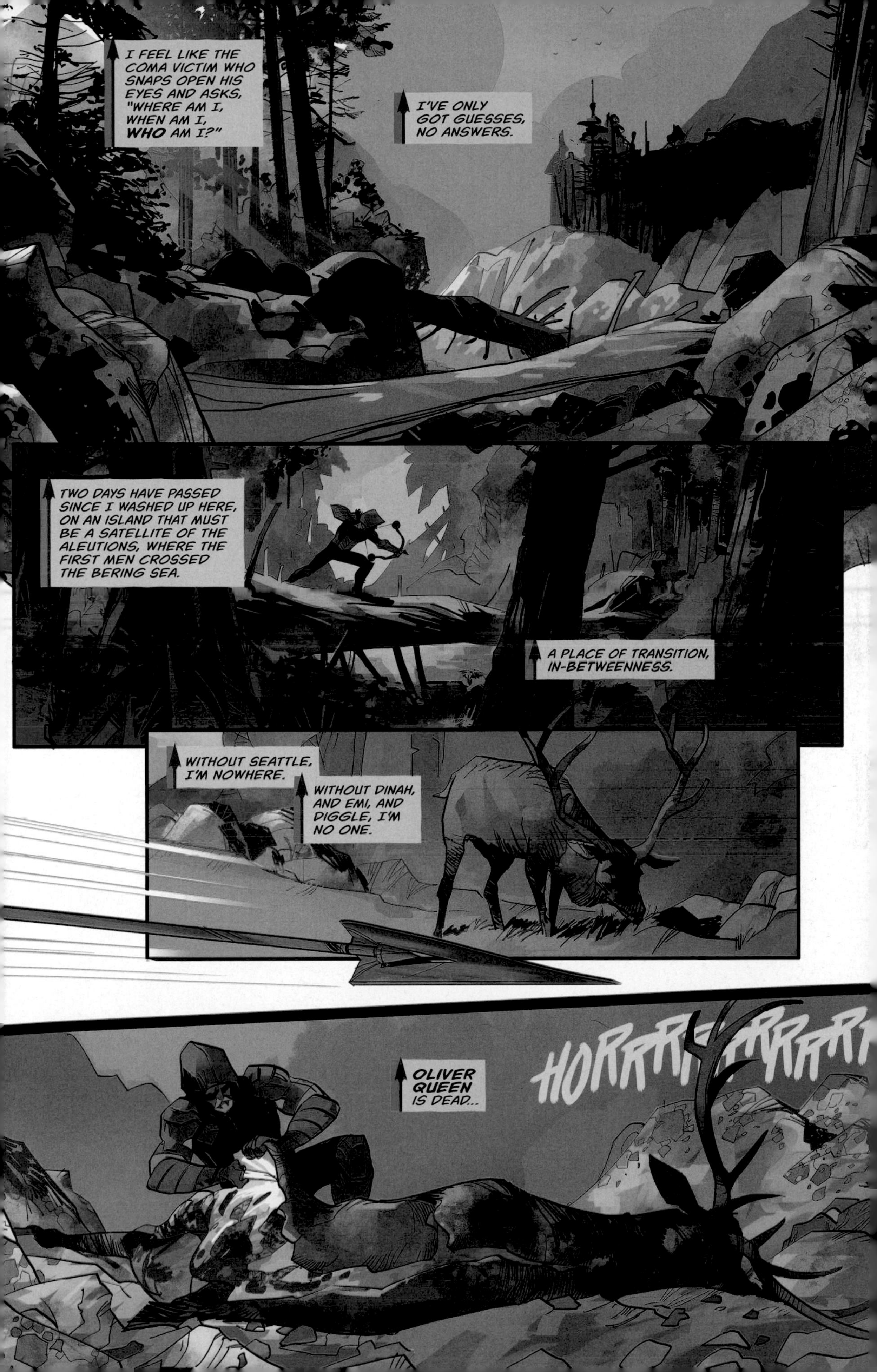
I FEEL LIKE THE COMA VICTIM WHO SNAPS OPEN HIS EYES AND ASKS, "WHERE AM I, WHEN AM I, **WHO** AM I?"
I'VE ONLY GOT GUESSES, NO ANSWERS.
TWO DAYS HAVE PASSED SINCE I WASHED UP HERE, ON AN ISLAND THAT MUST BE A SATELLITE OF THE ALEUTIONS, WHERE THE FIRST MEN CROSSED THE BERING SEA.
A PLACE OF TRANSITION, IN-BETWEENNESS.
WITHOUT SEATTLE, I'M NOWHERE.
WITHOUT DINAH, AND EMI, AND DIGGLE, I'M NO ONE.
HORRRRRRRRRR
OLIVER QUEEN IS DEAD...

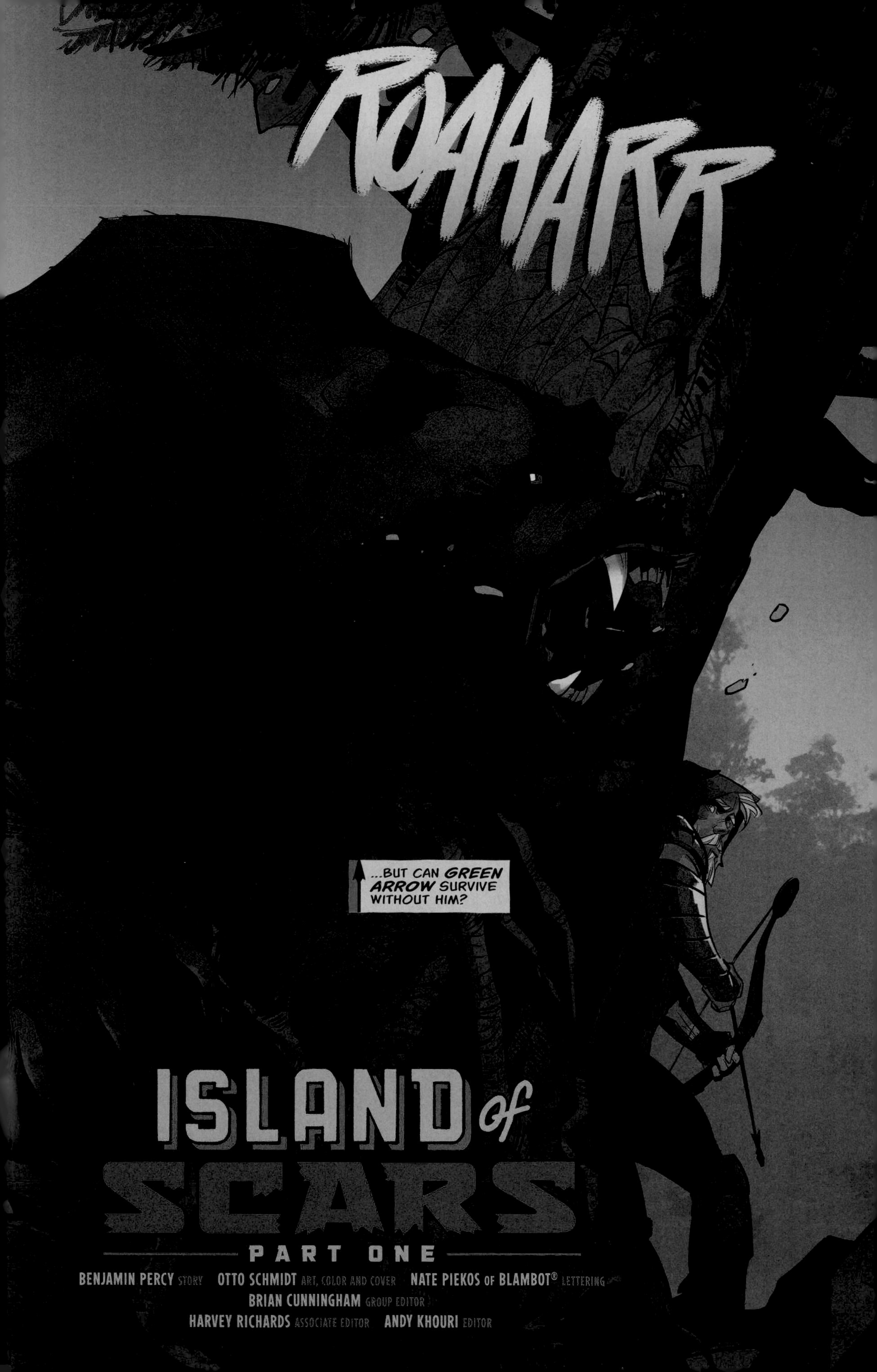
ROAAARR
...BUT CAN GREEN ARROW SURVIVE WITHOUT HIM?
ISLAND of SCARS
PART ONE
BENJAMIN PERCY STORY OTTO SCHMIDT ART, COLOR AND COVER NATE PIEKOS OF BLAMBOT® LETTERING
BRIAN CUNNINGHAM GROUP EDITOR
HARVEY RICHARDS ASSOCIATE EDITOR ANDY KHOURI EDITOR

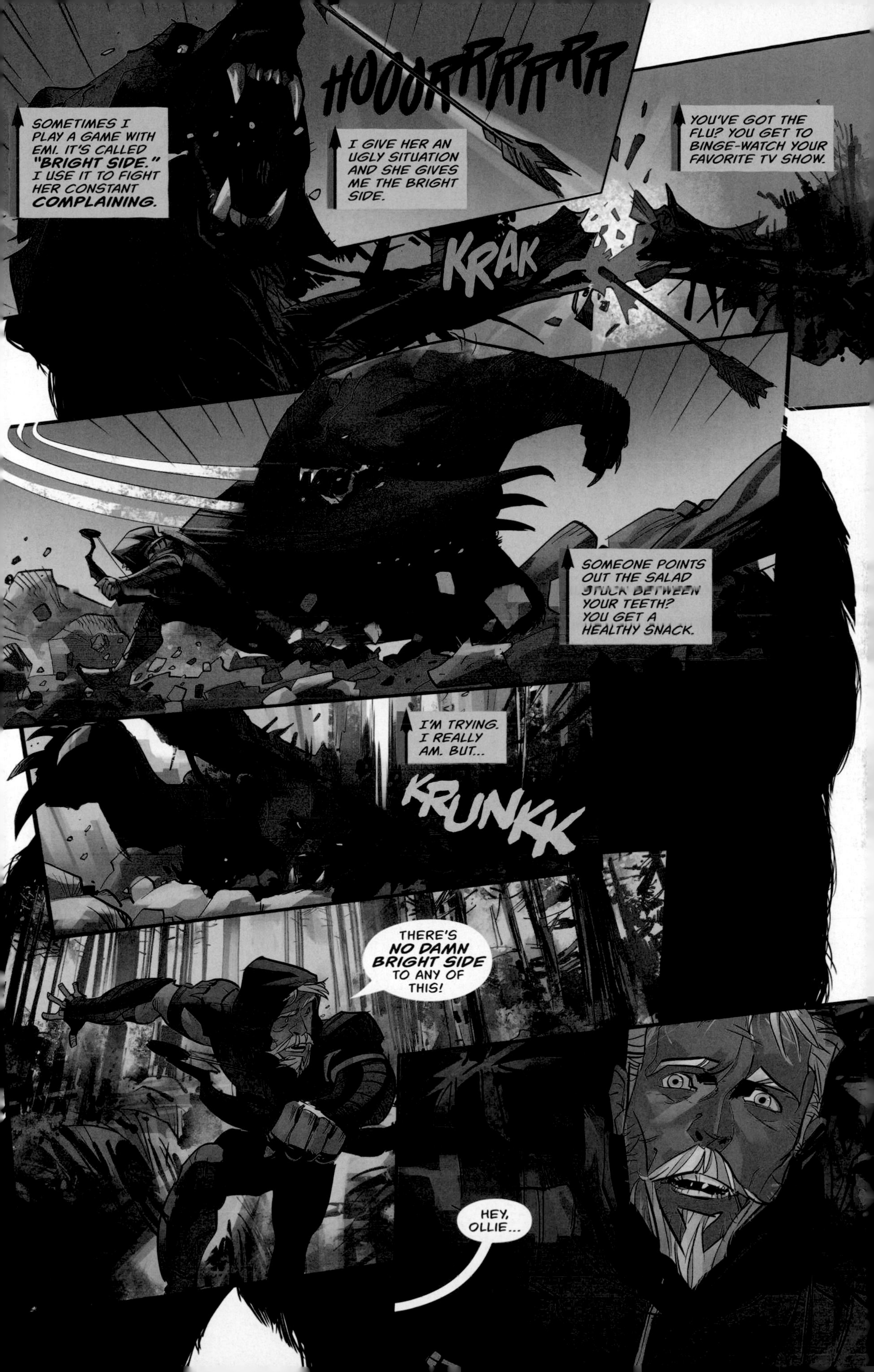
HOOOURRRRRRR
SOMETIMES I PLAY A GAME WITH EMI. IT'S CALLED "BRIGHT SIDE." I USE IT TO FIGHT HER CONSTANT COMPLAINING.
I GIVE HER AN UGLY SITUATION AND SHE GIVES ME THE BRIGHT SIDE.
YOU'VE GOT THE FLU? YOU GET TO BINGE-WATCH YOUR FAVORITE TV SHOW.
KRAK
SOMEONE POINTS OUT THE SALAD STUCK BETWEEN YOUR TEETH? YOU GET A HEALTHY SNACK.
I'M TRYING. I REALLY AM. BUT...
KRUNKK
THERE'S NO DAMN BRIGHT SIDE TO ANY OF THIS!
HEY, OLLIE...

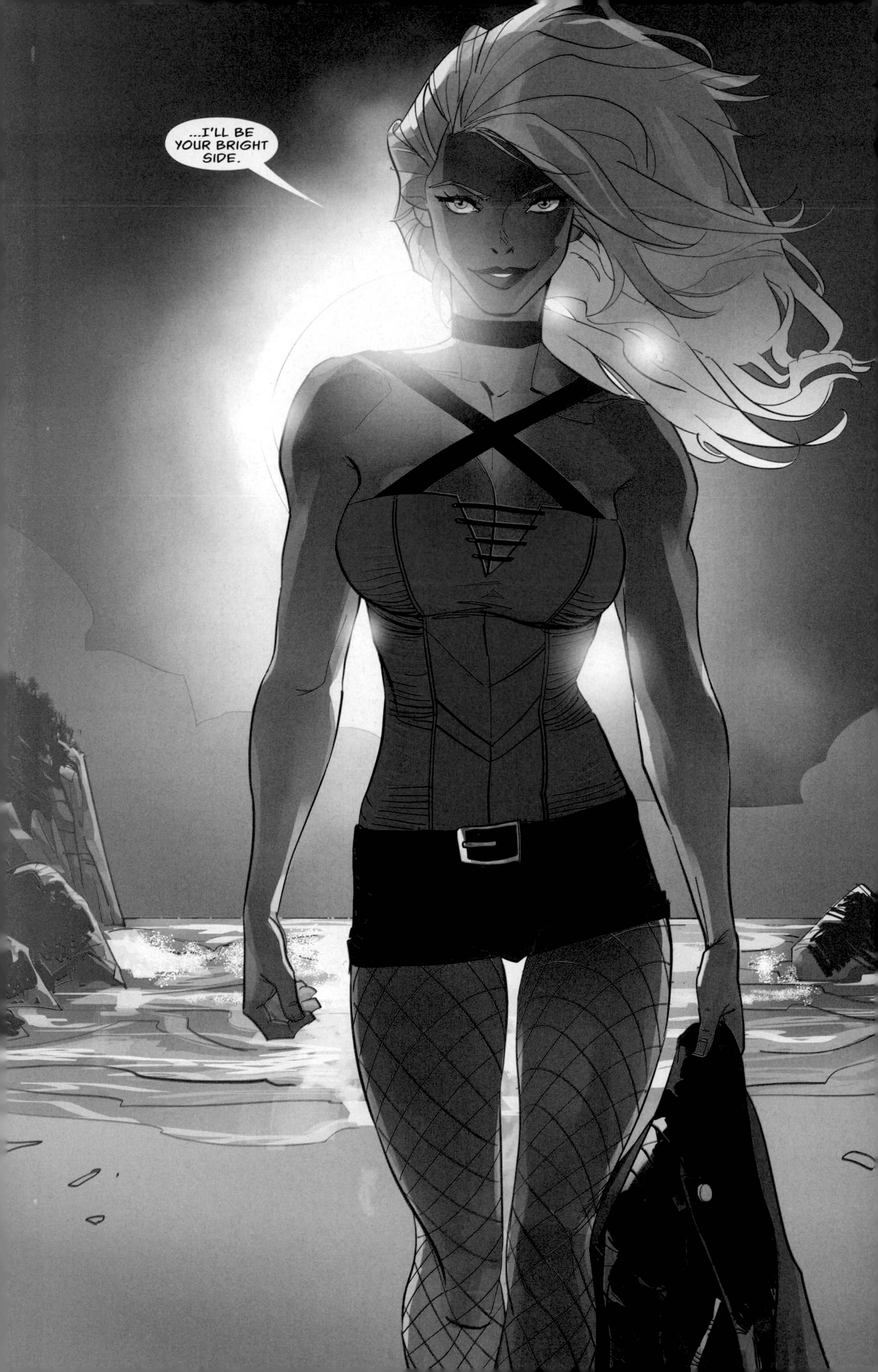
...I'LL BE YOUR BRIGHT SIDE.

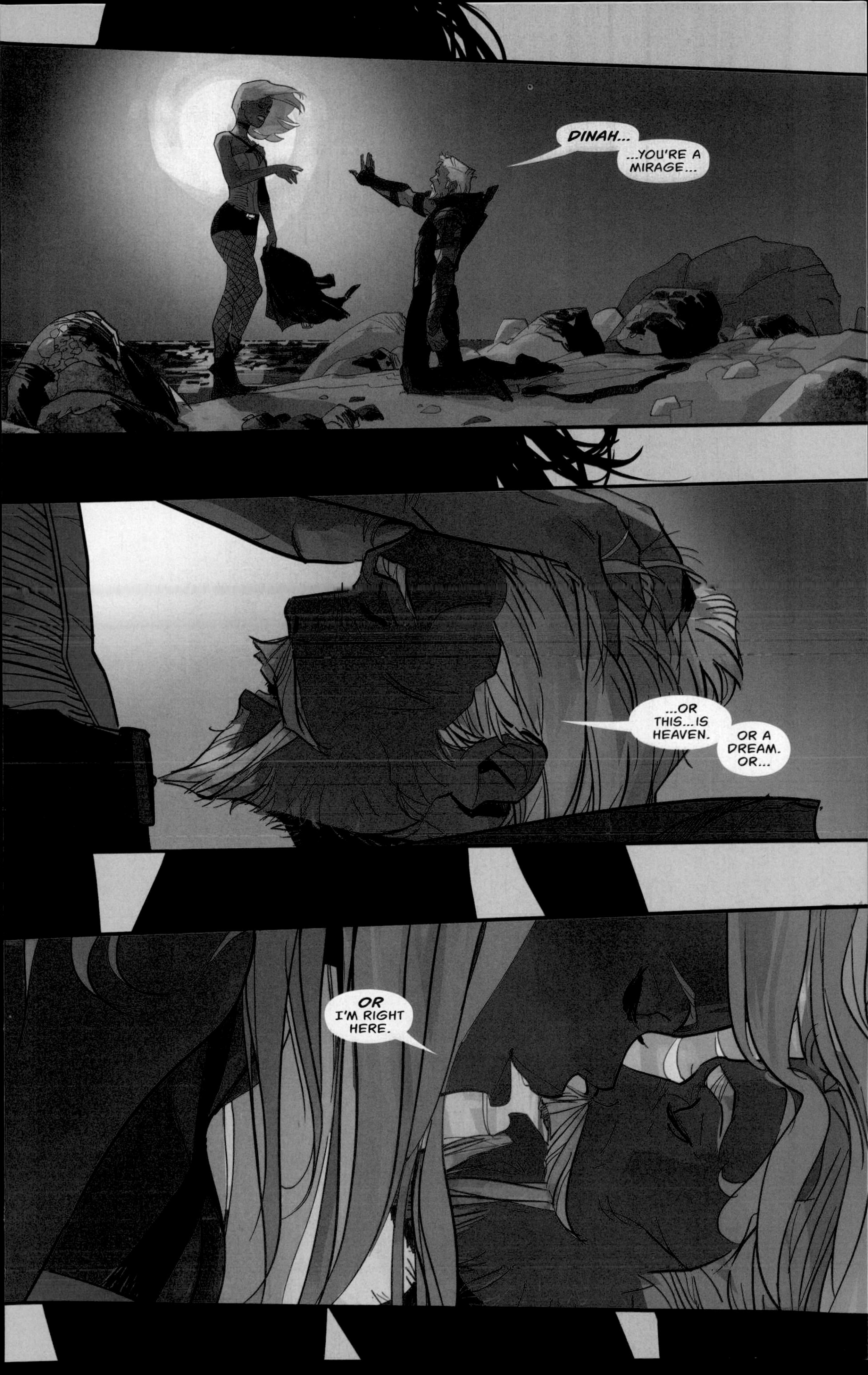
DINAH...
...YOU'RE A MIRAGE...
...OR THIS...IS HEAVEN.
OR A DREAM. OR...
OR I'M RIGHT HERE.

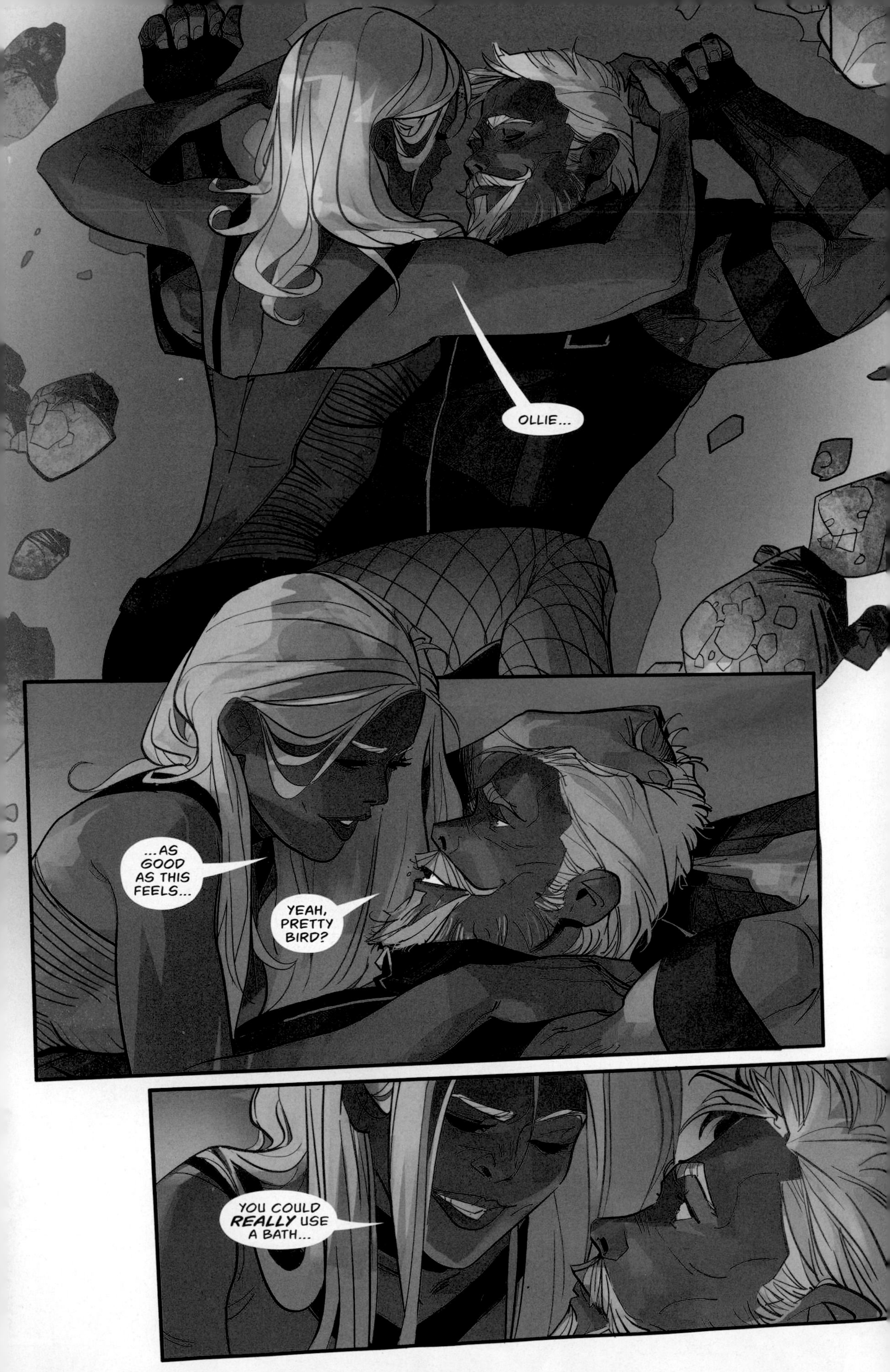
OLLIE...
...AS GOOD AS THIS FEELS...
YEAH, PRETTY BIRD?
YOU COULD REALLY USE A BATH...

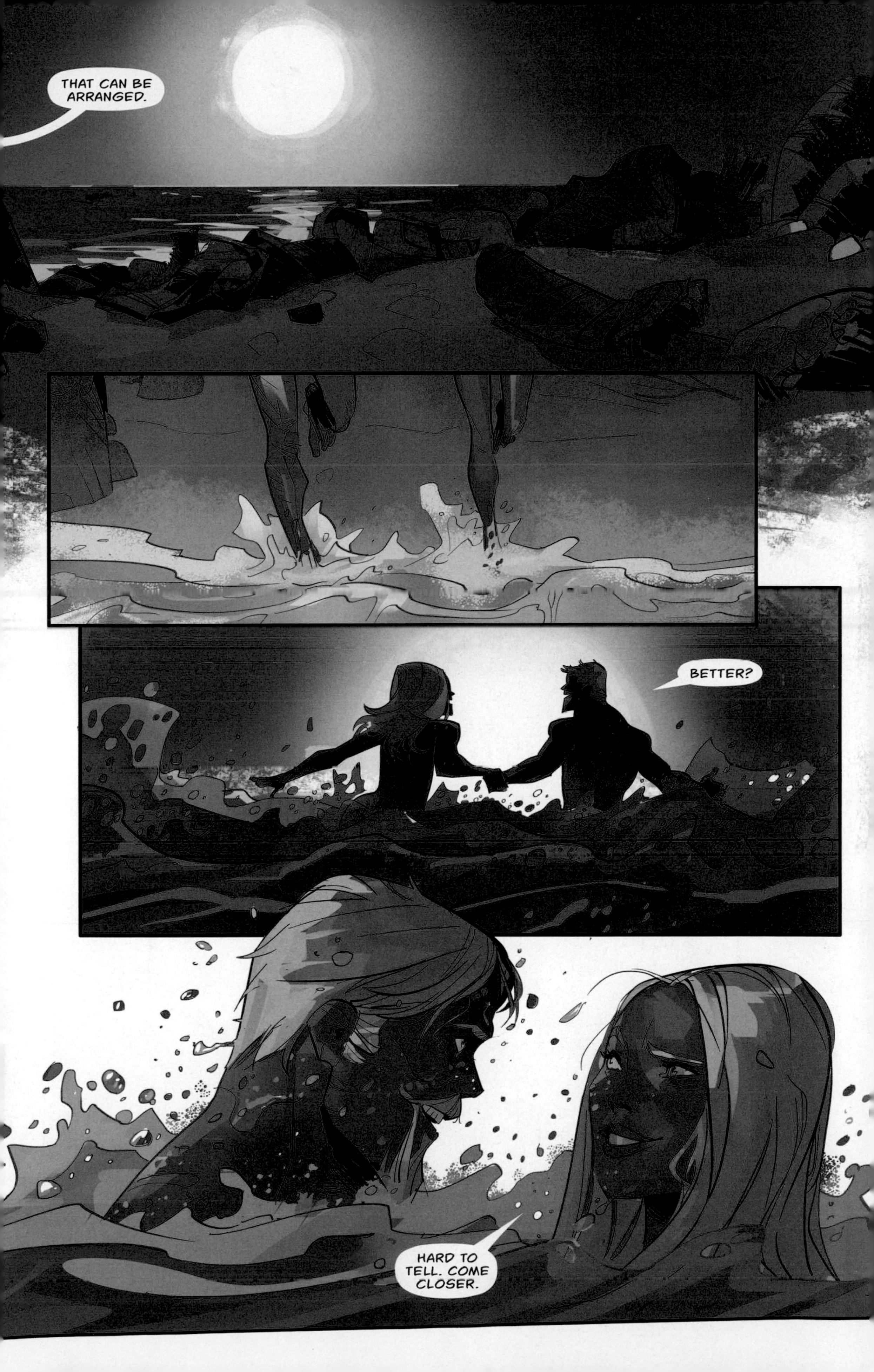
THAT CAN BE ARRANGED.
BETTER?
HARD TO TELL. COME CLOSER.

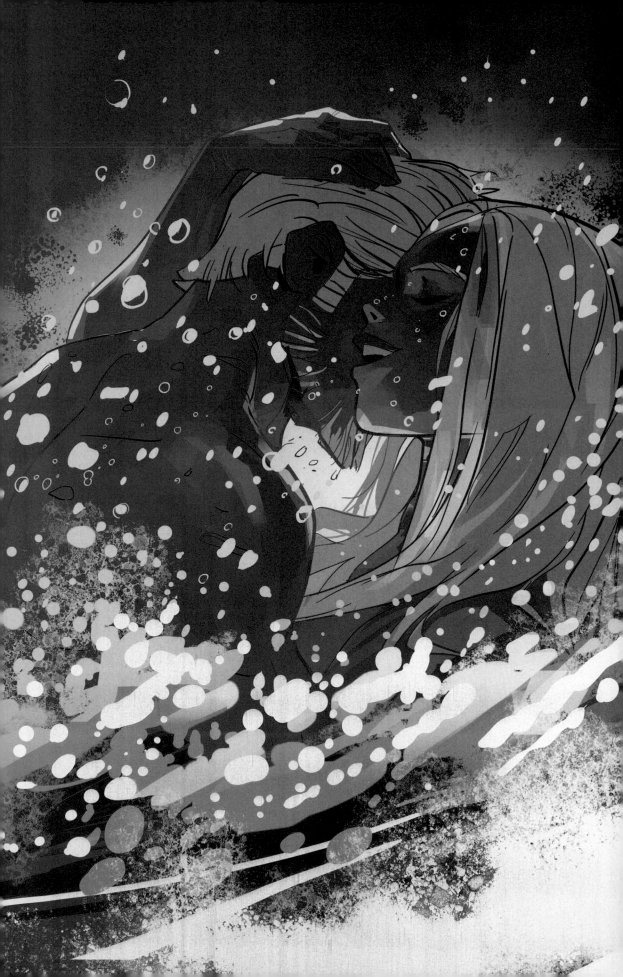

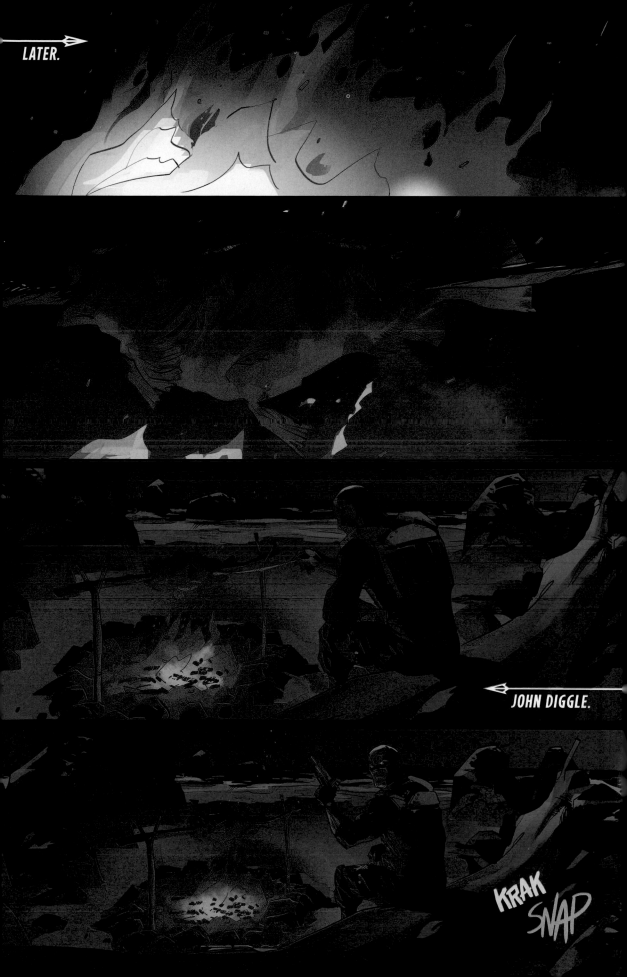

LATER.

JOHN DIGGLE.

KRAK
SNAP

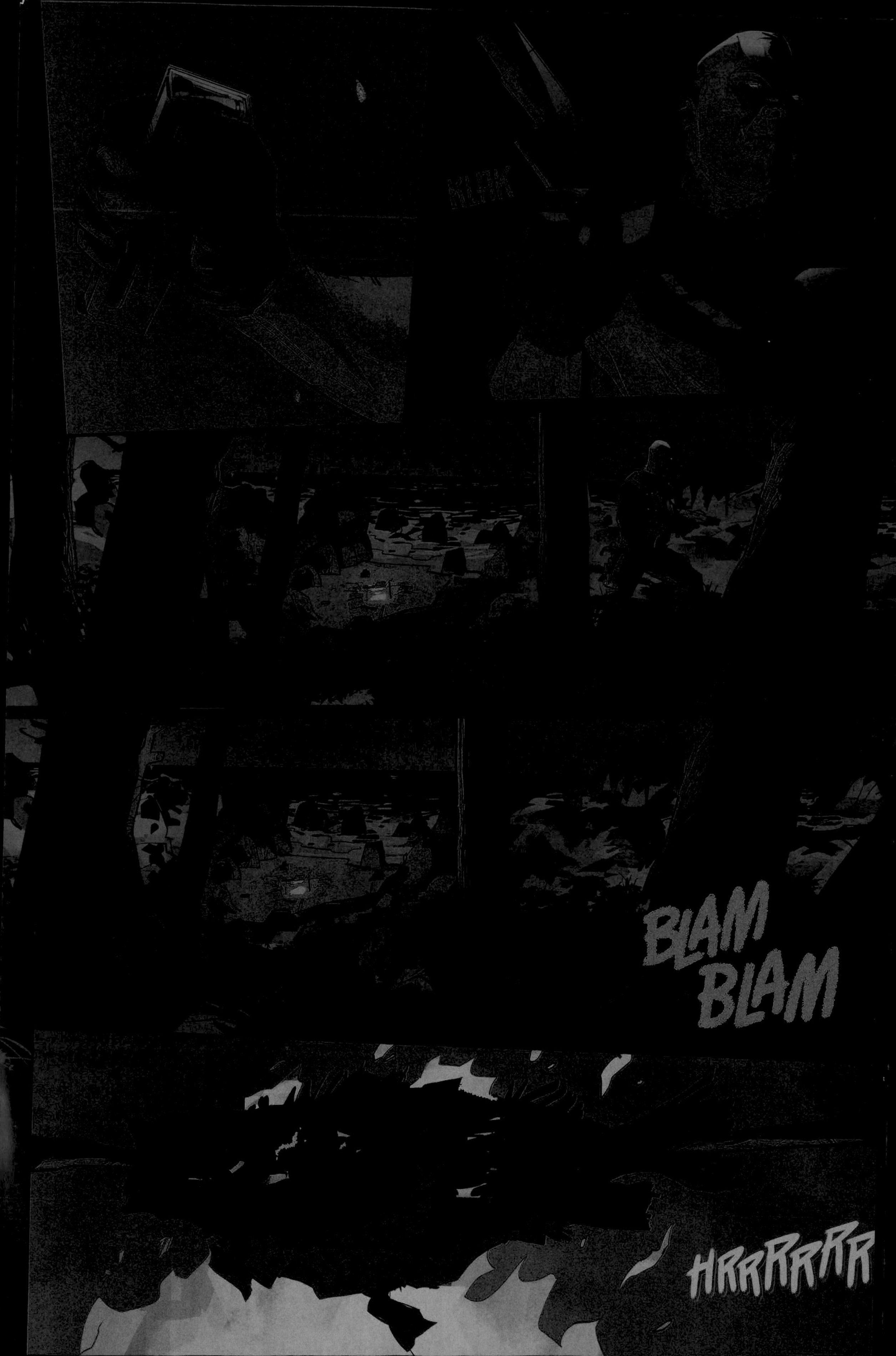
KLIK
BLAM BLAM
HRRRRRR

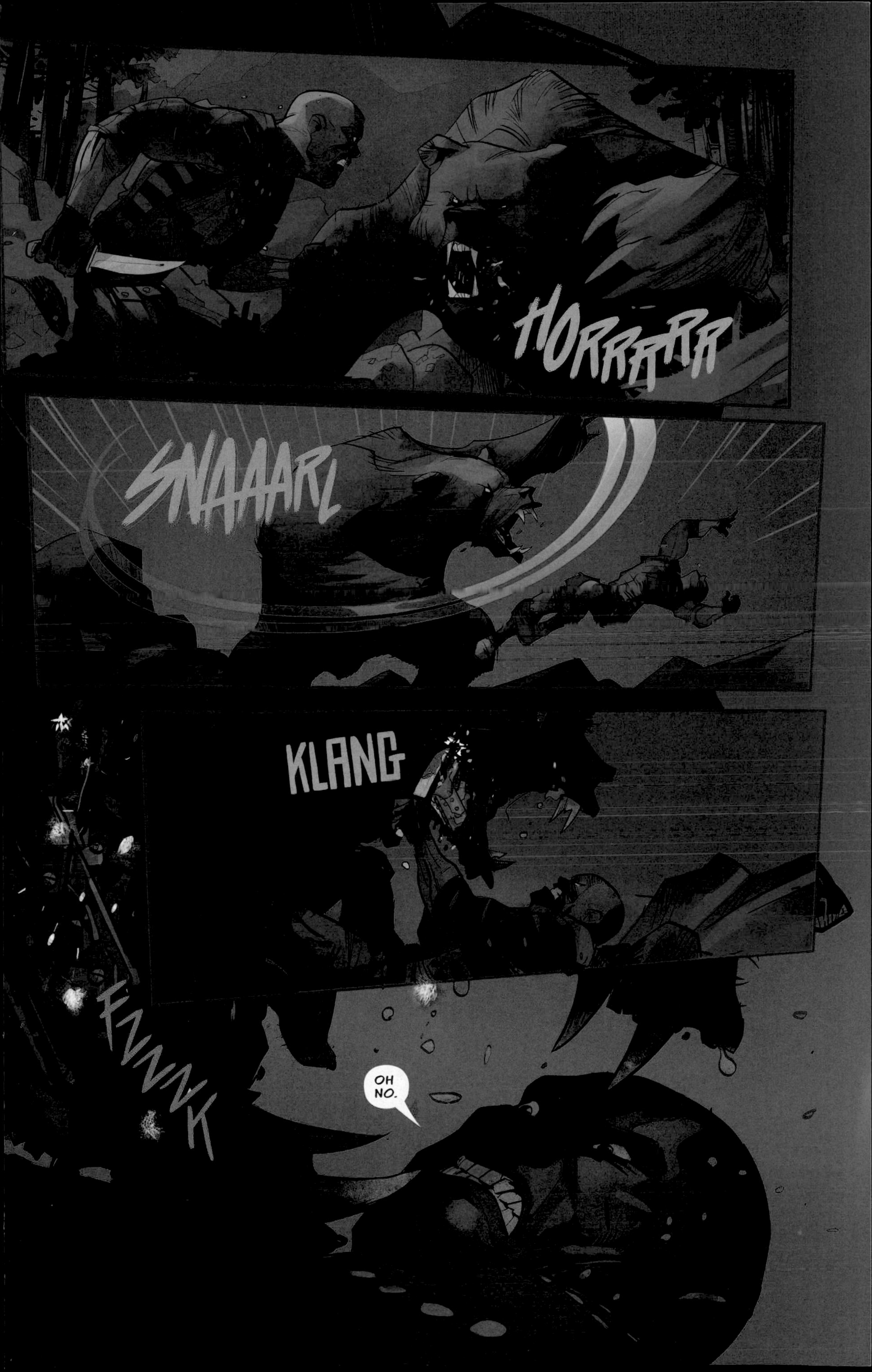
HORRRRRR
SNAAARL
KLANG
FZZZNK
OH NO.

RRAAA
HOLY HELL!
YOU'RE MADE OF METAL, BUT YOU SMELL LIKE A SHEEP SMOKING A CIGAR!
PSSSH
URRGH!
WHOEVER THE HELL YOU PEOPLE ARE, CALL OFF THE TERMINATOR TEDDY BEAR.
LET ME DOWN, DAMN IT!

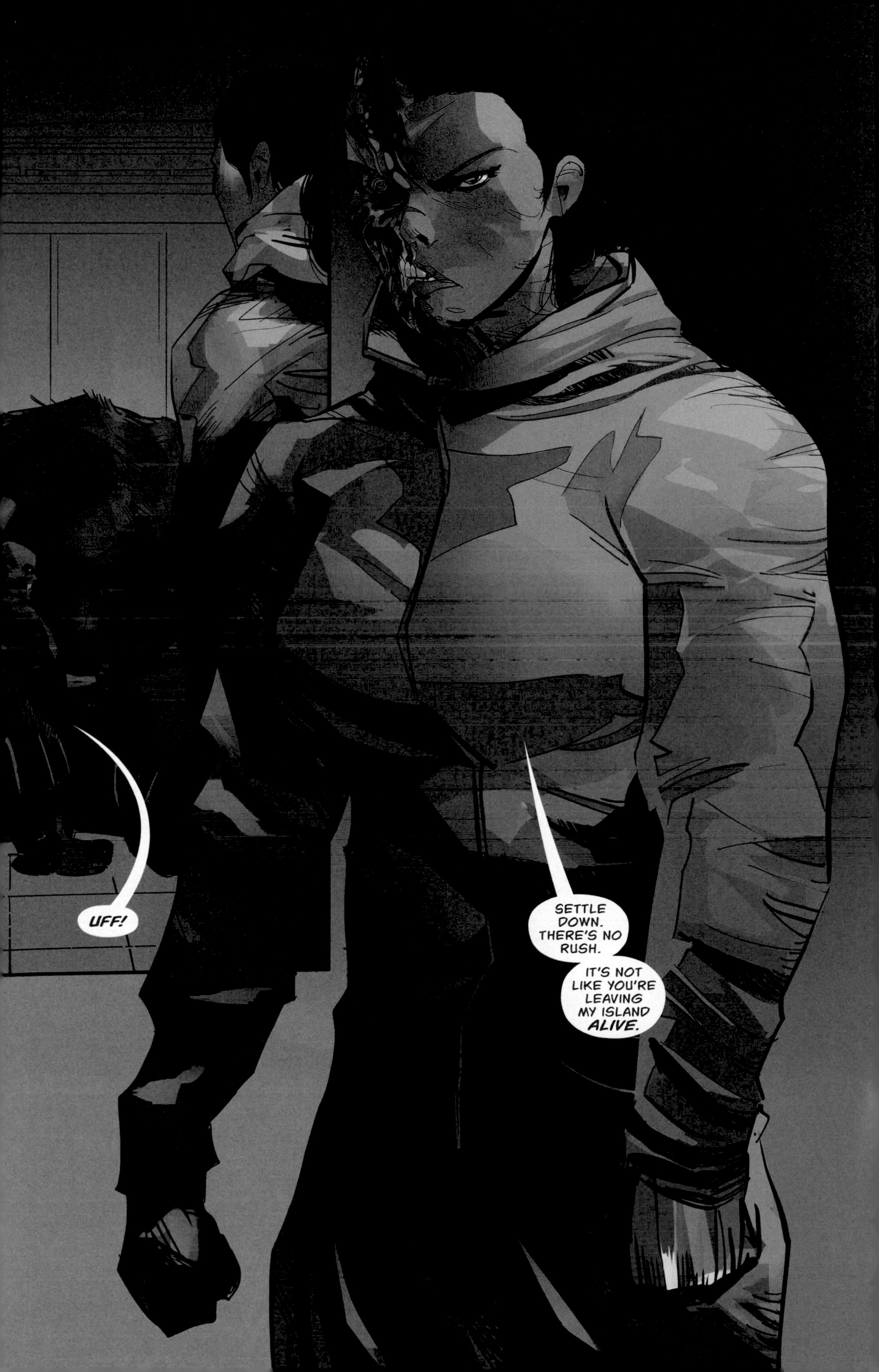
UFF!
SETTLE DOWN. THERE'S NO RUSH.
IT'S NOT LIKE YOU'RE LEAVING MY ISLAND ALIVE.

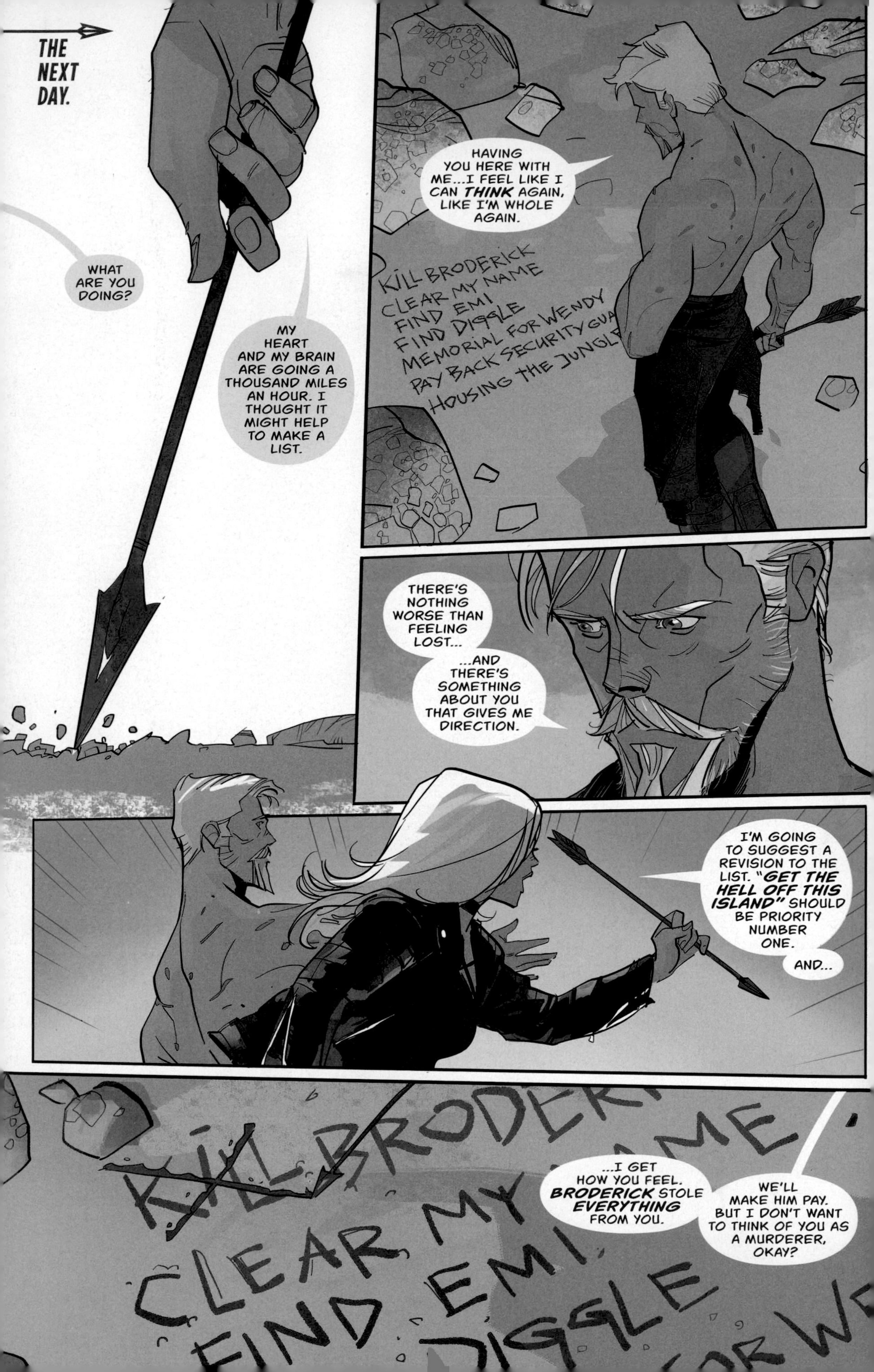
THE NEXT DAY.
WHAT ARE YOU DOING?
MY HEART AND MY BRAIN ARE GOING A THOUSAND MILES AN HOUR. I THOUGHT IT MIGHT HELP TO MAKE A LIST.
HAVING YOU HERE WITH ME...I FEEL LIKE I CAN THINK AGAIN, LIKE I'M WHOLE AGAIN.
KILL BRODERICK
CLEAR MY NAME
FIND EMI
FIND DIGGLE
MEMORIAL FOR WENDY
PAY BACK SECURITY GUA
HOUSING THE JUNGLE
THERE'S NOTHING WORSE THAN FEELING LOST...
...AND THERE'S SOMETHING ABOUT YOU THAT GIVES ME DIRECTION.
I'M GOING TO SUGGEST A REVISION TO THE LIST. "GET THE HELL OFF THIS ISLAND" SHOULD BE PRIORITY NUMBER ONE.
AND...
...I GET HOW YOU FEEL. BRODERICK STOLE EVERYTHING FROM YOU.
WE'LL MAKE HIM PAY. BUT I DON'T WANT TO THINK OF YOU AS A MURDERER, OKAY?

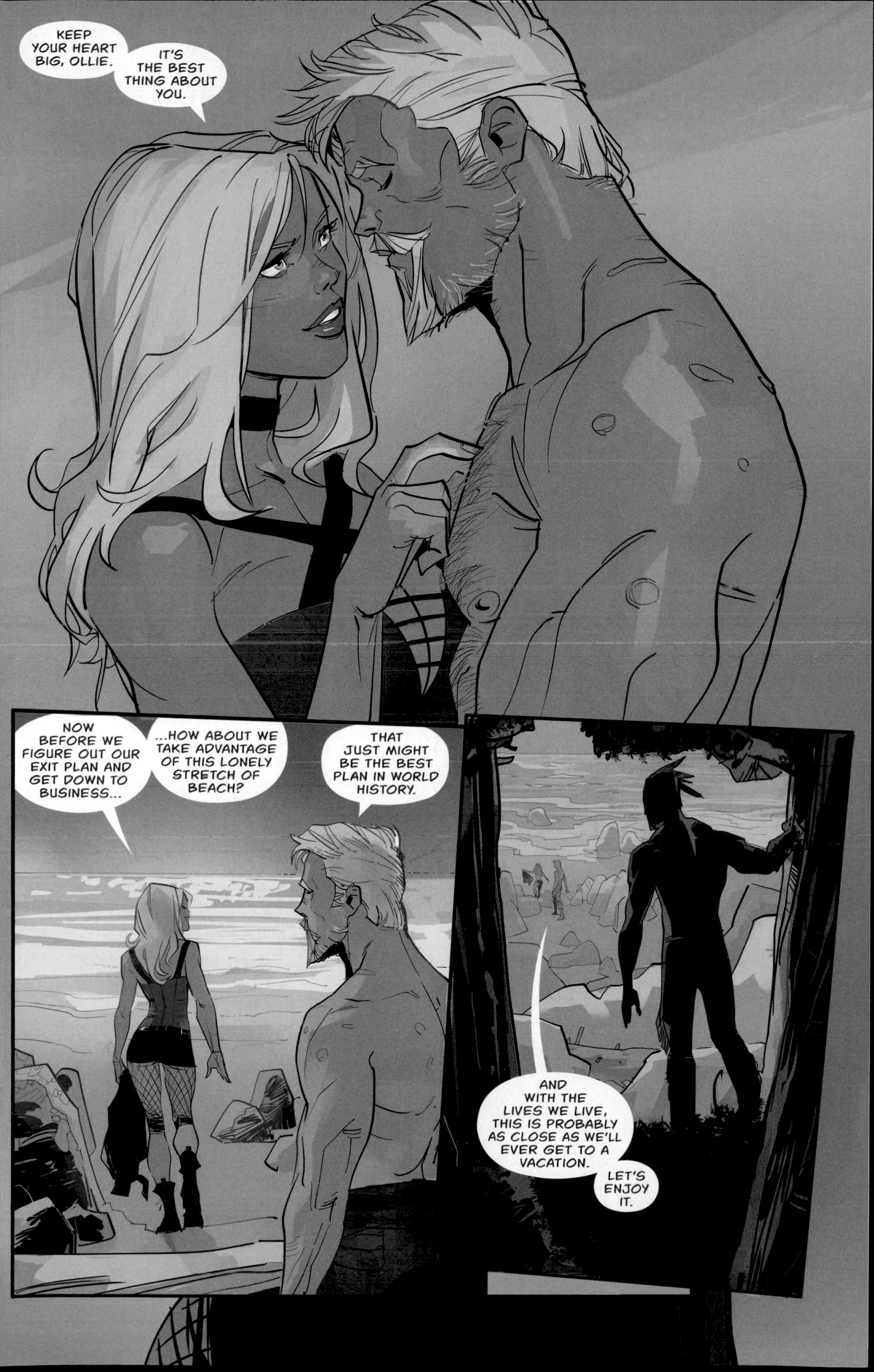
KEEP YOUR HEART BIG, OLLIE.
IT'S THE BEST THING ABOUT YOU.
NOW BEFORE WE FIGURE OUT OUR EXIT PLAN AND GET DOWN TO BUSINESS...
...HOW ABOUT WE TAKE ADVANTAGE OF THIS LONELY STRETCH OF BEACH?
THAT JUST MIGHT BE THE BEST PLAN IN WORLD HISTORY.
AND WITH THE LIVES WE LIVE, THIS IS PROBABLY AS CLOSE AS WE'LL EVER GET TO A VACATION.
LET'S ENJOY IT.

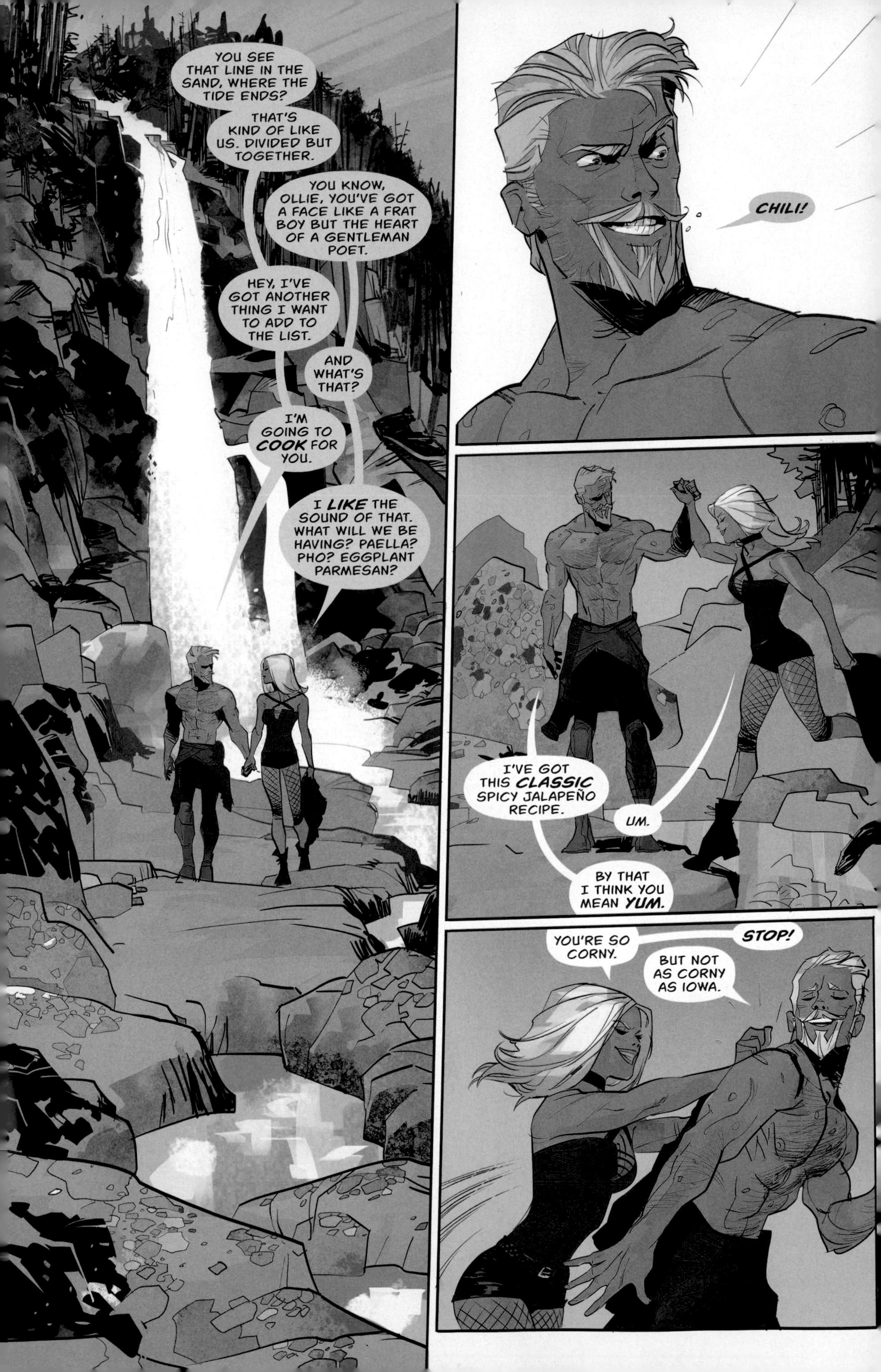
YOU SEE THAT LINE IN THE SAND, WHERE THE TIDE ENDS?
THAT'S KIND OF LIKE US. DIVIDED BUT TOGETHER.
YOU KNOW, OLLIE, YOU'VE GOT A FACE LIKE A FRAT BOY BUT THE HEART OF A GENTLEMAN POET.
HEY, I'VE GOT ANOTHER THING I WANT TO ADD TO THE LIST.
AND WHAT'S THAT?
I'M GOING TO COOK FOR YOU.
I LIKE THE SOUND OF THAT. WHAT WILL WE BE HAVING? PAELLA? PHO? EGGPLANT PARMESAN?
CHILI!
I'VE GOT THIS CLASSIC SPICY JALAPEÑO RECIPE.
UM.
BY THAT I THINK YOU MEAN YUM.
YOU'RE SO CORNY.
STOP!
BUT NOT AS CORNY AS IOWA.

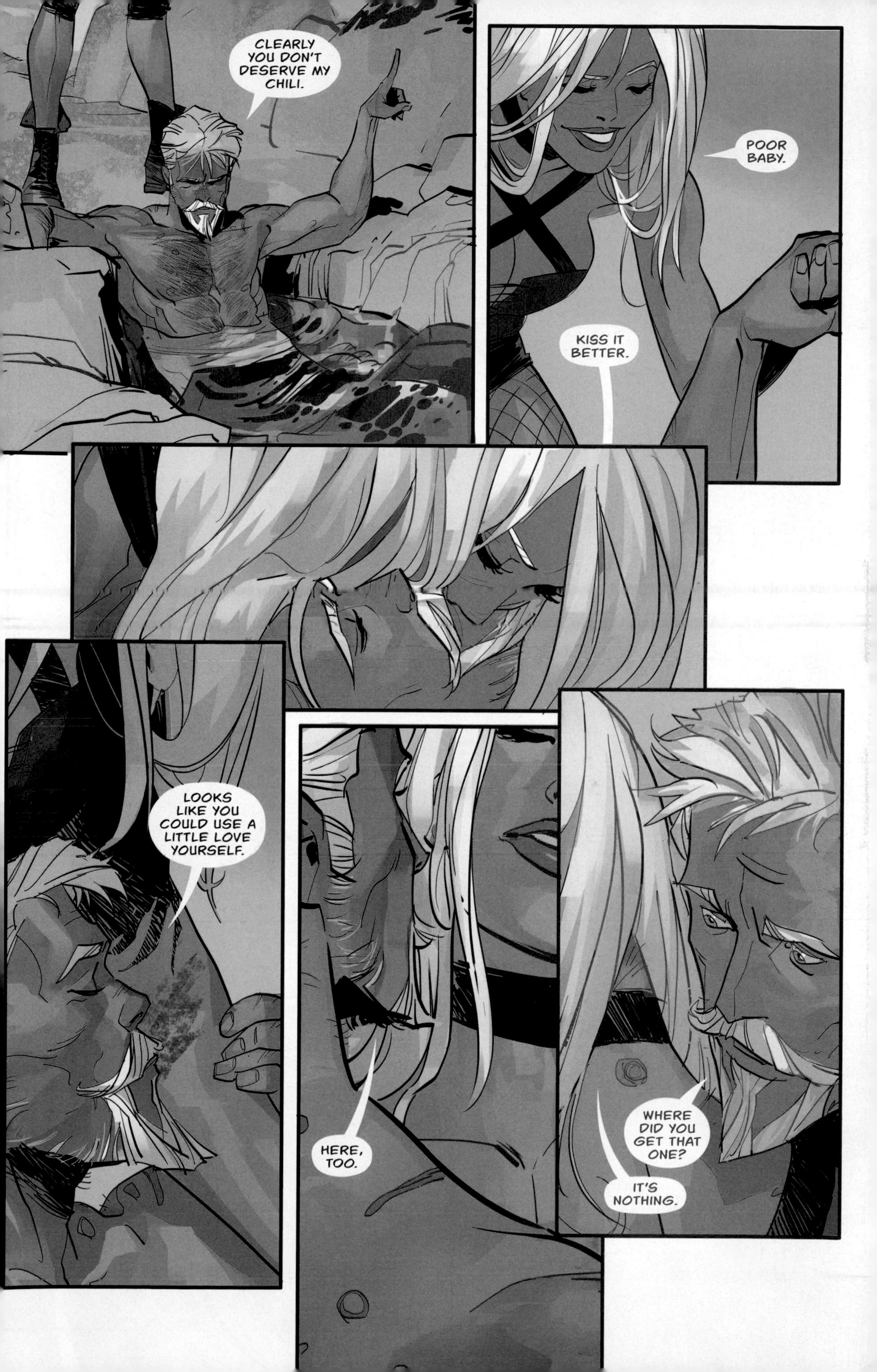
CLEARLY YOU DON'T DESERVE MY CHILI.
POOR BABY.
KISS IT BETTER.
LOOKS LIKE YOU COULD USE A LITTLE LOVE YOURSELF.
HERE, TOO.
WHERE DID YOU GET THAT ONE?
IT'S NOTHING.

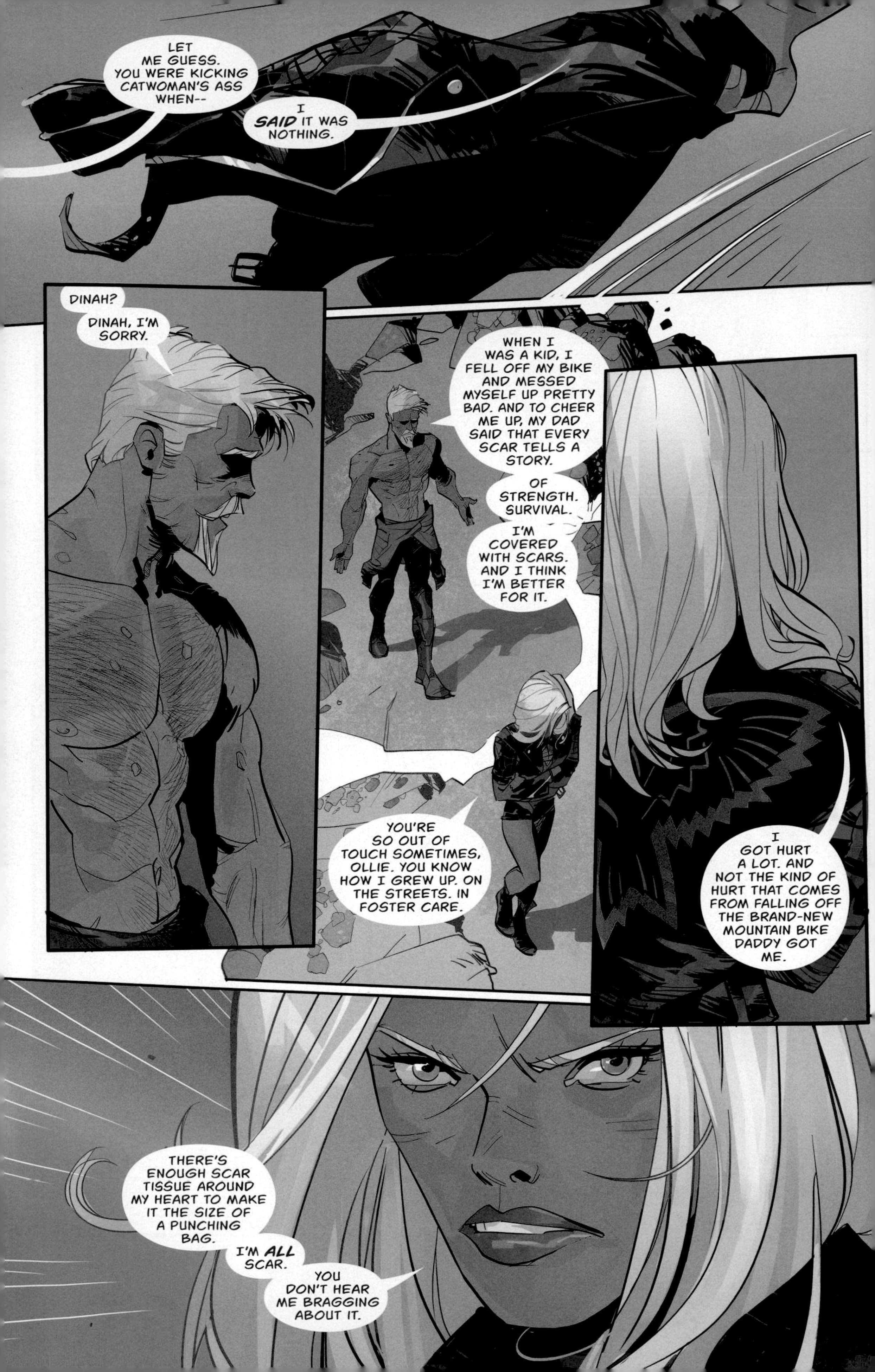

LET ME GUESS. YOU WERE KICKING CATWOMAN'S ASS WHEN--
I *SAID* IT WAS NOTHING.
DINAH?
DINAH, I'M SORRY.
WHEN I WAS A KID, I FELL OFF MY BIKE AND MESSED MYSELF UP PRETTY BAD. AND TO CHEER ME UP, MY DAD SAID THAT EVERY SCAR TELLS A STORY.
OF STRENGTH. SURVIVAL.
I'M COVERED WITH SCARS. AND I THINK I'M BETTER FOR IT.
YOU'RE SO OUT OF TOUCH SOMETIMES, OLLIE. YOU KNOW HOW I GREW UP. ON THE STREETS. IN FOSTER CARE.
I GOT HURT A LOT. AND NOT THE KIND OF HURT THAT COMES FROM FALLING OFF THE BRAND-NEW MOUNTAIN BIKE DADDY GOT ME.
THERE'S ENOUGH SCAR TISSUE AROUND MY HEART TO MAKE IT THE SIZE OF A PUNCHING BAG.
I'M *ALL* SCAR.
YOU DON'T HEAR ME BRAGGING ABOUT IT.

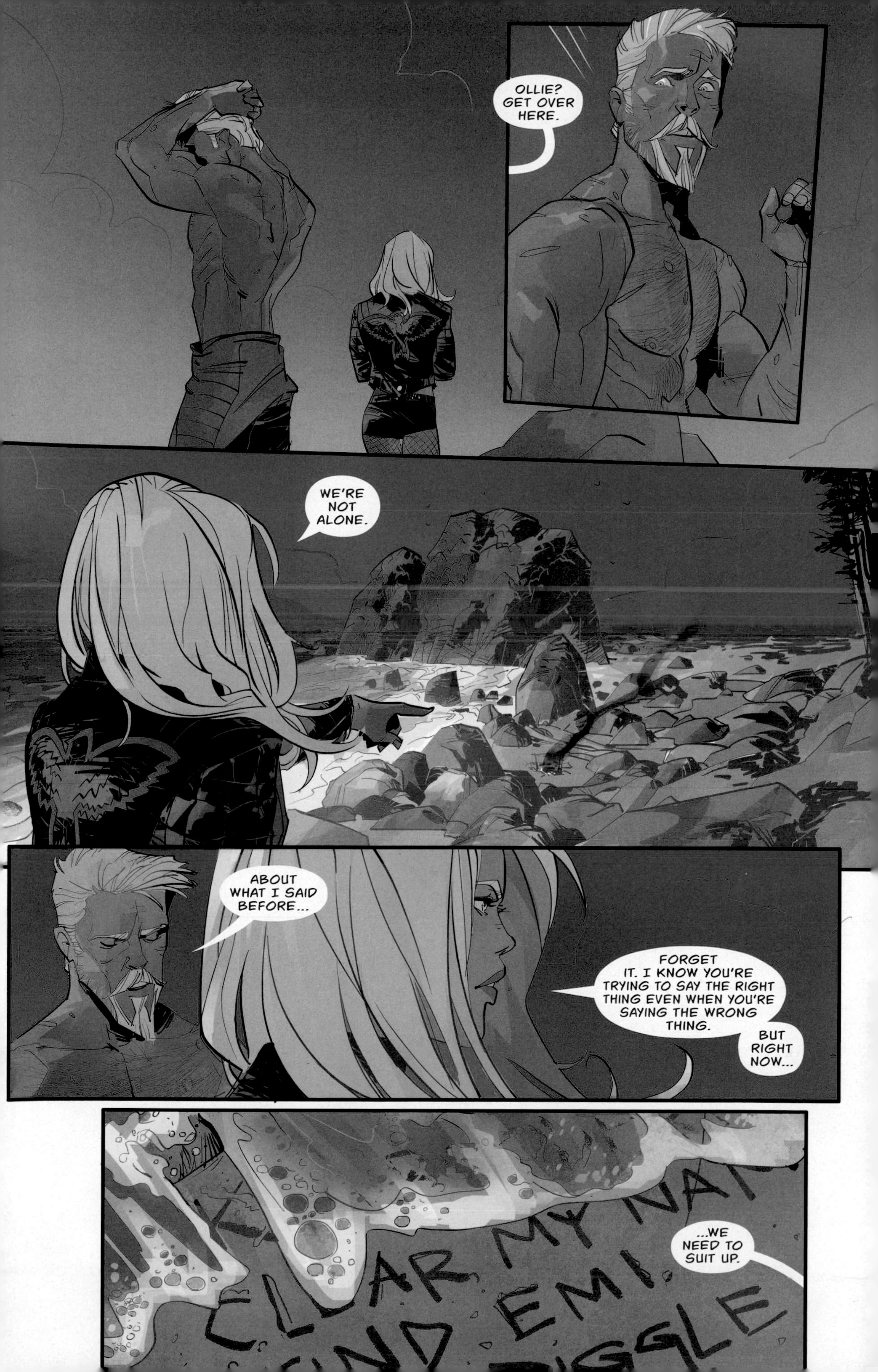
OLLIE? GET OVER HERE.
WE'RE NOT ALONE.
ABOUT WHAT I SAID BEFORE...
FORGET IT. I KNOW YOU'RE TRYING TO SAY THE RIGHT THING EVEN WHEN YOU'RE SAYING THE WRONG THING.
BUT RIGHT NOW...
...WE NEED TO SUIT UP.
CLEAR MY NA
FIND EMI
DIGGLE

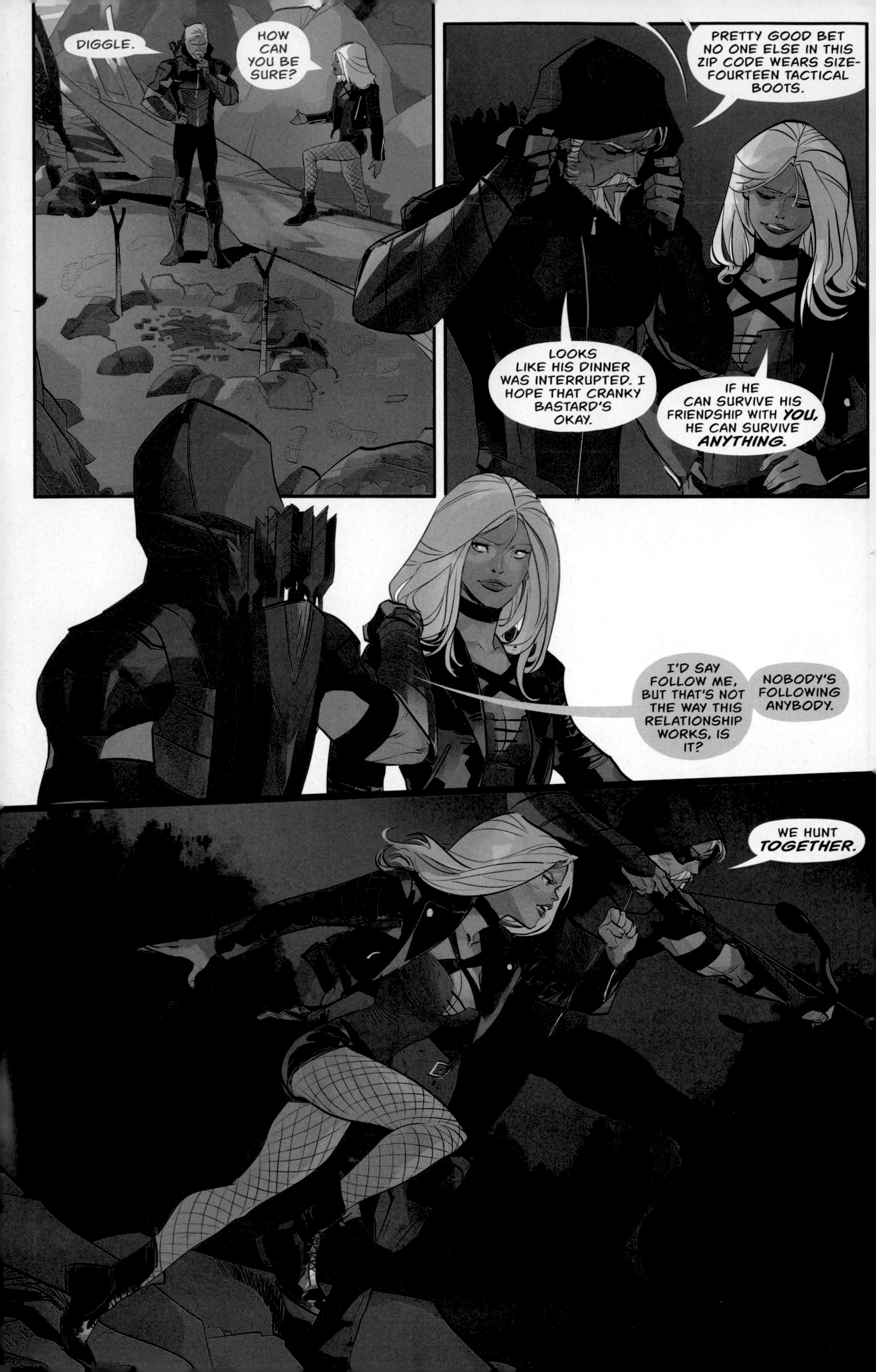
DIGGLE.
HOW CAN YOU BE SURE?
PRETTY GOOD BET NO ONE ELSE IN THIS ZIP CODE WEARS SIZE-FOURTEEN TACTICAL BOOTS.
LOOKS LIKE HIS DINNER WAS INTERRUPTED. I HOPE THAT CRANKY BASTARD'S OKAY.
IF HE CAN SURVIVE HIS FRIENDSHIP WITH *YOU,* HE CAN SURVIVE *ANYTHING.*
I'D SAY FOLLOW ME, BUT THAT'S NOT THE WAY THIS RELATIONSHIP WORKS, IS IT?
NOBODY'S FOLLOWING ANYBODY.
WE HUNT *TOGETHER.*

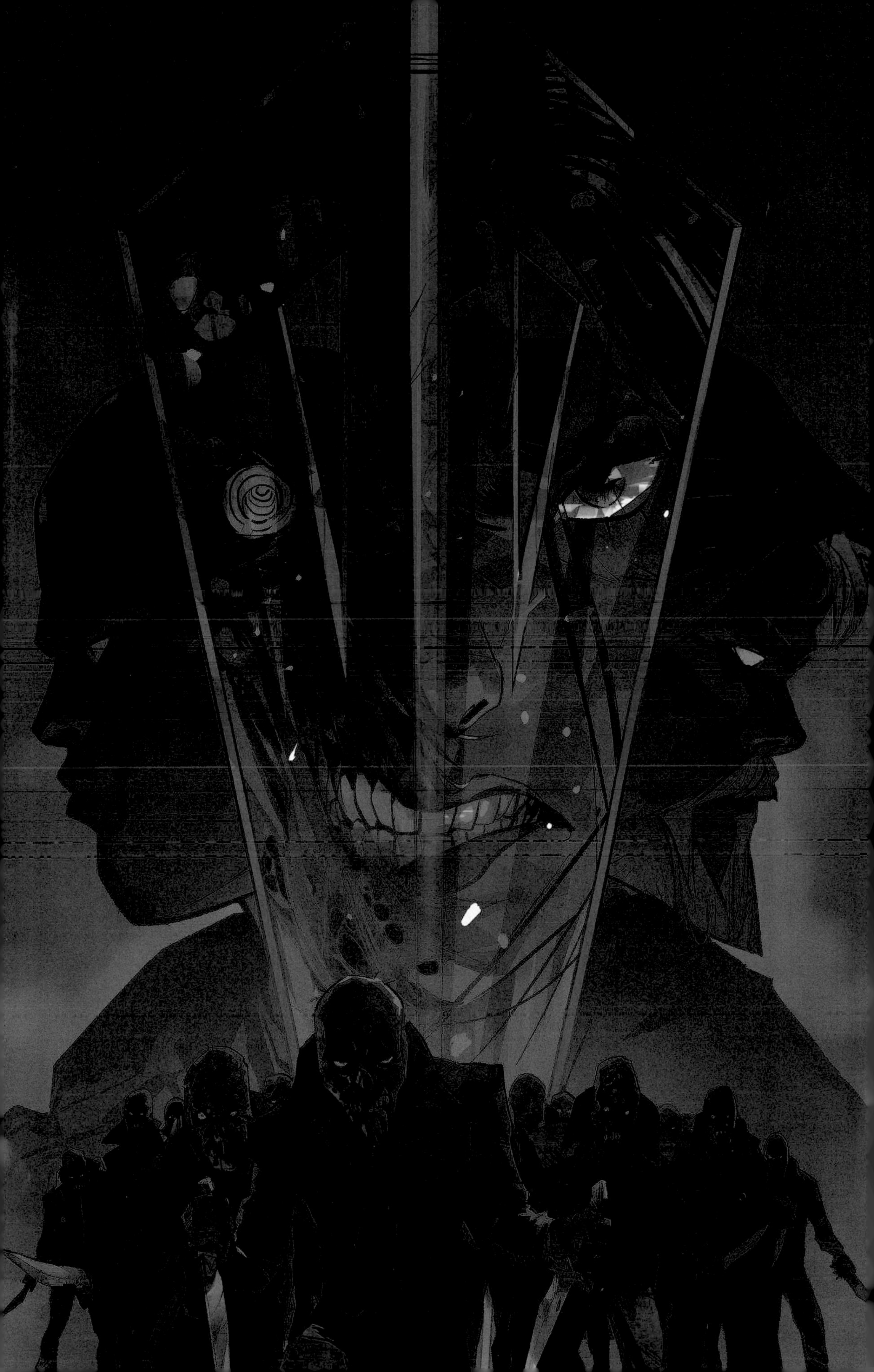

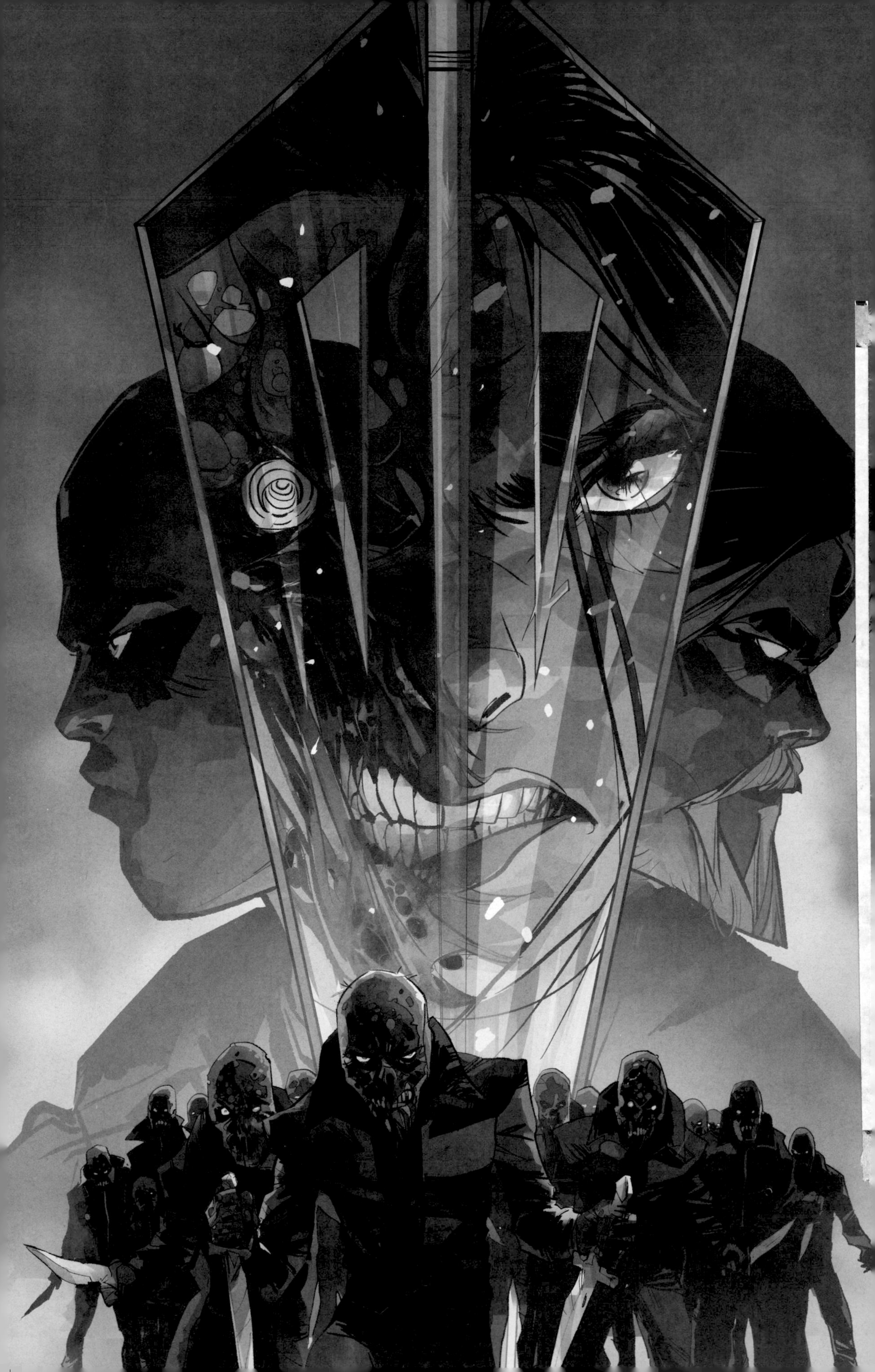

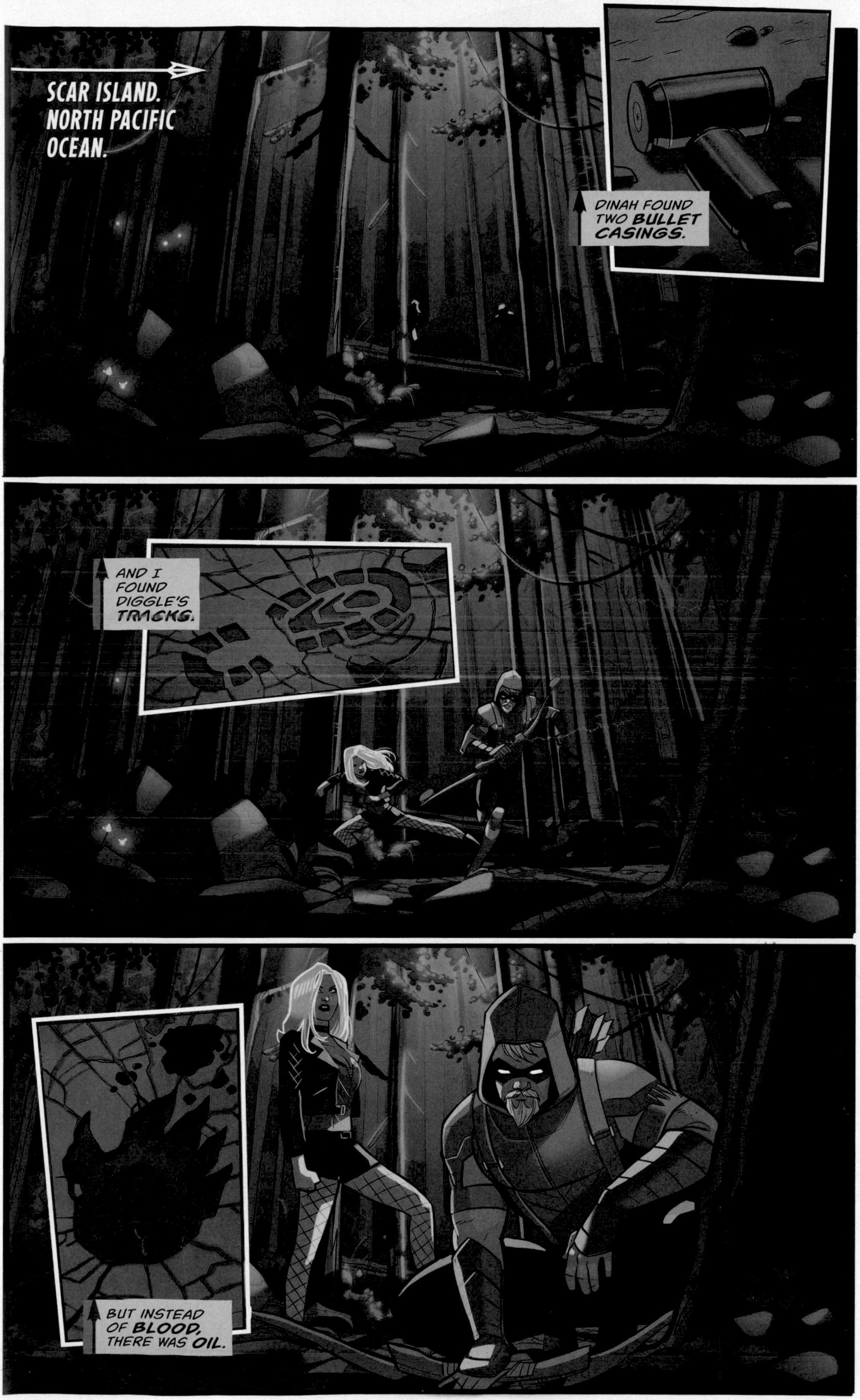
SCAR ISLAND. NORTH PACIFIC OCEAN.
DINAH FOUND TWO BULLET CASINGS.
AND I FOUND DIGGLE'S TRACKS.
BUT INSTEAD OF BLOOD, THERE WAS OIL.

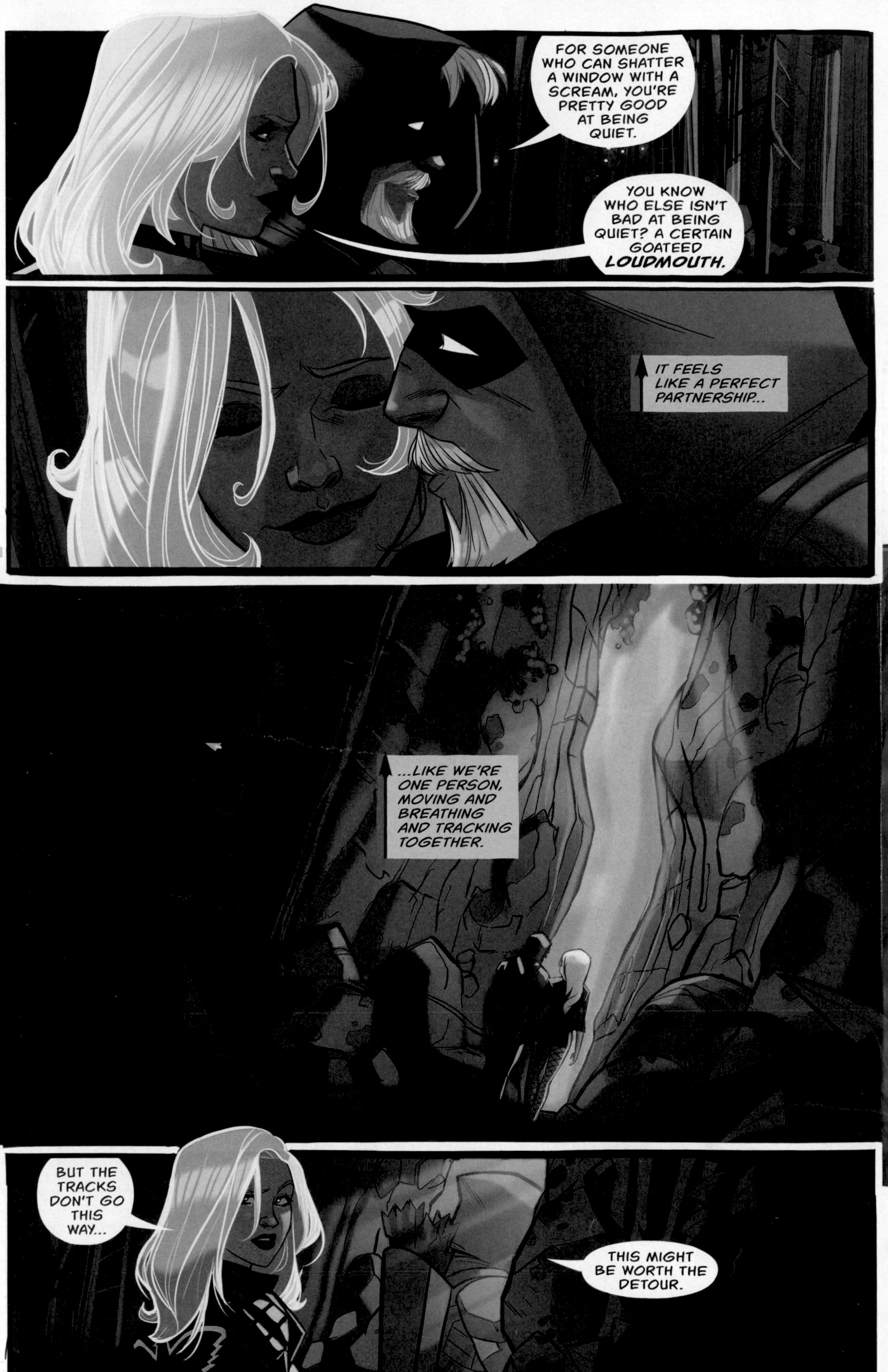
FOR SOMEONE WHO CAN SHATTER A WINDOW WITH A SCREAM, YOU'RE PRETTY GOOD AT BEING QUIET.
YOU KNOW WHO ELSE ISN'T BAD AT BEING QUIET? A CERTAIN GOATEED LOUDMOUTH.
IT FEELS LIKE A PERFECT PARTNERSHIP...
...LIKE WE'RE ONE PERSON, MOVING AND BREATHING AND TRACKING TOGETHER.
BUT THE TRACKS DON'T GO THIS WAY...
THIS MIGHT BE WORTH THE DETOUR.

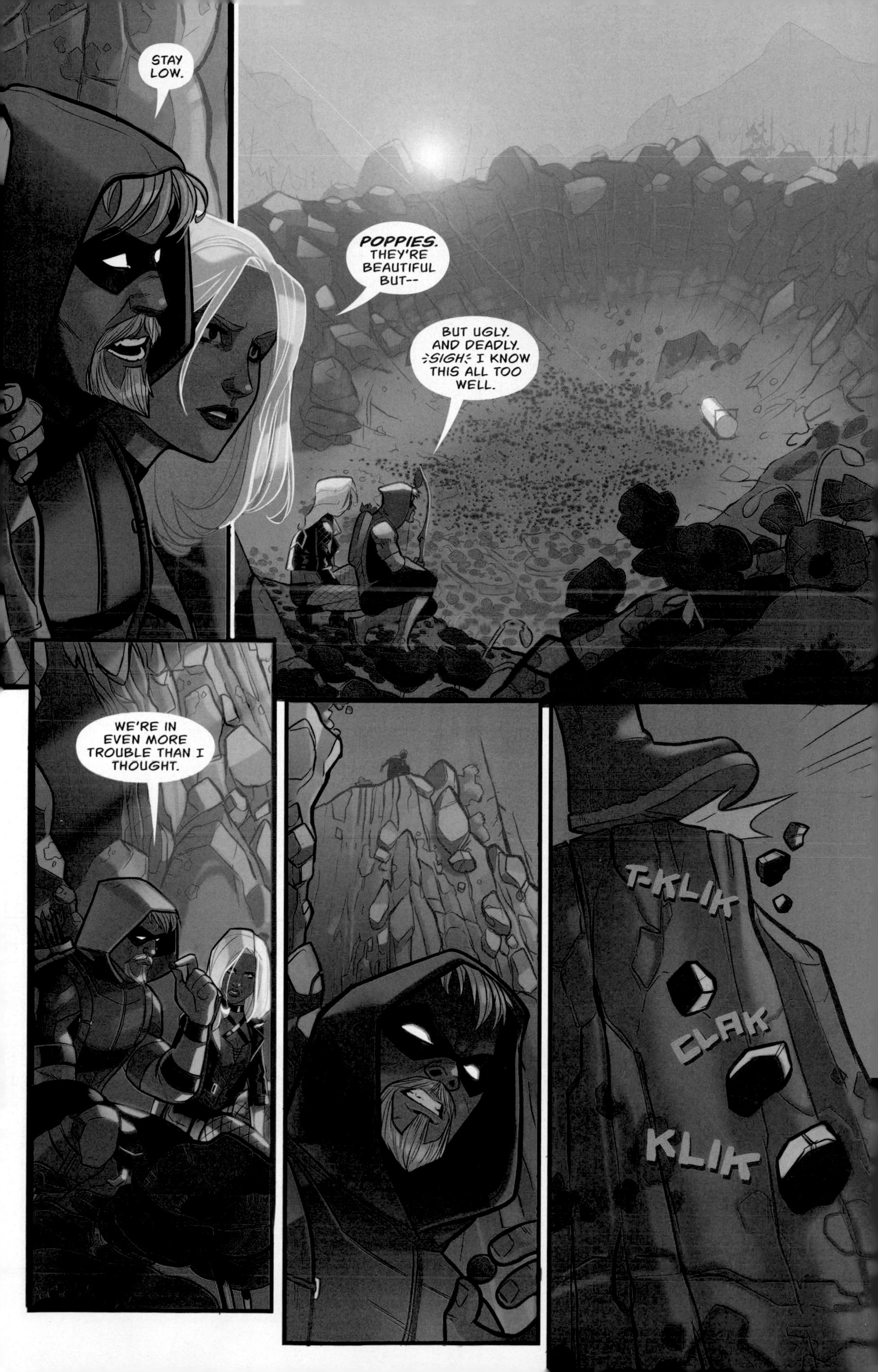
STAY LOW.
POPPIES. THEY'RE BEAUTIFUL BUT--
BUT UGLY. AND DEADLY. SIGH I KNOW THIS ALL TOO WELL.
WE'RE IN EVEN MORE TROUBLE THAN I THOUGHT.
T-KLIK
CLAK
KLIK

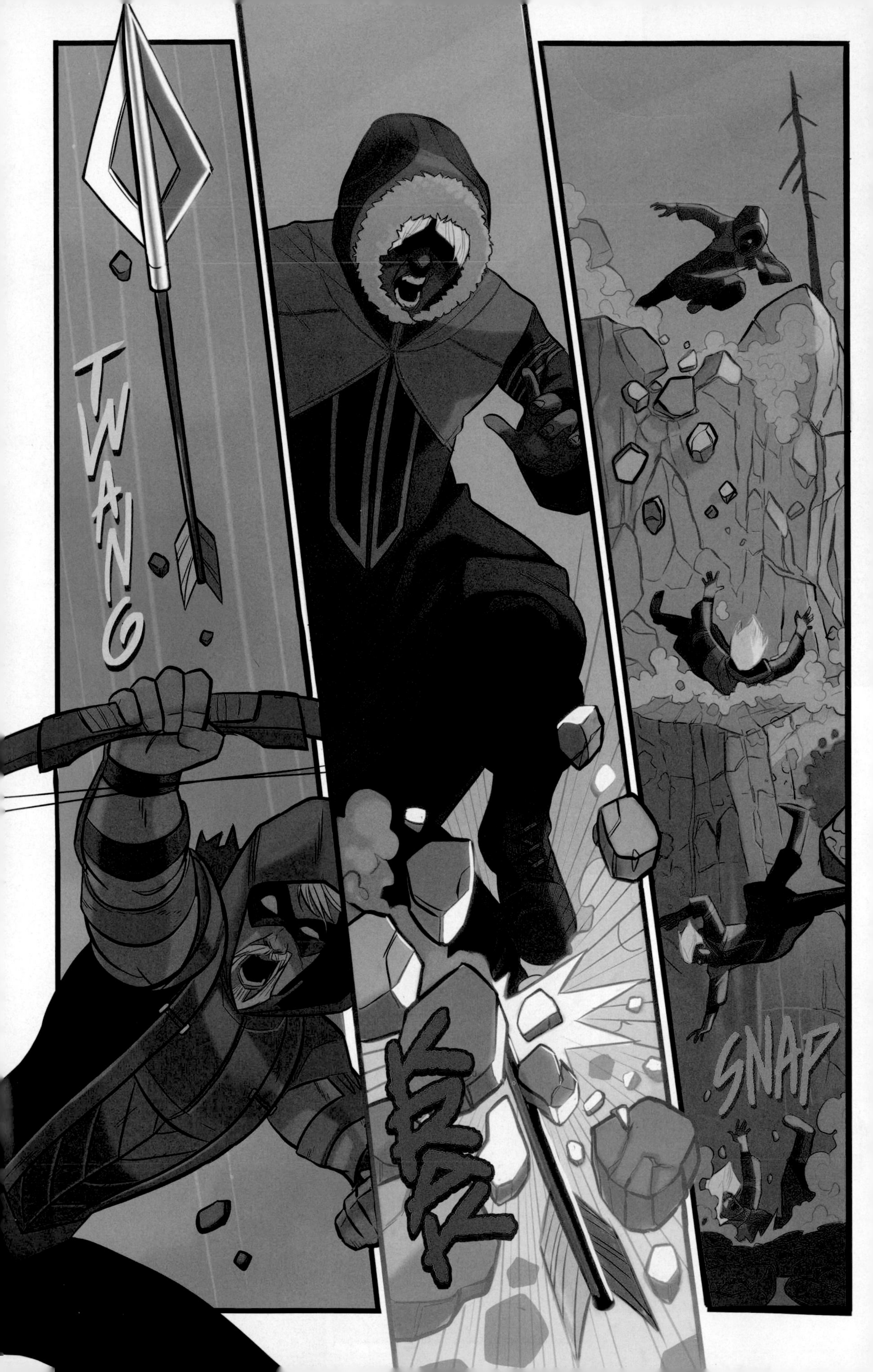
TWANG
KRAK
SNAP

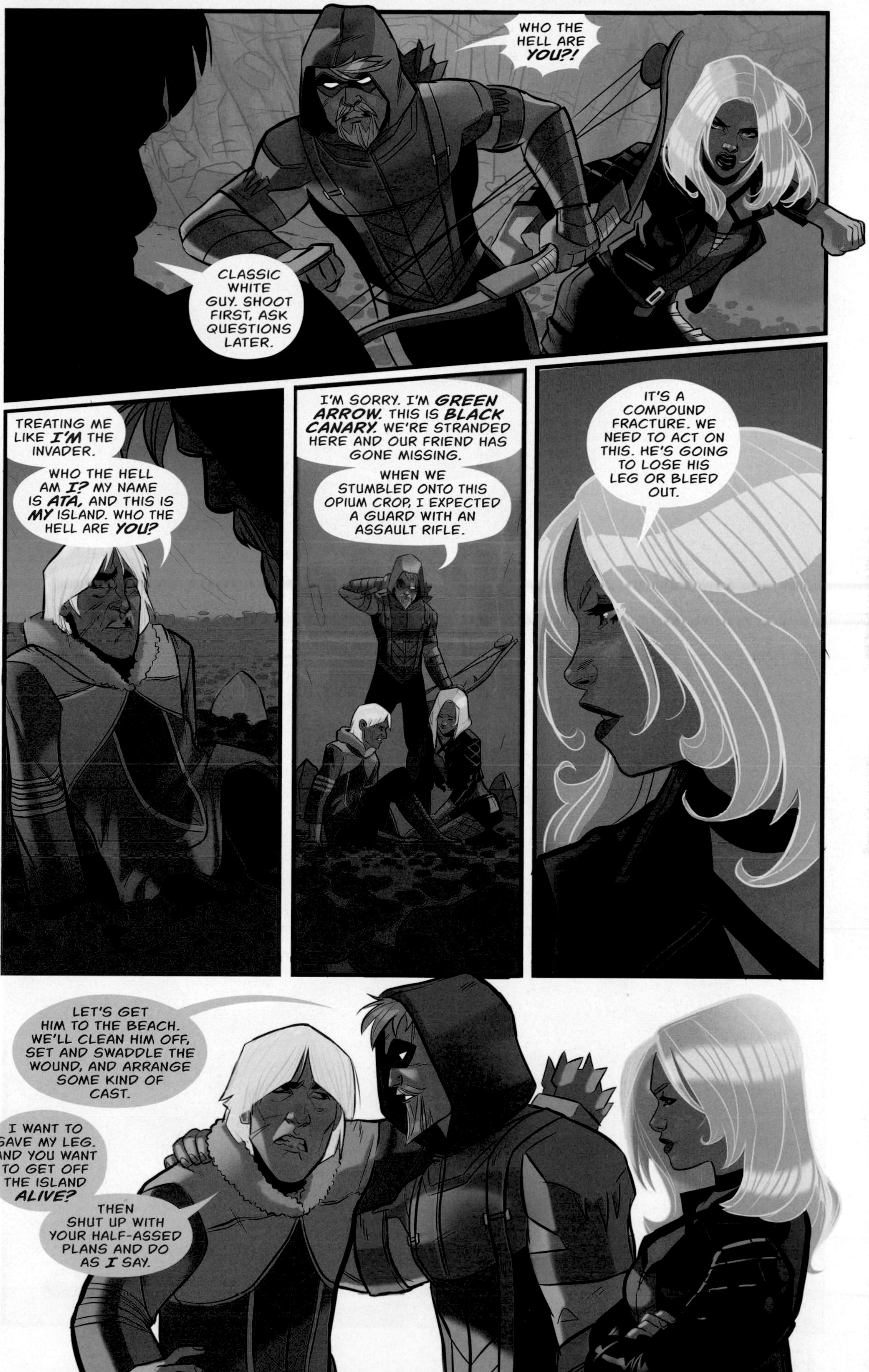
WHO THE HELL ARE *YOU?!*
CLASSIC WHITE GUY. SHOOT FIRST, ASK QUESTIONS LATER.
TREATING ME LIKE *I'M* THE INVADER.
WHO THE HELL AM *I?* MY NAME IS *ATA,* AND THIS IS *MY* ISLAND. WHO THE HELL ARE *YOU?*
I'M SORRY. I'M *GREEN ARROW.* THIS IS *BLACK CANARY.* WE'RE STRANDED HERE AND OUR FRIEND HAS GONE MISSING.
WHEN WE STUMBLED ONTO THIS OPIUM CROP, I EXPECTED A GUARD WITH AN ASSAULT RIFLE.
IT'S A COMPOUND FRACTURE. WE NEED TO ACT ON THIS. HE'S GOING TO LOSE HIS LEG OR BLEED OUT.
LET'S GET HIM TO THE BEACH. WE'LL CLEAN HIM OFF, SET AND SWADDLE THE WOUND, AND ARRANGE SOME KIND OF CAST.
I WANT TO SAVE MY LEG. AND YOU WANT TO GET OFF THE ISLAND *ALIVE?*
THEN SHUT UP WITH YOUR HALF-ASSED PLANS AND DO AS *I* SAY.

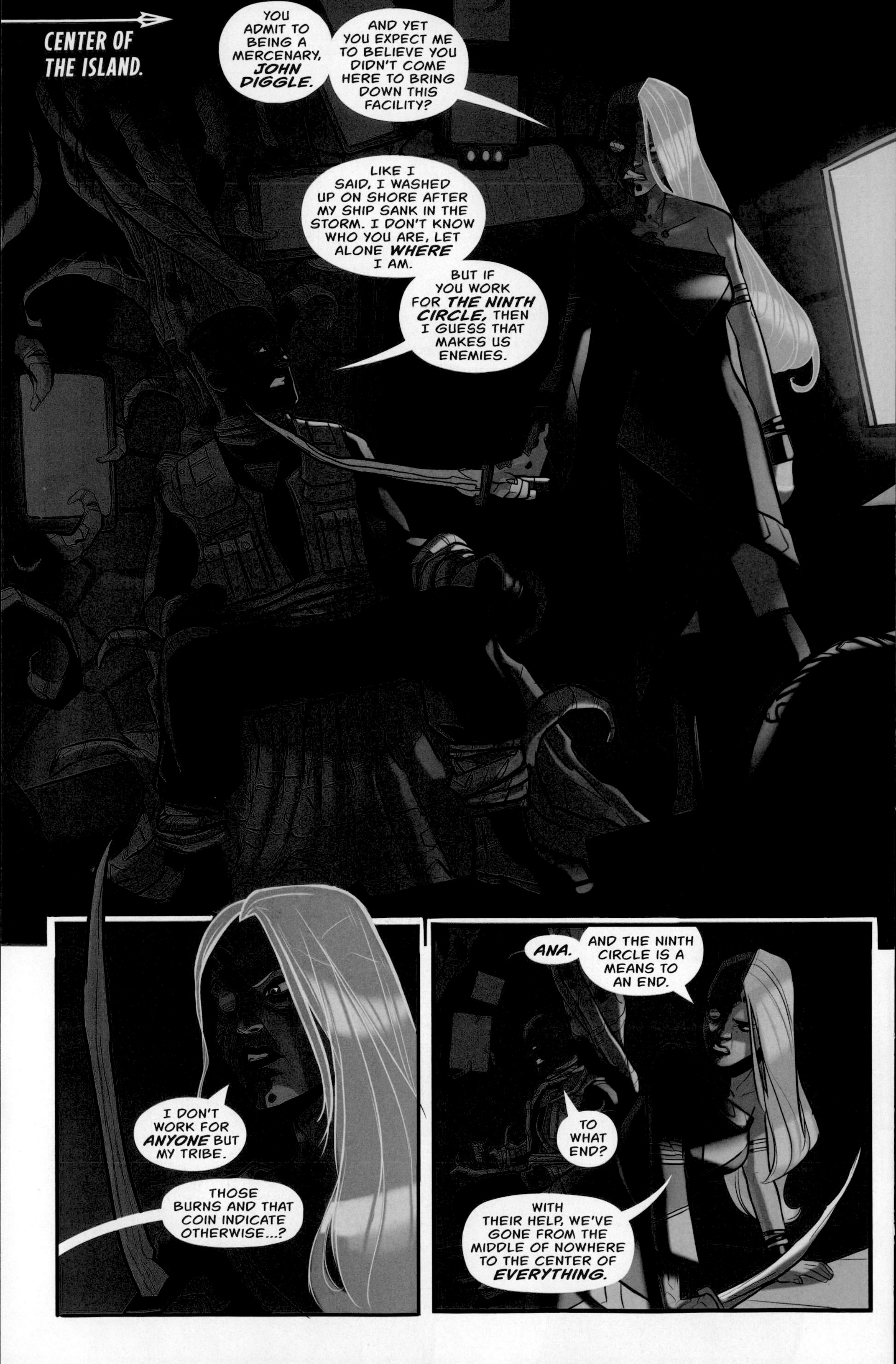

CENTER OF THE ISLAND.
YOU ADMIT TO BEING A MERCENARY, JOHN DIGGLE.
AND YET YOU EXPECT ME TO BELIEVE YOU DIDN'T COME HERE TO BRING DOWN THIS FACILITY?
LIKE I SAID, I WASHED UP ON SHORE AFTER MY SHIP SANK IN THE STORM. I DON'T KNOW WHO YOU ARE, LET ALONE WHERE I AM.
BUT IF YOU WORK FOR THE NINTH CIRCLE, THEN I GUESS THAT MAKES US ENEMIES.
I DON'T WORK FOR ANYONE BUT MY TRIBE.
THOSE BURNS AND THAT COIN INDICATE OTHERWISE...?
ANA.
AND THE NINTH CIRCLE IS A MEANS TO AN END.
TO WHAT END?
WITH THEIR HELP, WE'VE GONE FROM THE MIDDLE OF NOWHERE TO THE CENTER OF EVERYTHING.

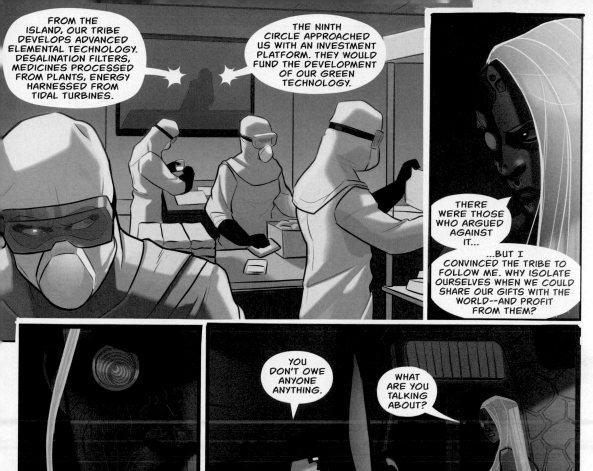

FROM THE ISLAND, OUR TRIBE DEVELOPS ADVANCED ELEMENTAL TECHNOLOGY. DESALINATION FILTERS, MEDICINES PROCESSED FROM PLANTS, ENERGY HARNESSED FROM TIDAL TURBINES.

THE NINTH CIRCLE APPROACHED US WITH AN INVESTMENT PLATFORM. THEY WOULD FUND THE DEVELOPMENT OF OUR GREEN TECHNOLOGY.

THERE WERE THOSE WHO ARGUED AGAINST IT...

...BUT I CONVINCED THE TRIBE TO FOLLOW ME. WHY ISOLATE OURSELVES WHEN WE COULD SHARE OUR GIFTS WITH THE WORLD--AND PROFIT FROM THEM?

YOU DON'T OWE ANYONE ANYTHING.

WHAT ARE YOU TALKING ABOUT?

BUT I DIDN'T REALIZE I HAD SIGNED THE CONTRACT WITH MY FLESH.

AND I DIDN'T PLAN ON PAYING BACK THE LOAN BY FARMING POPPIES AND PROCESSING A POWERFUL STRAIN OF HEROIN IN OUR MINERAL-RICH VOLCANIC SOIL.

KNOK KNOK

HAVEN'T BEEN COMPLETELY HONEST WITH YOU. THAT SHIP THAT SANK AND STRANDED ME HERE? IT WAS THE *INFERNO*.

DANTE IS DEAD. THE NINTH CIRCLE IS *FINISHED*.

EVEN IF DANTE IS DEAD...

...THE NINTH CIRCLE IS *MORE* THAN A MAN.

AND *YOU'RE* MORE THAN SOMEBODY'S TOOL.

YOU SOUND LIKE...

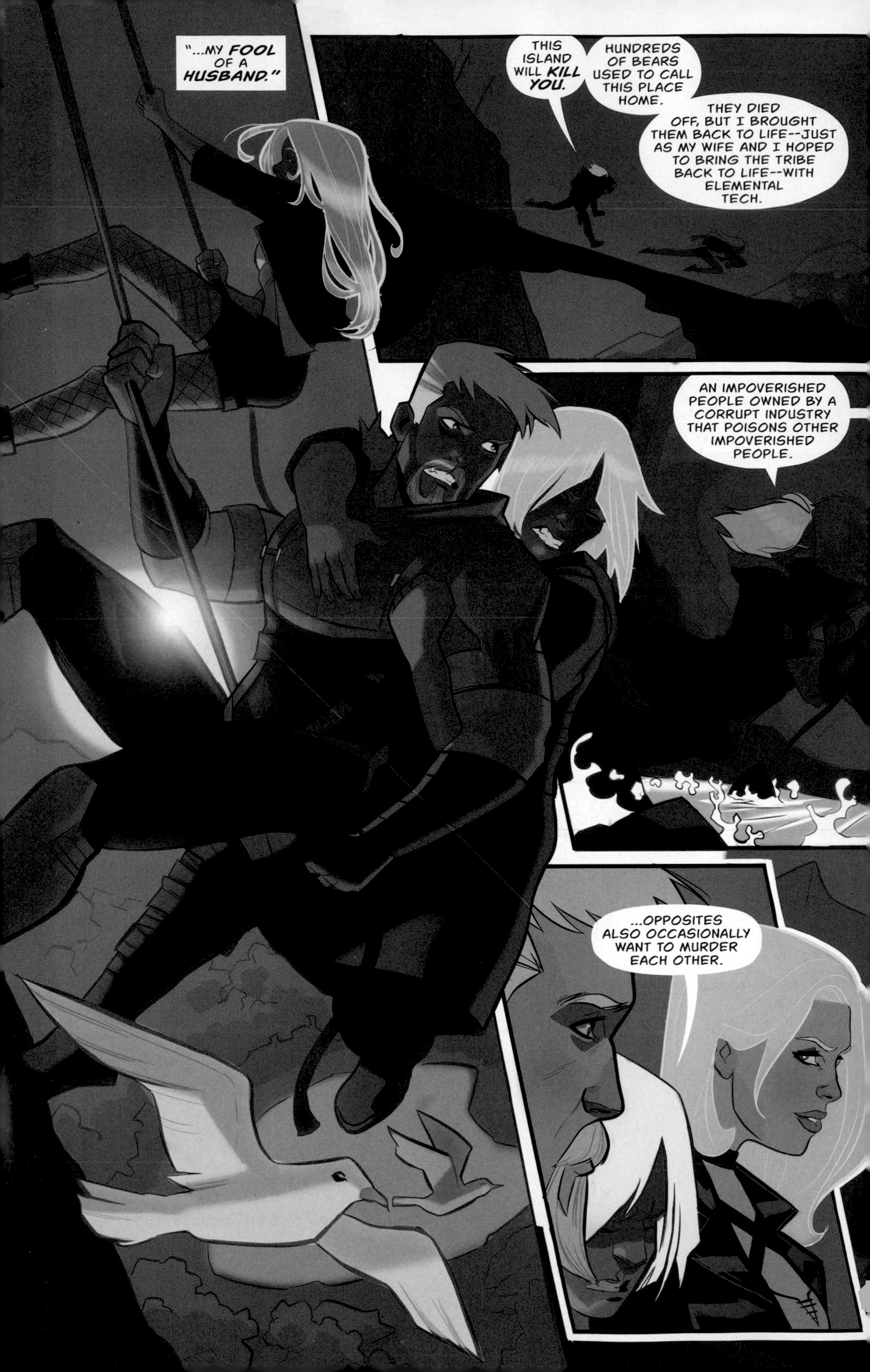
"...MY FOOL OF A HUSBAND."
THIS ISLAND WILL KILL YOU.
HUNDREDS OF BEARS USED TO CALL THIS PLACE HOME.
THEY DIED OFF, BUT I BROUGHT THEM BACK TO LIFE--JUST AS MY WIFE AND I HOPED TO BRING THE TRIBE BACK TO LIFE--WITH ELEMENTAL TECH.
AN IMPOVERISHED PEOPLE OWNED BY A CORRUPT INDUSTRY THAT POISONS OTHER IMPOVERISHED PEOPLE.
...OPPOSITES ALSO OCCASIONALLY WANT TO MURDER EACH OTHER.

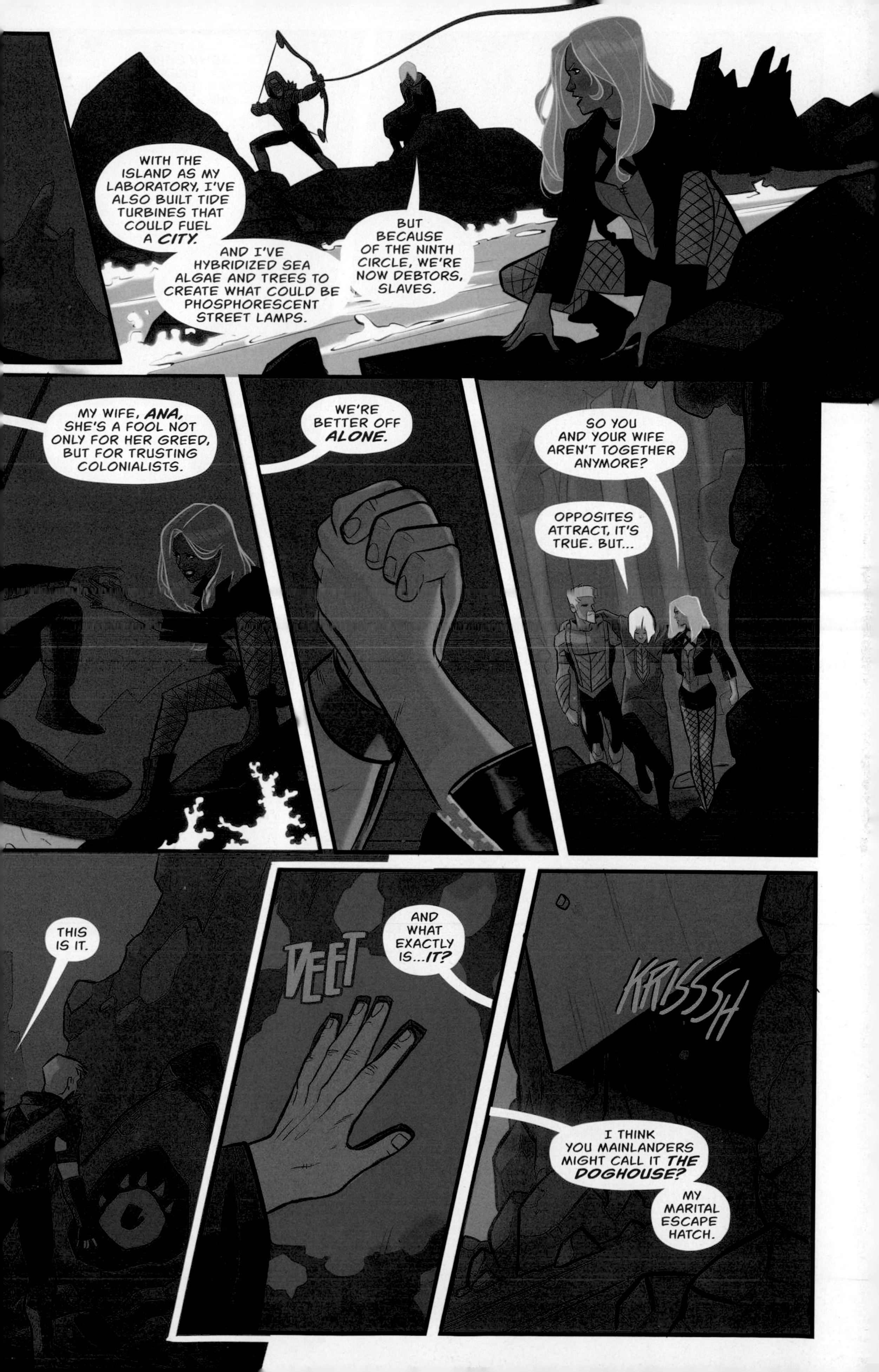
WITH THE ISLAND AS MY LABORATORY, I'VE ALSO BUILT TIDE TURBINES THAT COULD FUEL A CITY.
AND I'VE HYBRIDIZED SEA ALGAE AND TREES TO CREATE WHAT COULD BE PHOSPHORESCENT STREET LAMPS.
BUT BECAUSE OF THE NINTH CIRCLE, WE'RE NOW DEBTORS, SLAVES.
MY WIFE, ANA, SHE'S A FOOL NOT ONLY FOR HER GREED, BUT FOR TRUSTING COLONIALISTS.
WE'RE BETTER OFF ALONE.
SO YOU AND YOUR WIFE AREN'T TOGETHER ANYMORE?
OPPOSITES ATTRACT, IT'S TRUE. BUT...
THIS IS IT.
DEEET
AND WHAT EXACTLY IS...IT?
KRISSSH
I THINK YOU MAINLANDERS MIGHT CALL IT THE DOGHOUSE?
MY MARITAL ESCAPE HATCH.

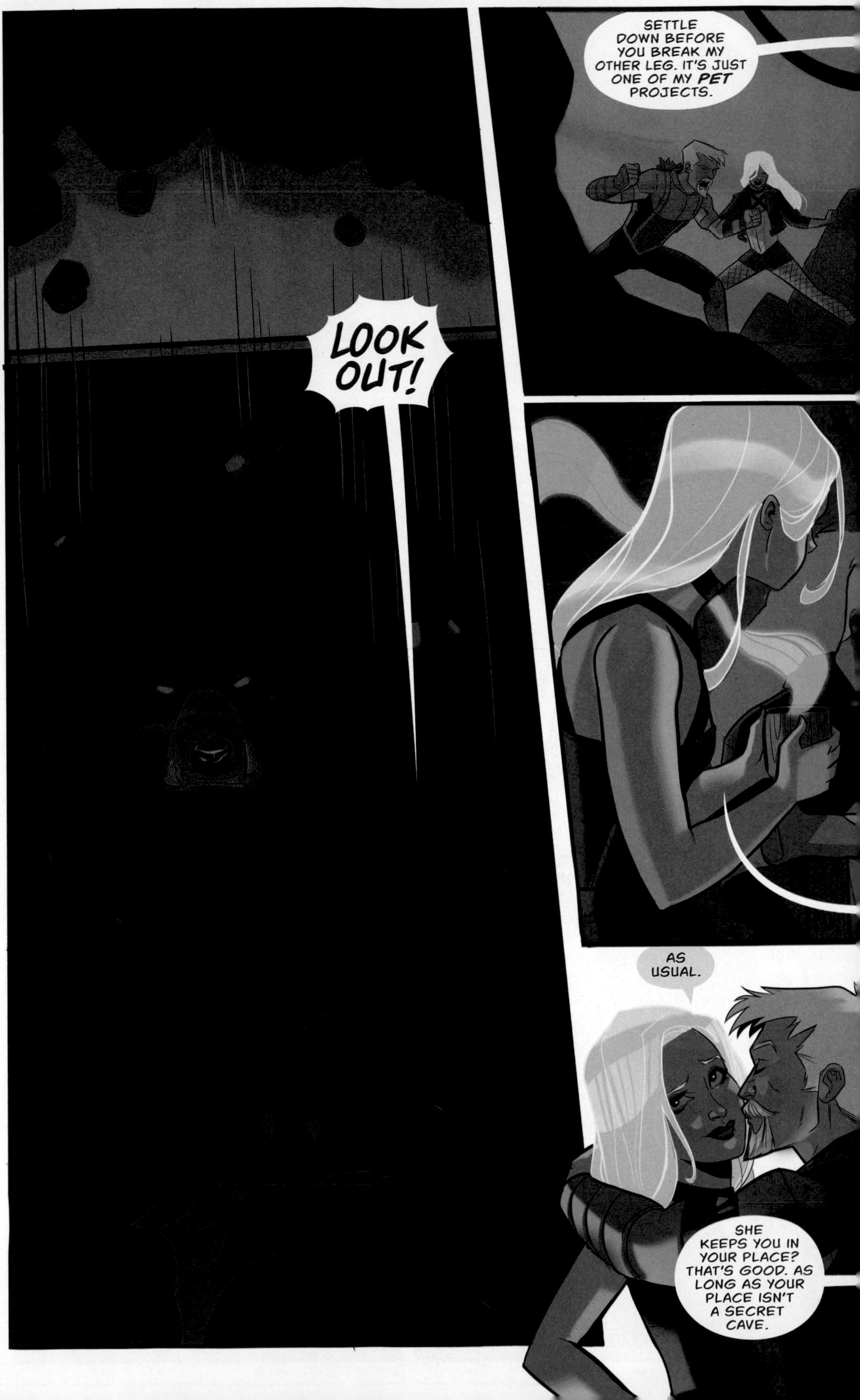
LOOK OUT!
SETTLE DOWN BEFORE YOU BREAK MY OTHER LEG. IT'S JUST ONE OF MY PET PROJECTS.
AS USUAL.
SHE KEEPS YOU IN YOUR PLACE? THAT'S GOOD. AS LONG AS YOUR PLACE ISN'T A SECRET CAVE.

HELP ME TO MY BED OVER THERE. I'LL NEED YOU TO FETCH SOME THINGS. OPIATES. A BONE GLUE MADE FROM GROUND-UP SHELLS. A CONCH FUNGUS POULTICE WITH ADVANCED HEALING PROPERTIES.

I WON'T BE BREAKDANCING ANYTIME SOON, BUT THIS WILL HELP.

AMAZING. I WISH I COULD INVEST IN SOME OF THESE PROJECTS, BUT MY COMPANY...

DON'T START FEELING SORRY FOR YOURSELF, OLLIE.

YOU'RE RIGHT.

I'VE BEEN KNOWN TO THINK OF MYSELF AS THE SELF-PITYING CENTER OF THE UNIVERSE.

OR SELF-AGGRANDIZING.

SHE HELPS CHECK THE BIG GREEN EGO.

FROM WHAT I'M HEARING, ATA, THE LAST THING YOU NEED IS A BUNCH OF MAINLANDERS INTERFERING WITH YOUR AFFAIRS.

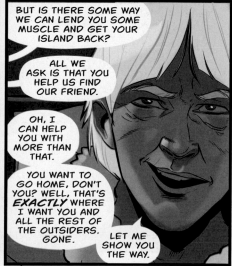

BUT IS THERE SOME WAY WE CAN LEND YOU SOME MUSCLE AND GET YOUR ISLAND BACK?

ALL WE ASK IS THAT YOU HELP US FIND OUR FRIEND.

OH, I CAN HELP YOU WITH MORE THAN THAT.

YOU WANT TO GO HOME, DON'T YOU? WELL, THAT'S EXACTLY WHERE I WANT YOU AND ALL THE REST OF THE OUTSIDERS GONE.

LET ME SHOW YOU THE WAY.

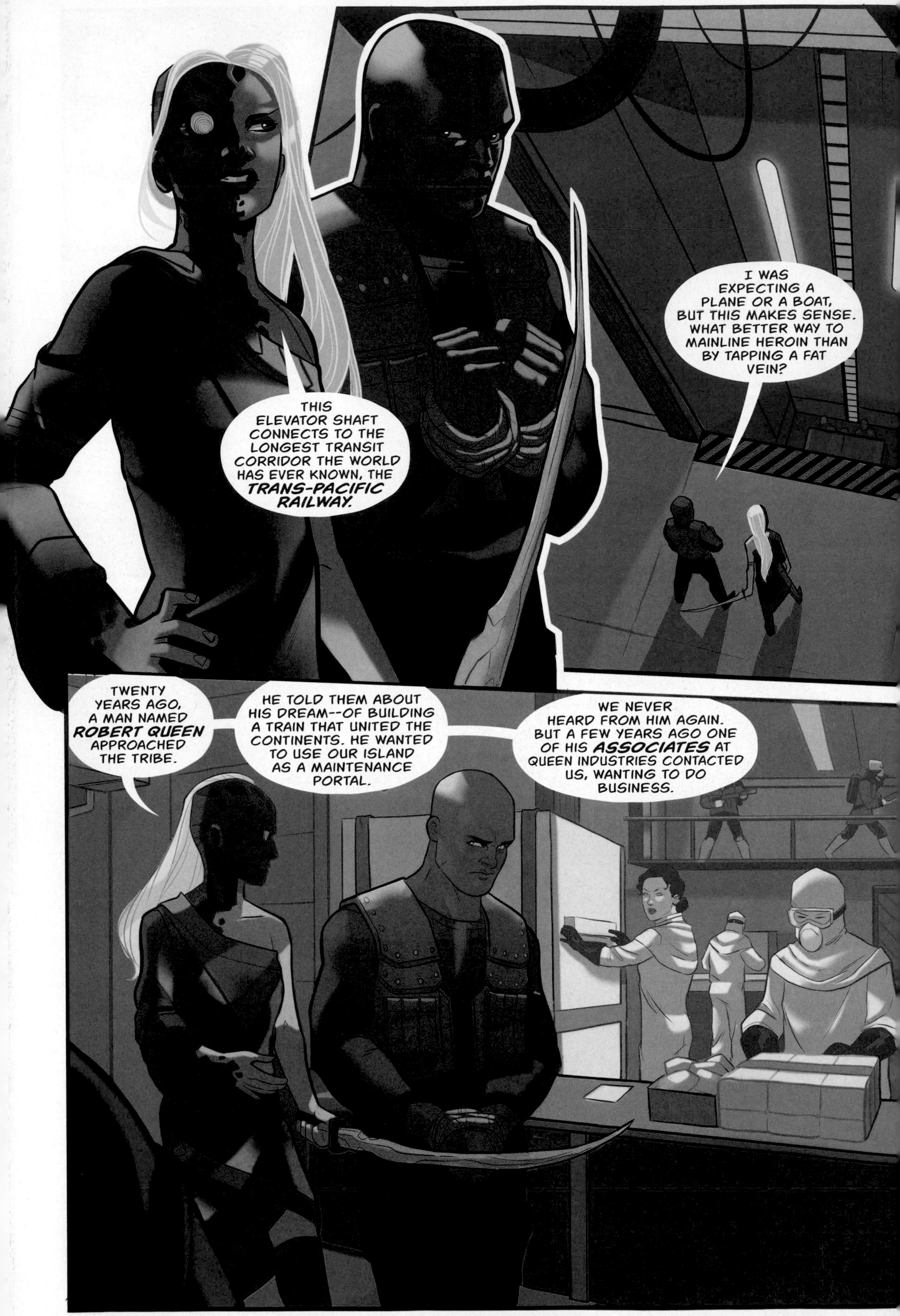

THIS ELEVATOR SHAFT CONNECTS TO THE LONGEST TRANSIT CORRIDOR THE WORLD HAS EVER KNOWN, THE ***TRANS-PACIFIC RAILWAY.***
I WAS EXPECTING A PLANE OR A BOAT, BUT THIS MAKES SENSE. WHAT BETTER WAY TO MAINLINE HEROIN THAN BY TAPPING A FAT VEIN?
TWENTY YEARS AGO, A MAN NAMED ***ROBERT QUEEN*** APPROACHED THE TRIBE.
HE TOLD THEM ABOUT HIS DREAM--OF BUILDING A TRAIN THAT UNITED THE CONTINENTS. HE WANTED TO USE OUR ISLAND AS A MAINTENANCE PORTAL.
WE NEVER HEARD FROM HIM AGAIN. BUT A FEW YEARS AGO ONE OF HIS ***ASSOCIATES*** AT QUEEN INDUSTRIES CONTACTED US, WANTING TO DO BUSINESS.

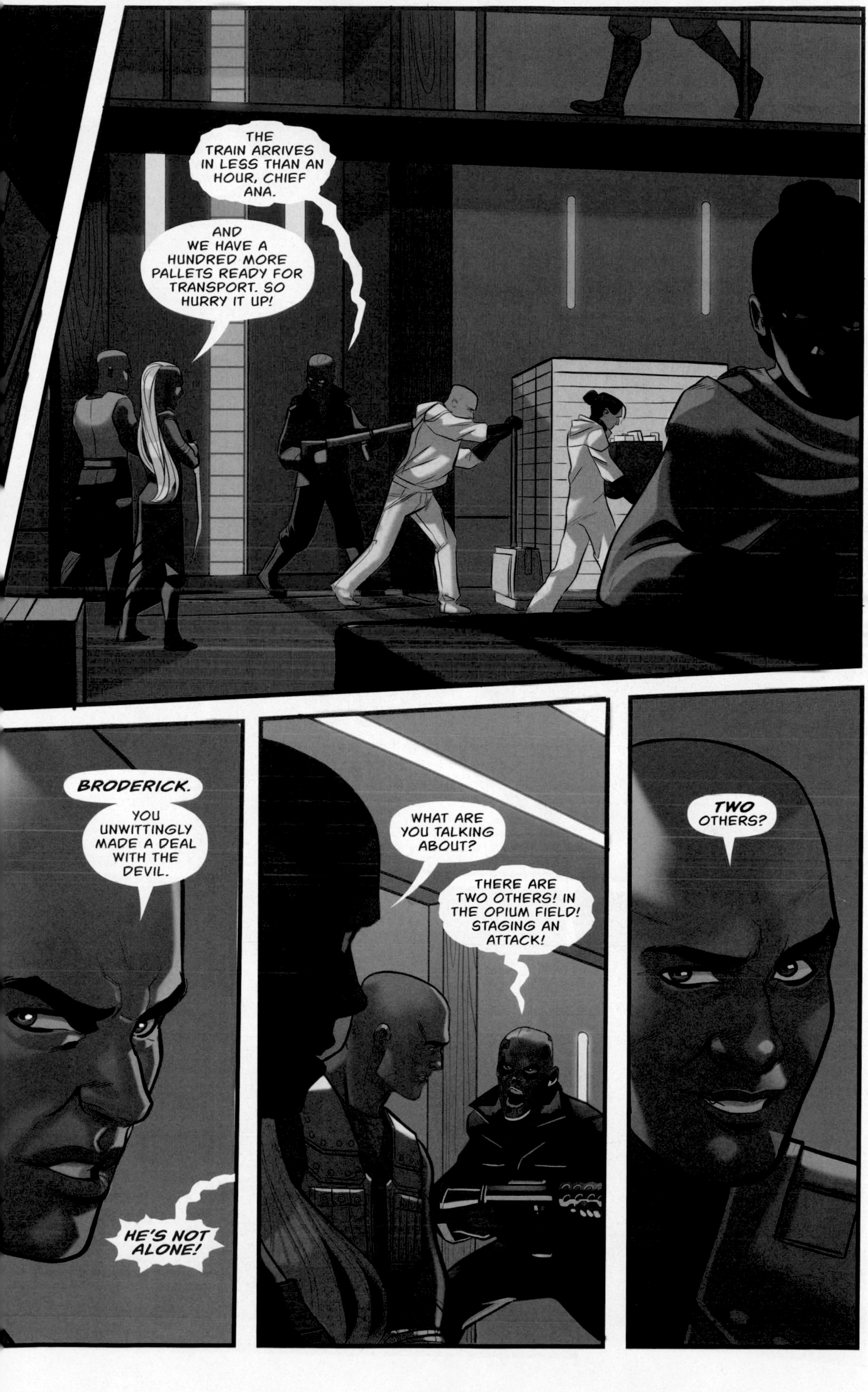
THE TRAIN ARRIVES IN LESS THAN AN HOUR, CHIEF ANA.
AND WE HAVE A HUNDRED MORE PALLETS READY FOR TRANSPORT. SO HURRY IT UP!
BRODERICK.
YOU UNWITTINGLY MADE A DEAL WITH THE DEVIL.
HE'S NOT ALONE!
WHAT ARE YOU TALKING ABOUT?
THERE ARE TWO OTHERS! IN THE OPIUM FIELD! STAGING AN ATTACK!
TWO OTHERS?

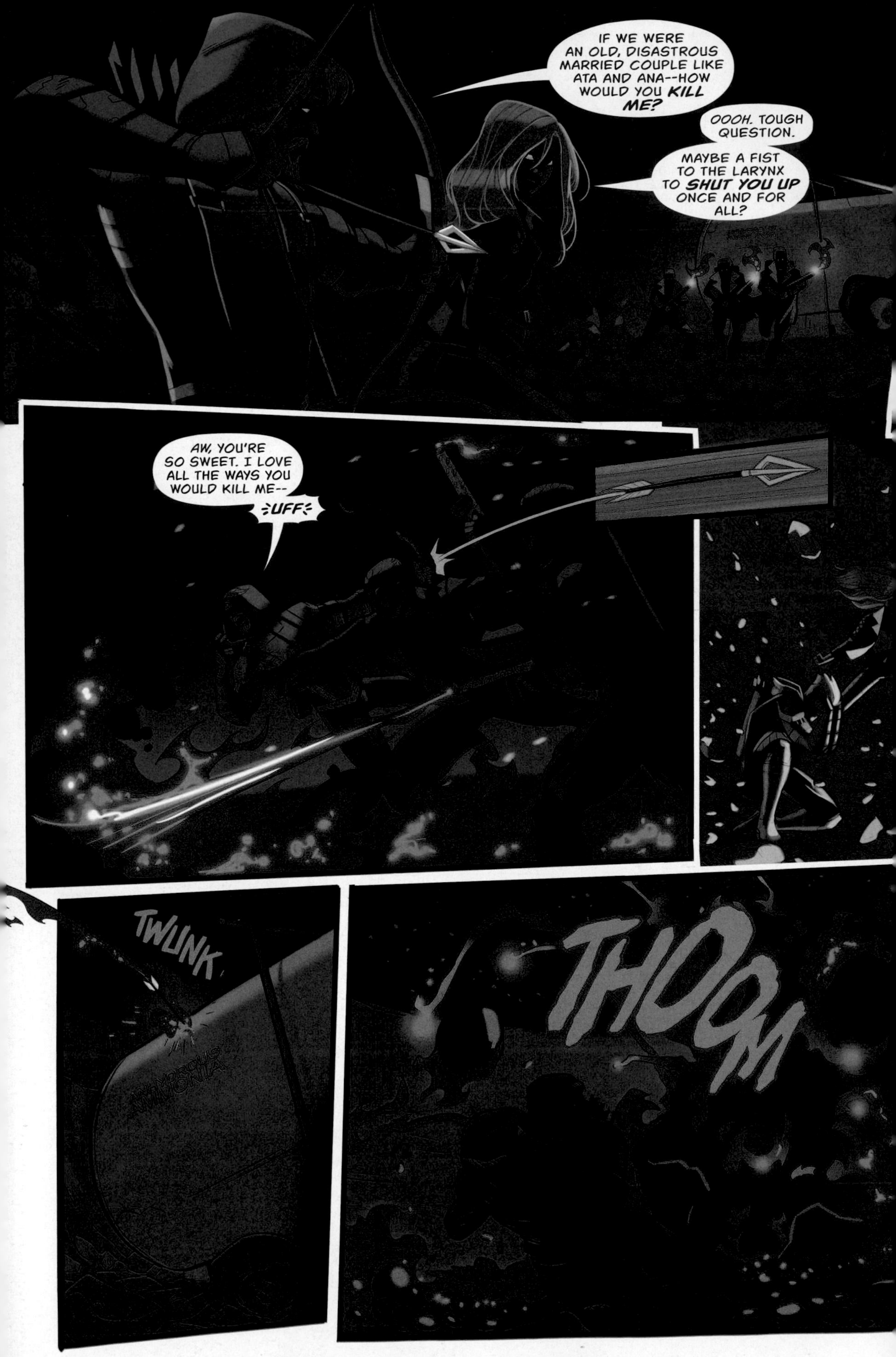
IF WE WERE AN OLD, DISASTROUS MARRIED COUPLE LIKE ATA AND ANA--HOW WOULD YOU KILL ME?
OOOH. TOUGH QUESTION.
MAYBE A FIST TO THE LARYNX TO SHUT YOU UP ONCE AND FOR ALL?
AW, YOU'RE SO SWEET. I LOVE ALL THE WAYS YOU WOULD KILL ME--
UFF
TWUNK
THOOM

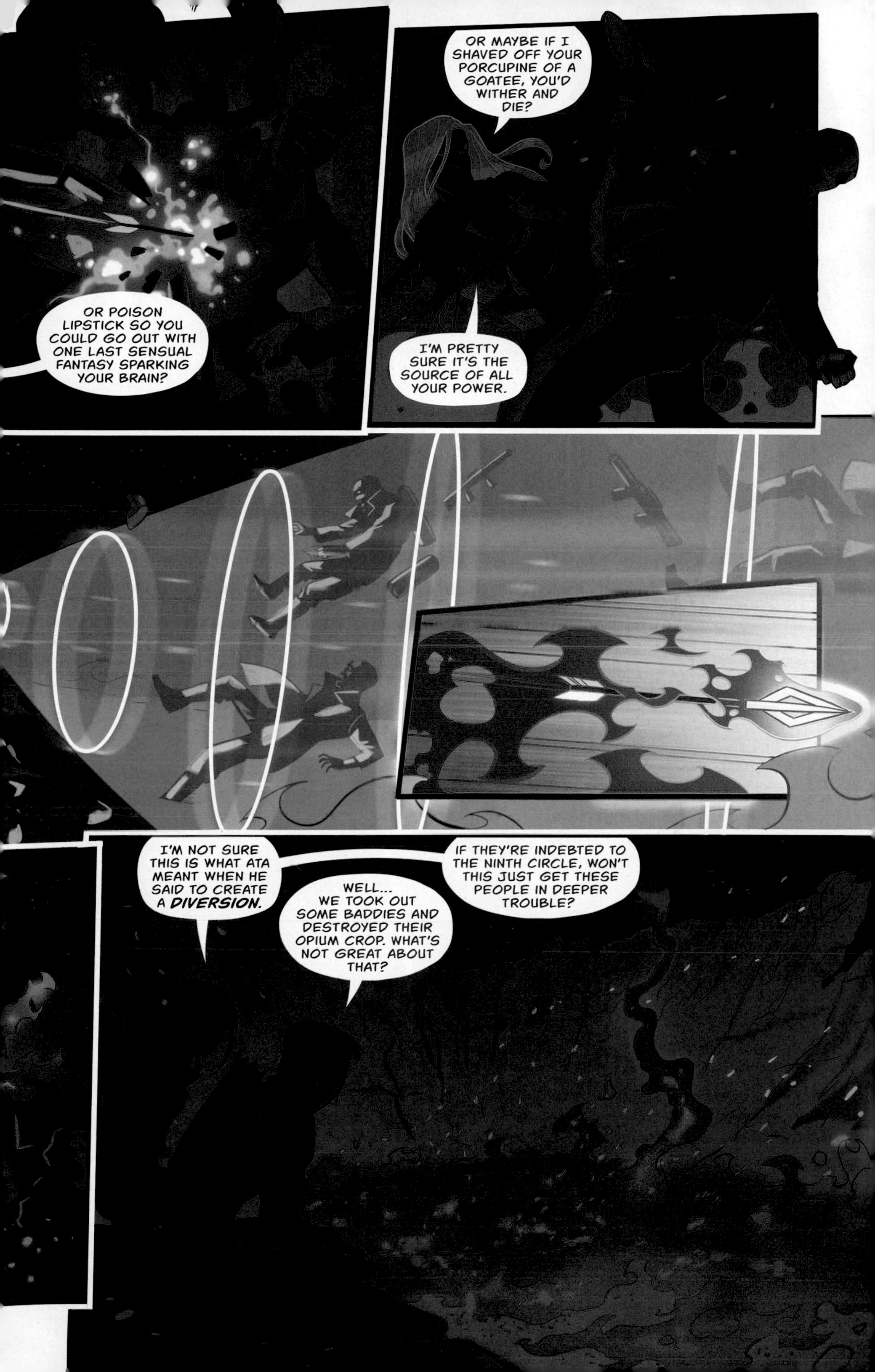
OR POISON LIPSTICK SO YOU COULD GO OUT WITH ONE LAST SENSUAL FANTASY SPARKING YOUR BRAIN?
OR MAYBE IF I SHAVED OFF YOUR PORCUPINE OF A GOATEE, YOU'D WITHER AND DIE?
I'M PRETTY SURE IT'S THE SOURCE OF ALL YOUR POWER.
I'M NOT SURE THIS IS WHAT ATA MEANT WHEN HE SAID TO CREATE A DIVERSION.
IF THEY'RE INDEBTED TO THE NINTH CIRCLE, WON'T THIS JUST GET THESE PEOPLE IN DEEPER TROUBLE?
WELL... WE TOOK OUT SOME BADDIES AND DESTROYED THEIR OPIUM CROP. WHAT'S NOT GREAT ABOUT THAT?

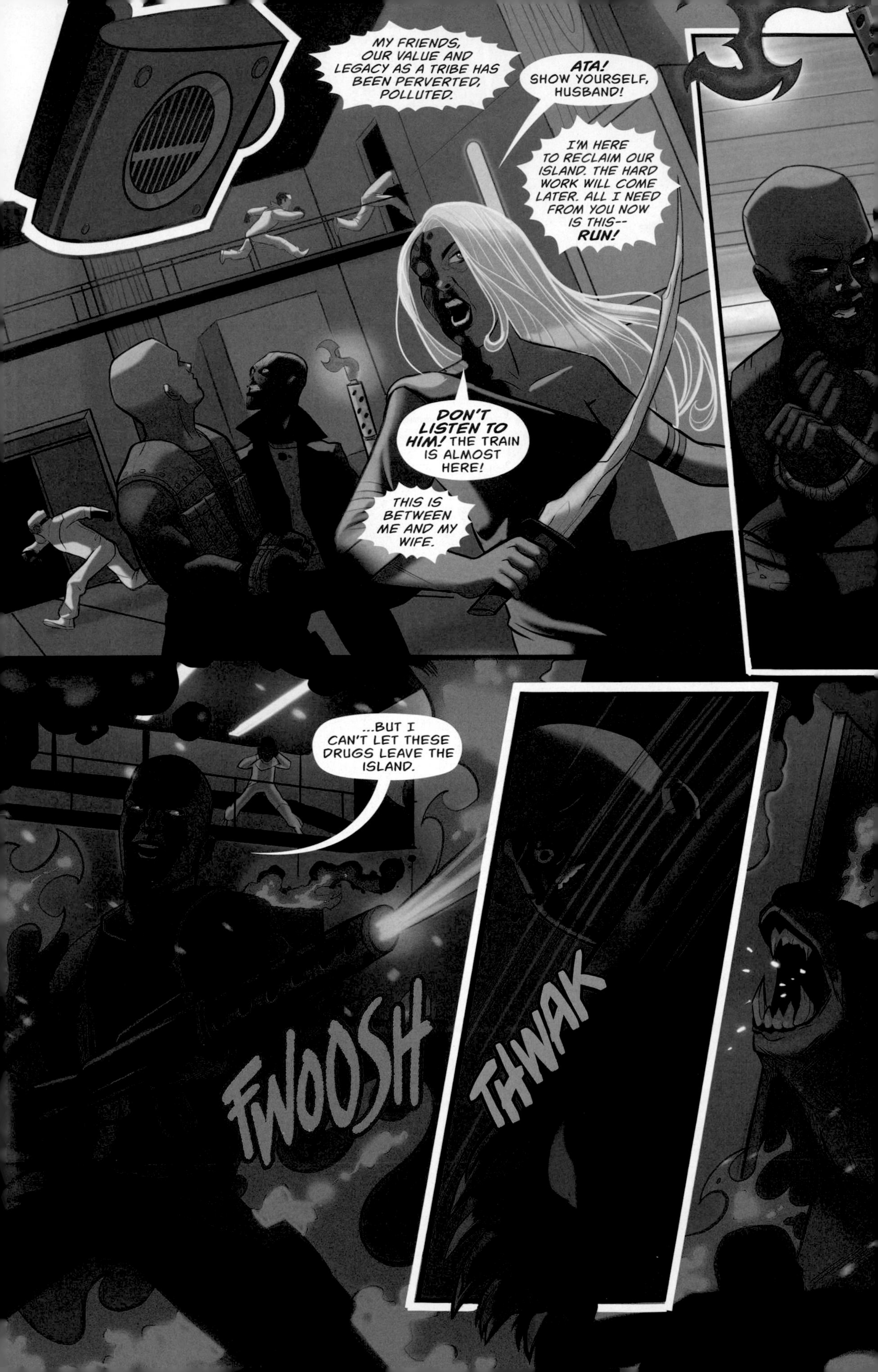
MY FRIENDS, OUR VALUE AND LEGACY AS A TRIBE HAS BEEN PERVERTED, POLLUTED.
ATA! SHOW YOURSELF, HUSBAND!
I'M HERE TO RECLAIM OUR ISLAND. THE HARD WORK WILL COME LATER. ALL I NEED FROM YOU NOW IS THIS-- RUN!
DON'T LISTEN TO HIM! THE TRAIN IS ALMOST HERE!
THIS IS BETWEEN ME AND MY WIFE.
...BUT I CAN'T LET THESE DRUGS LEAVE THE ISLAND.
FWOOSH
THWAK

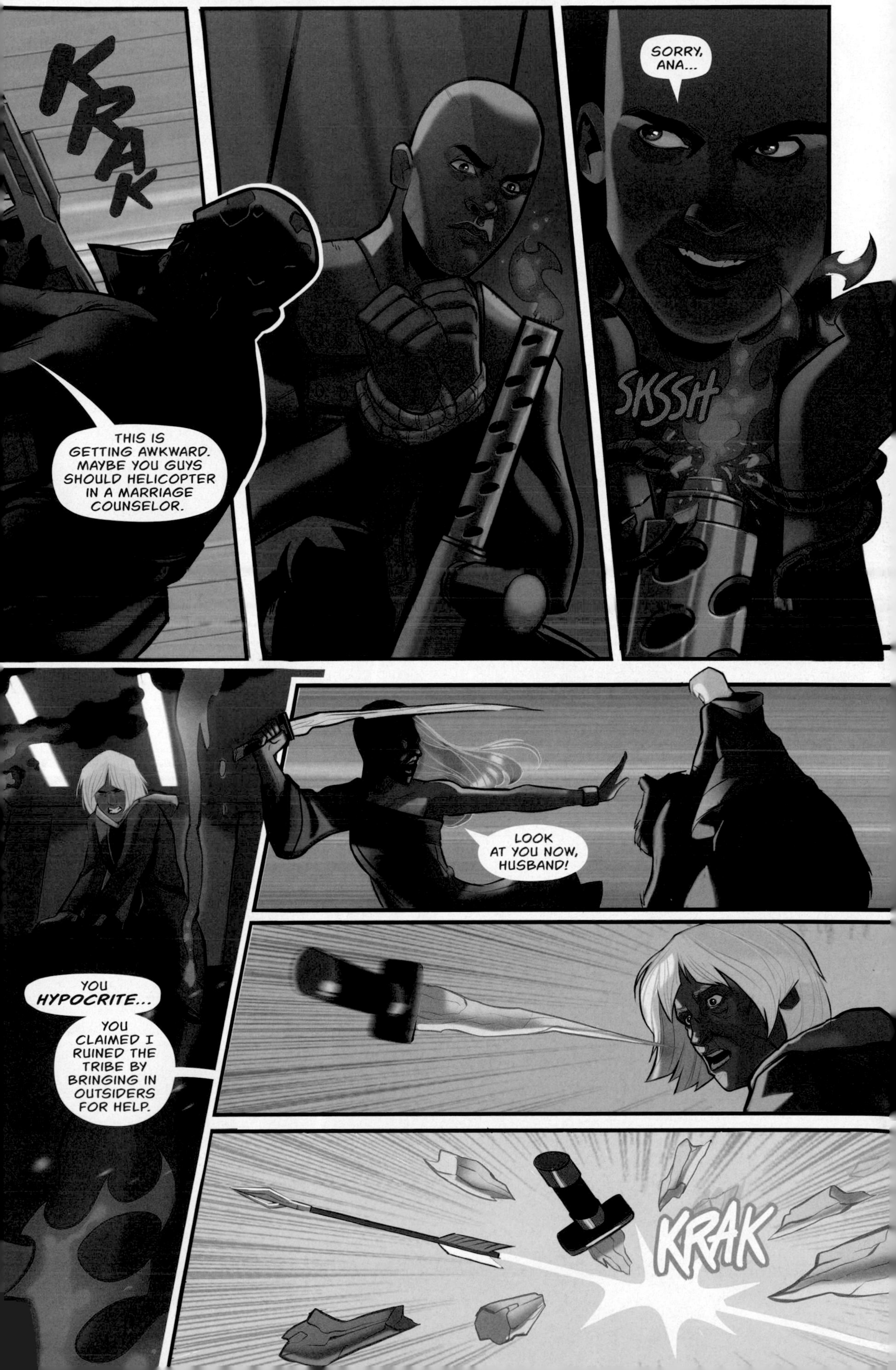
KRAK
THIS IS GETTING AWKWARD. MAYBE YOU GUYS SHOULD HELICOPTER IN A MARRIAGE COUNSELOR.
SORRY, ANA...
SKSSH
LOOK AT YOU NOW, HUSBAND!
YOU *HYPOCRITE...*
YOU CLAIMED I RUINED THE TRIBE BY BRINGING IN OUTSIDERS FOR HELP.
KRAK

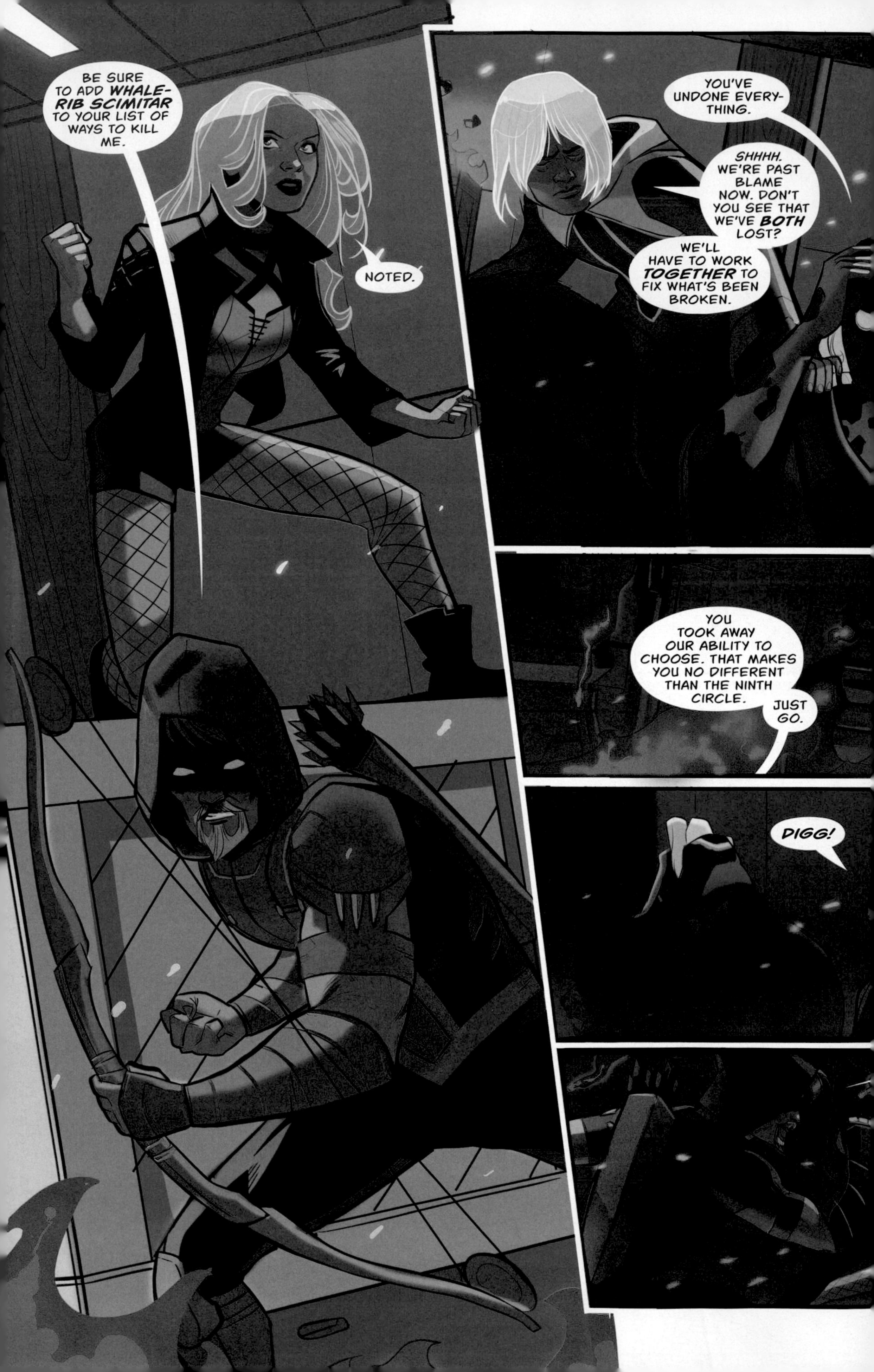
BE SURE TO ADD *WHALE-RIB SCIMITAR* TO YOUR LIST OF WAYS TO KILL ME.
NOTED.
YOU'VE UNDONE EVERY-THING.
SHHHH. WE'RE PAST BLAME NOW. DON'T YOU SEE THAT WE'VE *BOTH* LOST?
WE'LL HAVE TO WORK *TOGETHER* TO FIX WHAT'S BEEN BROKEN.
YOU TOOK AWAY OUR ABILITY TO CHOOSE. THAT MAKES YOU NO DIFFERENT THAN THE NINTH CIRCLE.
JUST GO.
DIGG!

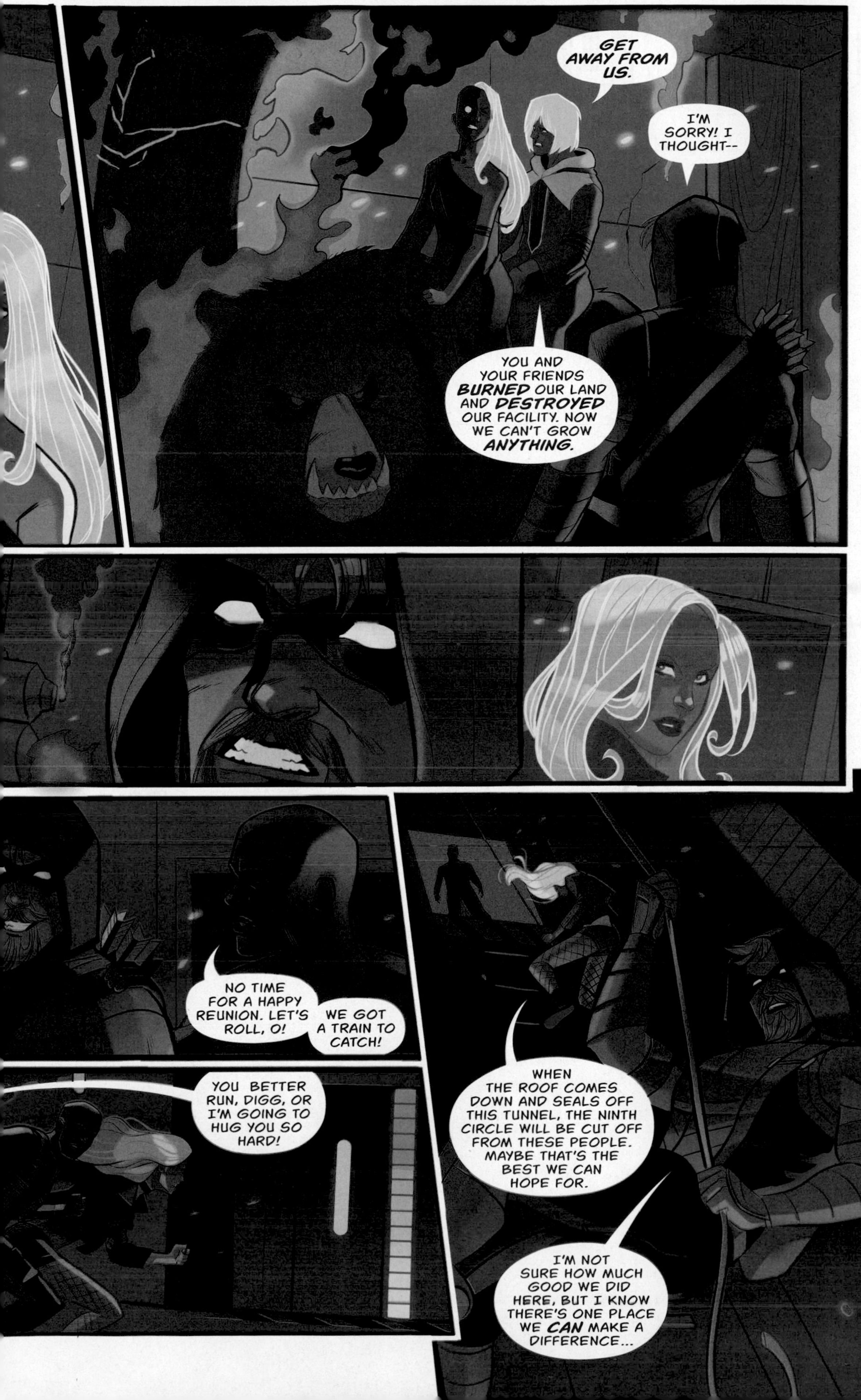

GET AWAY FROM US.
I'M SORRY! I THOUGHT--
YOU AND YOUR FRIENDS BURNED OUR LAND AND DESTROYED OUR FACILITY. NOW WE CAN'T GROW ANYTHING.
NO TIME FOR A HAPPY REUNION. LET'S ROLL, O!
WE GOT A TRAIN TO CATCH!
YOU BETTER RUN, DIGG, OR I'M GOING TO HUG YOU SO HARD!
WHEN THE ROOF COMES DOWN AND SEALS OFF THIS TUNNEL, THE NINTH CIRCLE WILL BE CUT OFF FROM THESE PEOPLE. MAYBE THAT'S THE BEST WE CAN HOPE FOR.
I'M NOT SURE HOW MUCH GOOD WE DID HERE, BUT I KNOW THERE'S ONE PLACE WE CAN MAKE A DIFFERENCE...

ISLAND of SCARS
PART TWO: TRACKS
BENJAMIN PERCY STORY STEPHEN BYRNE ART AND COLOR NATE PIEKOS OF BLAMBOT® LETTERING
BRIAN CUNNINGHAM GROUP EDITOR
HARVEY RICHARDS ASSOCIATE EDITOR ANDY KHOURI EDITOR
...SEATTLE.
ALMOST HOME.
BUT SOMETIMES THE LIGHT AT THE END OF THE TUNNEL...
...TURNS OUT TO BE AN APPROACHING TRAIN.

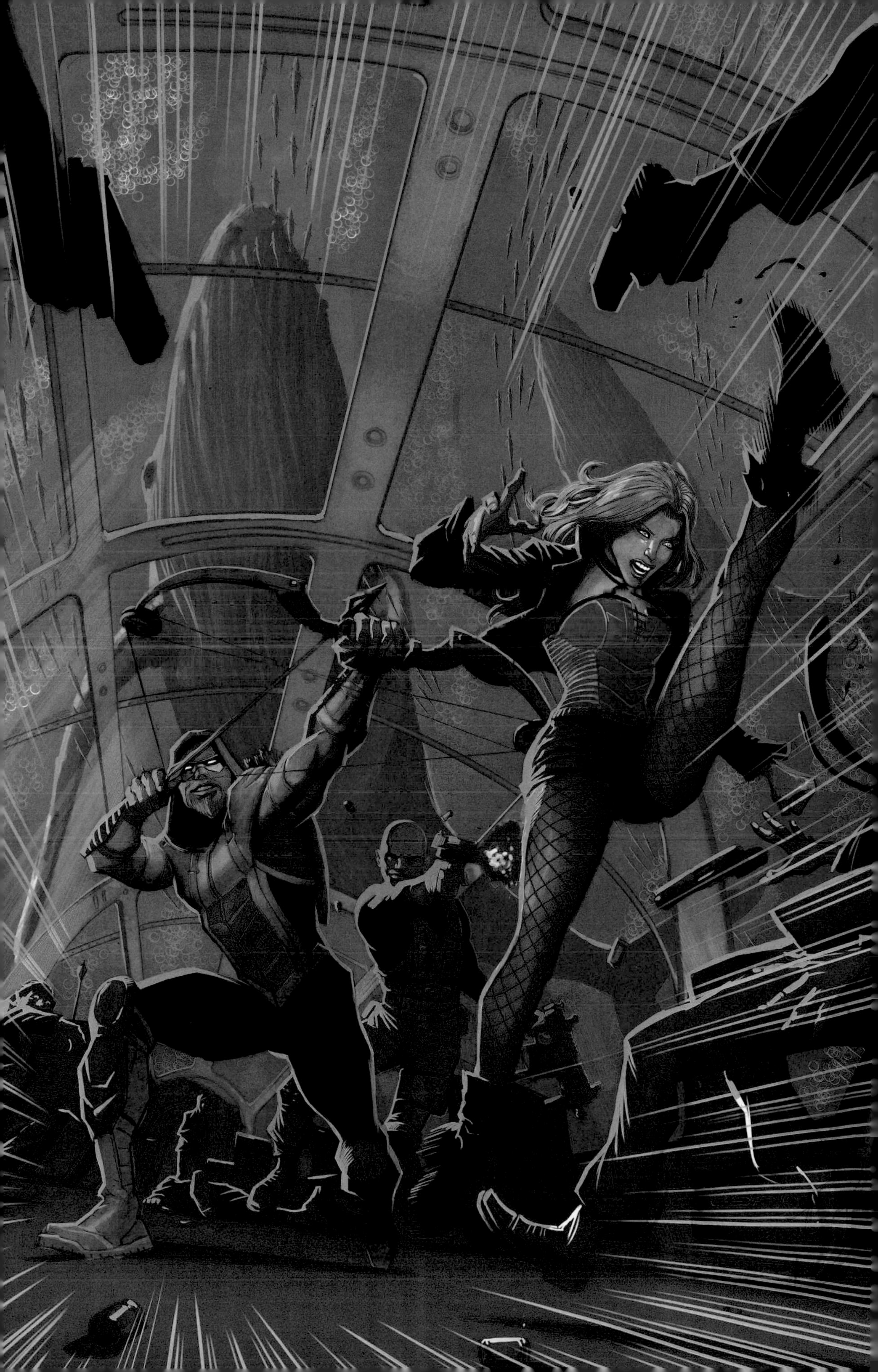

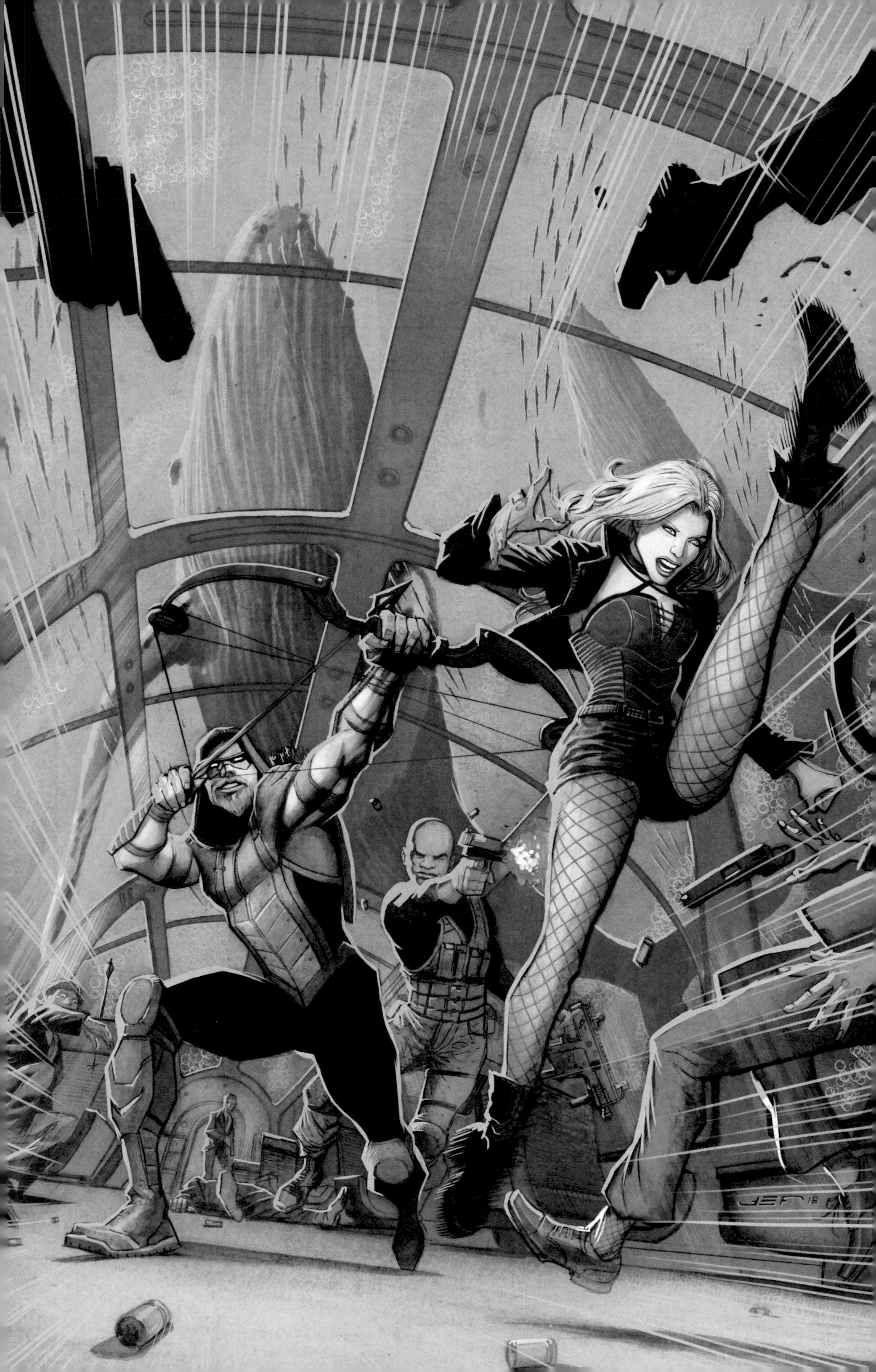

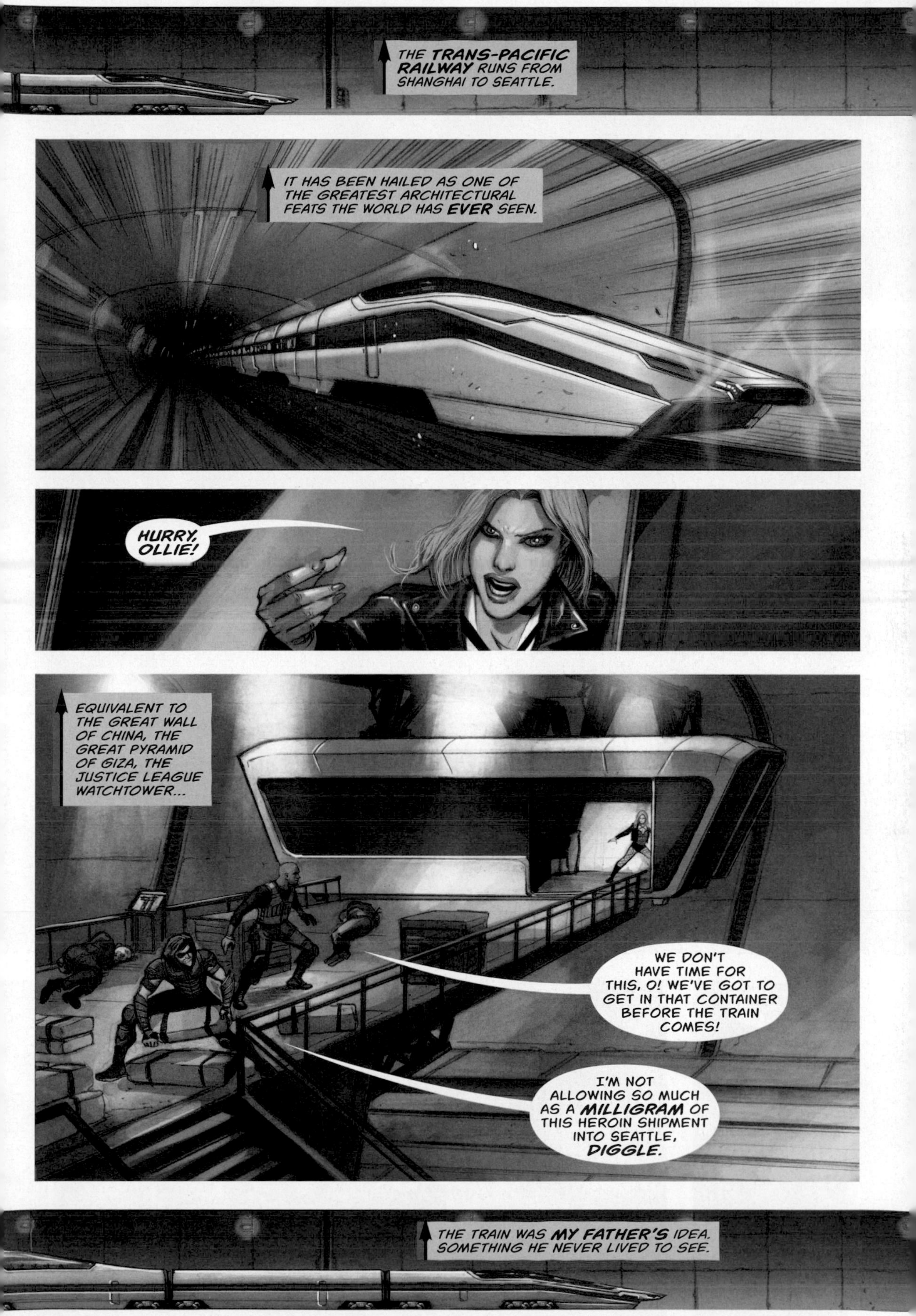
THE TRANS-PACIFIC RAILWAY RUNS FROM SHANGHAI TO SEATTLE.
IT HAS BEEN HAILED AS ONE OF THE GREATEST ARCHITECTURAL FEATS THE WORLD HAS EVER SEEN.
HURRY, OLLIE!
EQUIVALENT TO THE GREAT WALL OF CHINA, THE GREAT PYRAMID OF GIZA, THE JUSTICE LEAGUE WATCHTOWER...
WE DON'T HAVE TIME FOR THIS, O! WE'VE GOT TO GET IN THAT CONTAINER BEFORE THE TRAIN COMES!
I'M NOT ALLOWING SO MUCH AS A MILLIGRAM OF THIS HEROIN SHIPMENT INTO SEATTLE, DIGGLE.
THE TRAIN WAS MY FATHER'S IDEA. SOMETHING HE NEVER LIVED TO SEE.

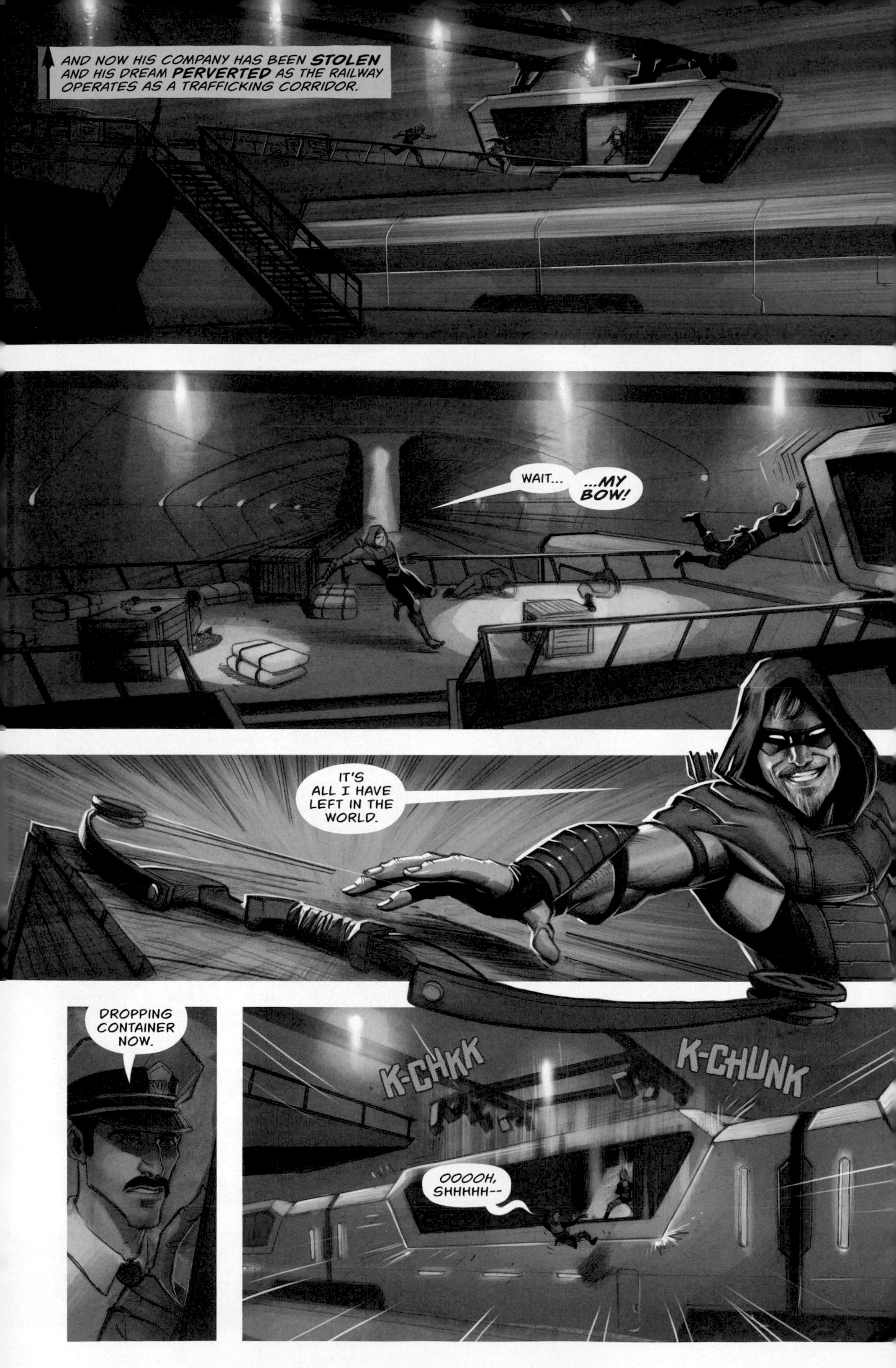
AND NOW HIS COMPANY HAS BEEN STOLEN AND HIS DREAM PERVERTED AS THE RAILWAY OPERATES AS A TRAFFICKING CORRIDOR.
WAIT...
...MY BOW!
IT'S ALL I HAVE LEFT IN THE WORLD.
DROPPING CONTAINER NOW.
K-CHKK
K-CHUNK
OOOOH, SHHHHH--

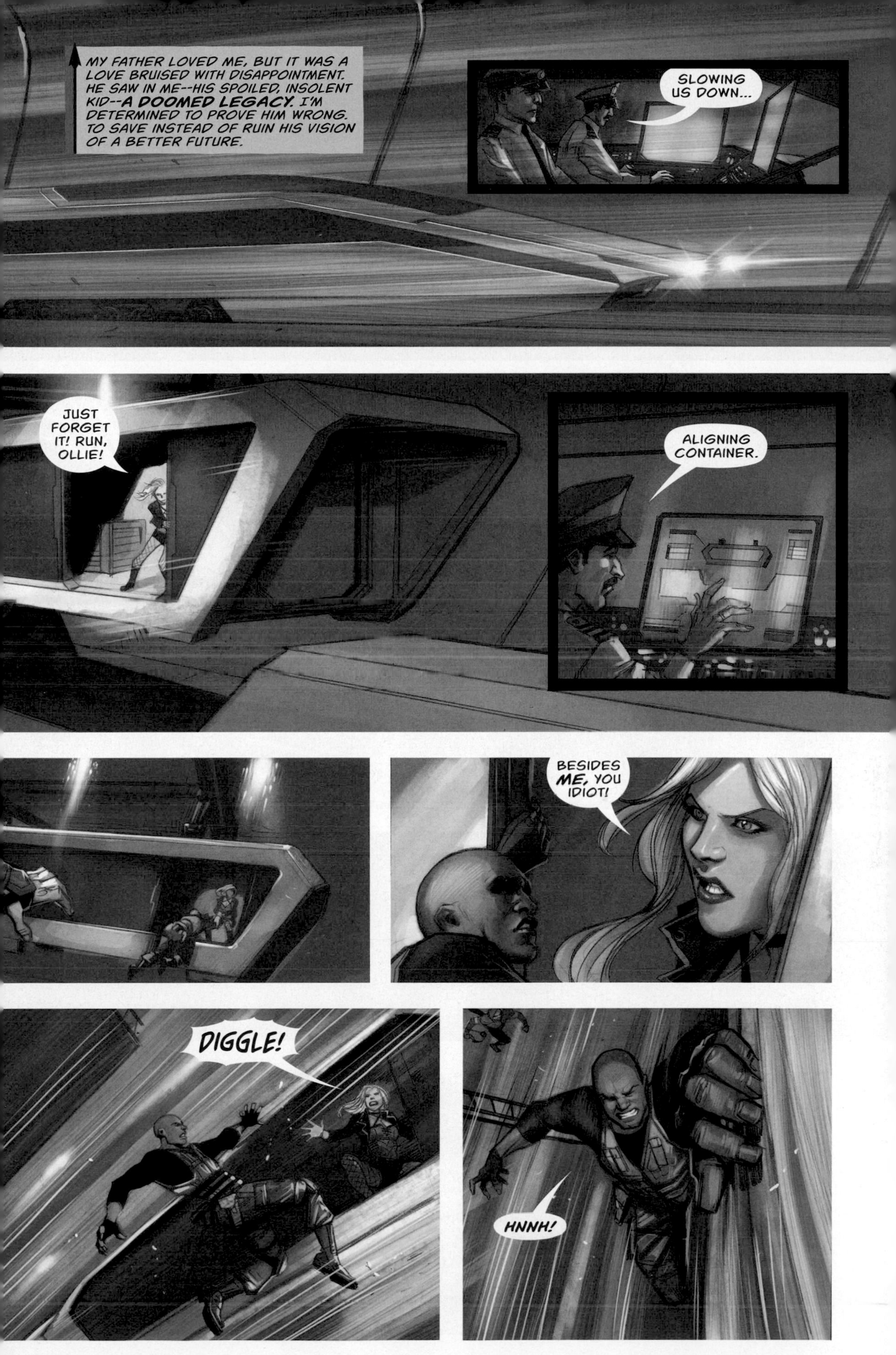

MY FATHER LOVED ME, BUT IT WAS A LOVE BRUISED WITH DISAPPOINTMENT. HE SAW IN ME--HIS SPOILED, INSOLENT KID--**A DOOMED LEGACY.** I'M DETERMINED TO PROVE HIM WRONG. TO SAVE INSTEAD OF RUIN HIS VISION OF A BETTER FUTURE.
SLOWING US DOWN...
JUST FORGET IT! RUN, OLLIE!
ALIGNING CONTAINER.
BESIDES **ME,** YOU IDIOT!
DIGGLE!
HNNH!

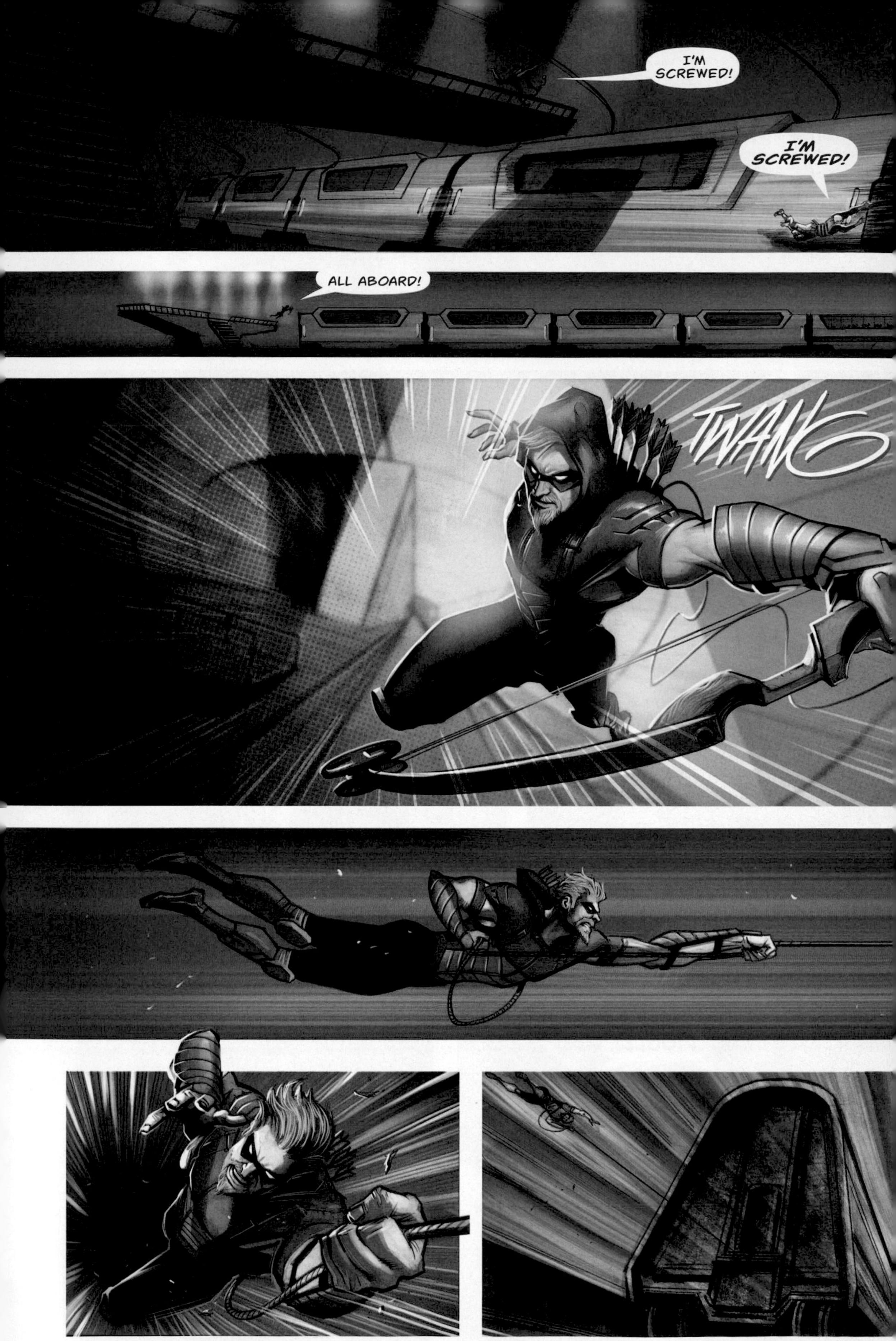
I'M SCREWED!
I'M SCREWED!
ALL ABOARD!
TWANG

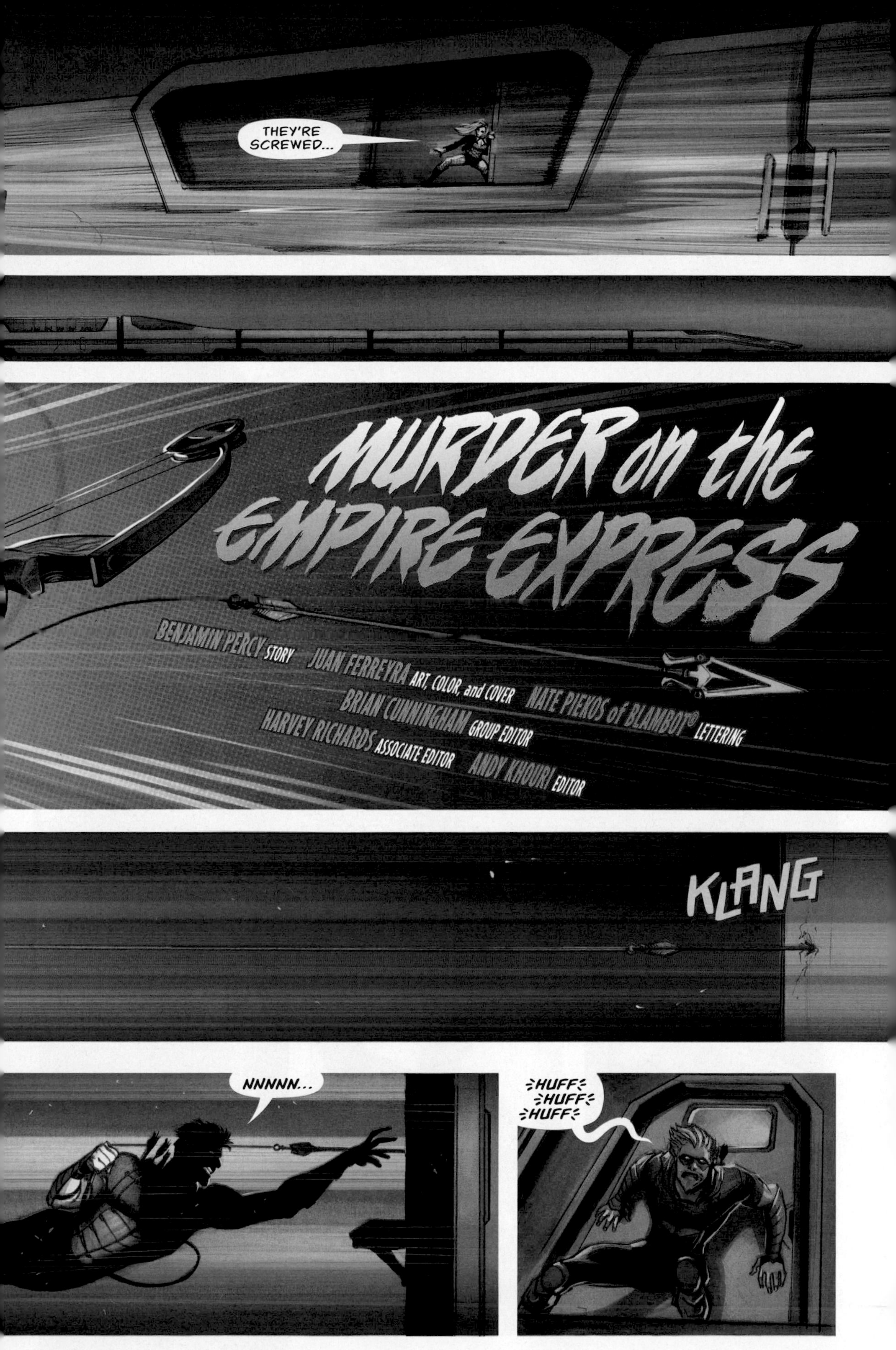
THEY'RE SCREWED...
MURDER on the EMPIRE EXPRESS
BENJAMIN PERCY STORY
JUAN FERREYRA ART, COLOR, and COVER
NATE PIEKOS of BLAMBOT® LETTERING
BRIAN CUNNINGHAM GROUP EDITOR
HARVEY RICHARDS ASSOCIATE EDITOR
ANDY KHOURI EDITOR
KLANG
NNNNN...
HUFF HUFF HUFF

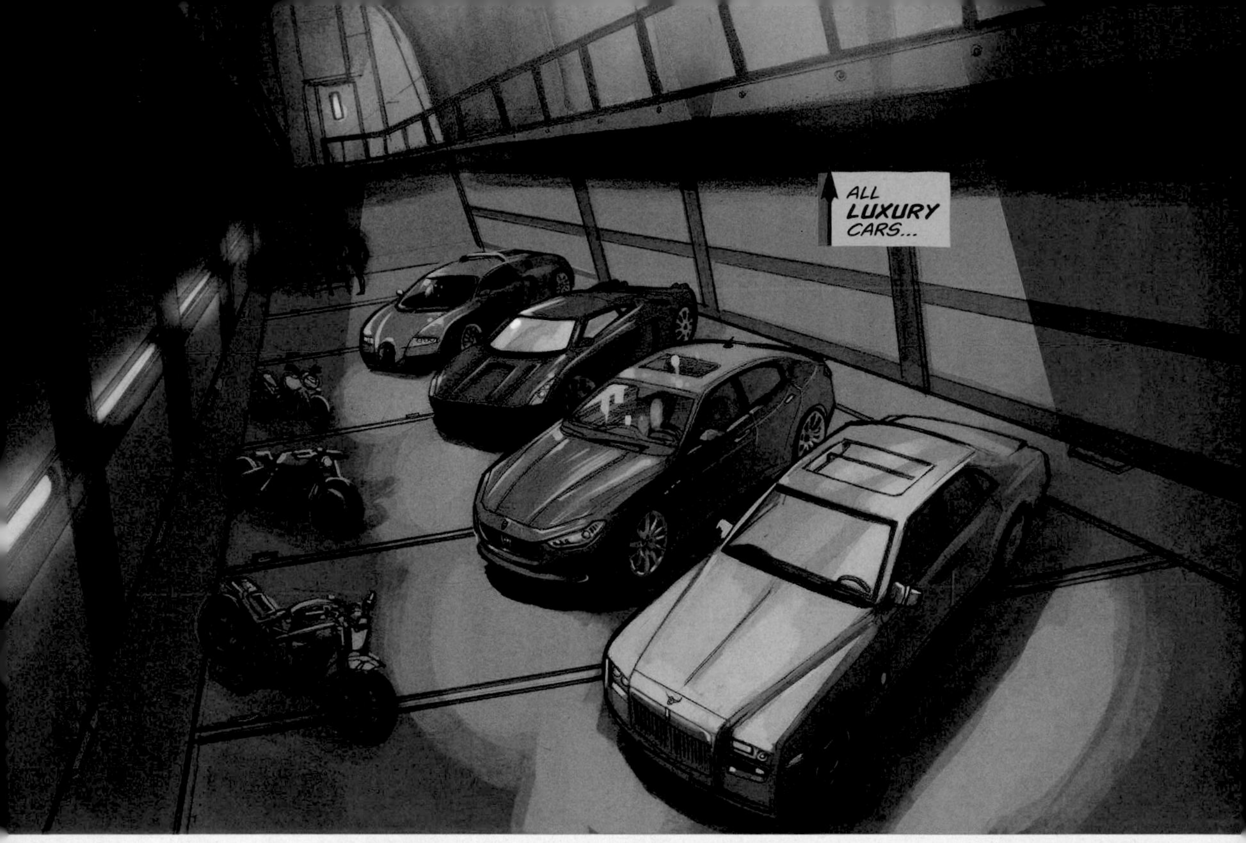
ALL LUXURY CARS...
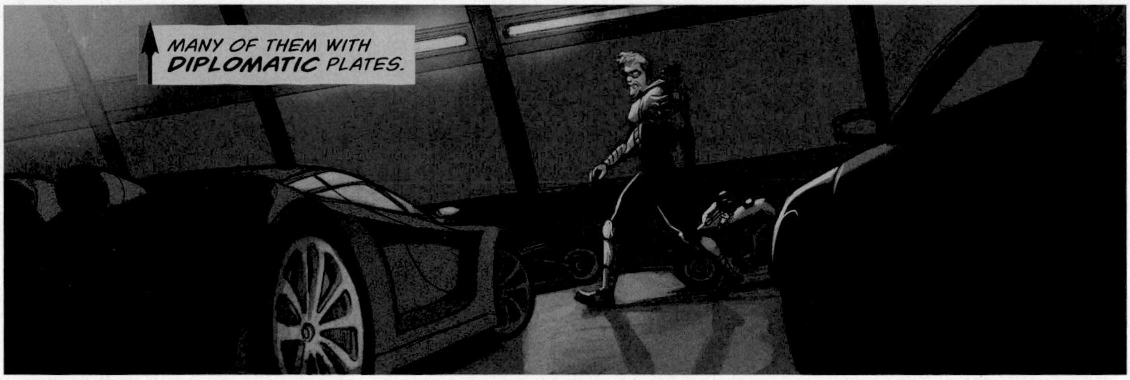
MANY OF THEM WITH DIPLOMATIC PLATES.
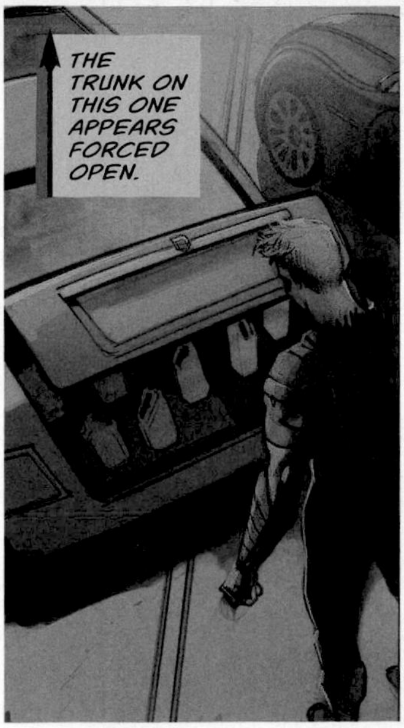
THE TRUNK ON THIS ONE APPEARS FORCED OPEN.
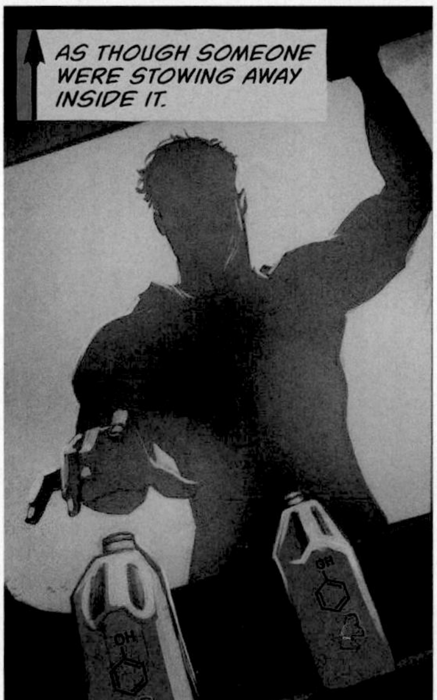
AS THOUGH SOMEONE WERE STOWING AWAY INSIDE IT.
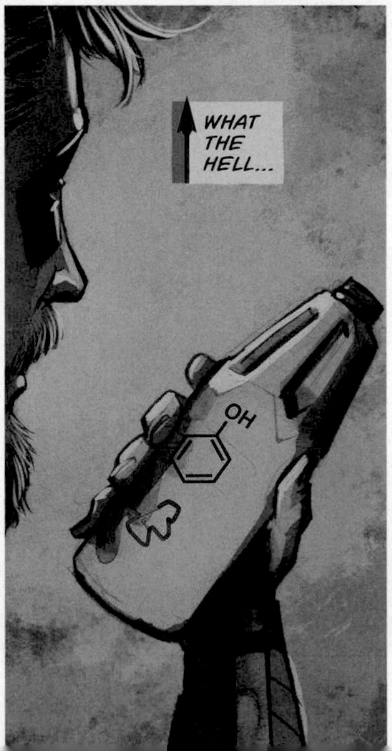
WHAT THE HELL...
OH

...IS HAPPENING ON BOARD THIS TRAIN?

NNNH!

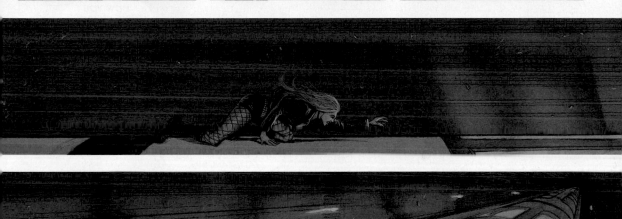

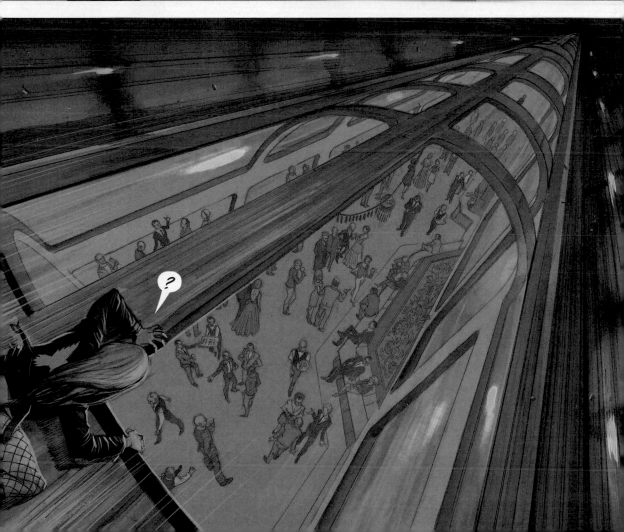

?

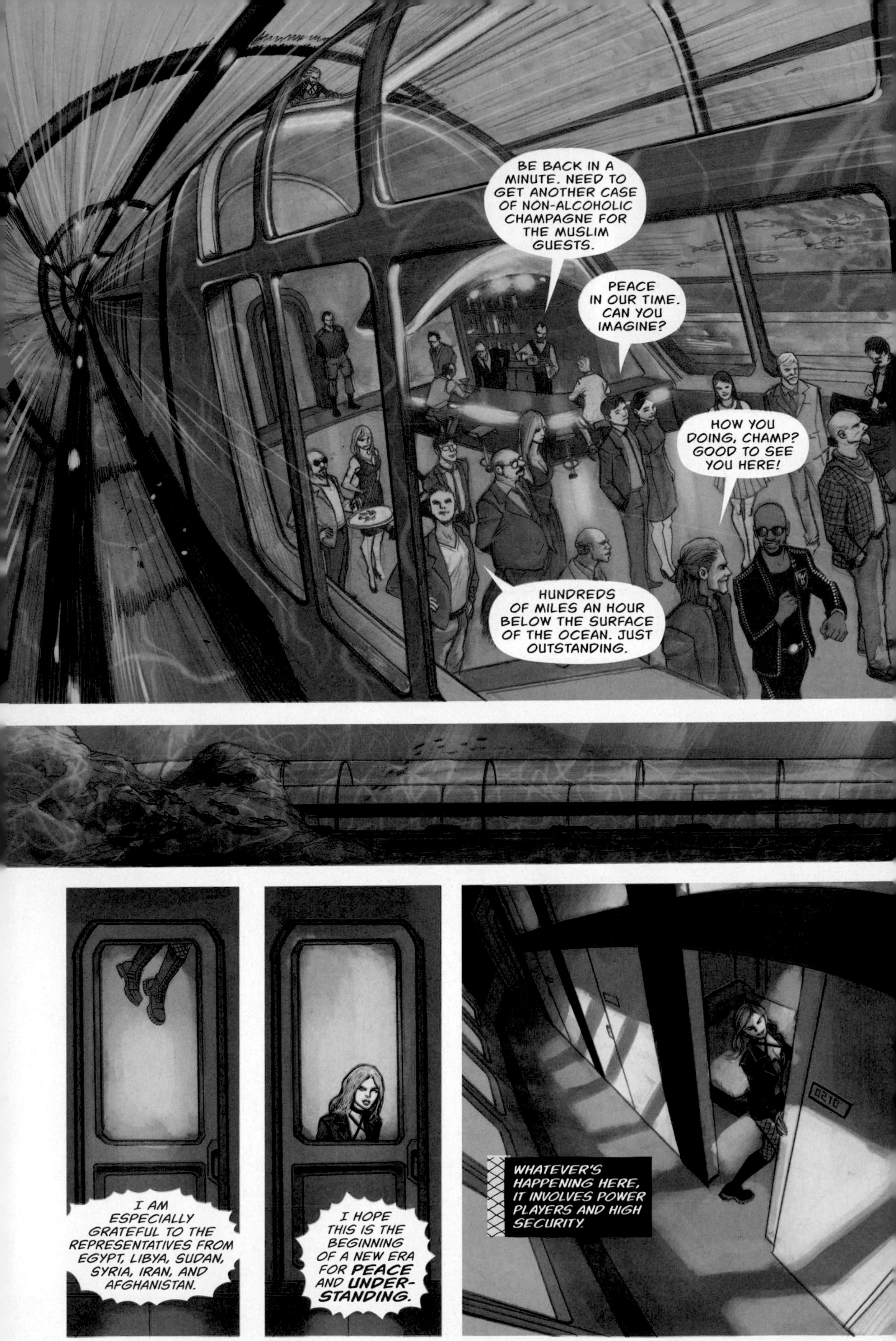
BE BACK IN A MINUTE. NEED TO GET ANOTHER CASE OF NON-ALCOHOLIC CHAMPAGNE FOR THE MUSLIM GUESTS.
PEACE IN OUR TIME. CAN YOU IMAGINE?
HOW YOU DOING, CHAMP? GOOD TO SEE YOU HERE!
HUNDREDS OF MILES AN HOUR BELOW THE SURFACE OF THE OCEAN. JUST OUTSTANDING.
I AM ESPECIALLY GRATEFUL TO THE REPRESENTATIVES FROM EGYPT, LIBYA, SUDAN, SYRIA, IRAN, AND AFGHANISTAN.
I HOPE THIS IS THE BEGINNING OF A NEW ERA FOR PEACE AND UNDER-STANDING.
WHATEVER'S HAPPENING HERE, IT INVOLVES POWER PLAYERS AND HIGH SECURITY.

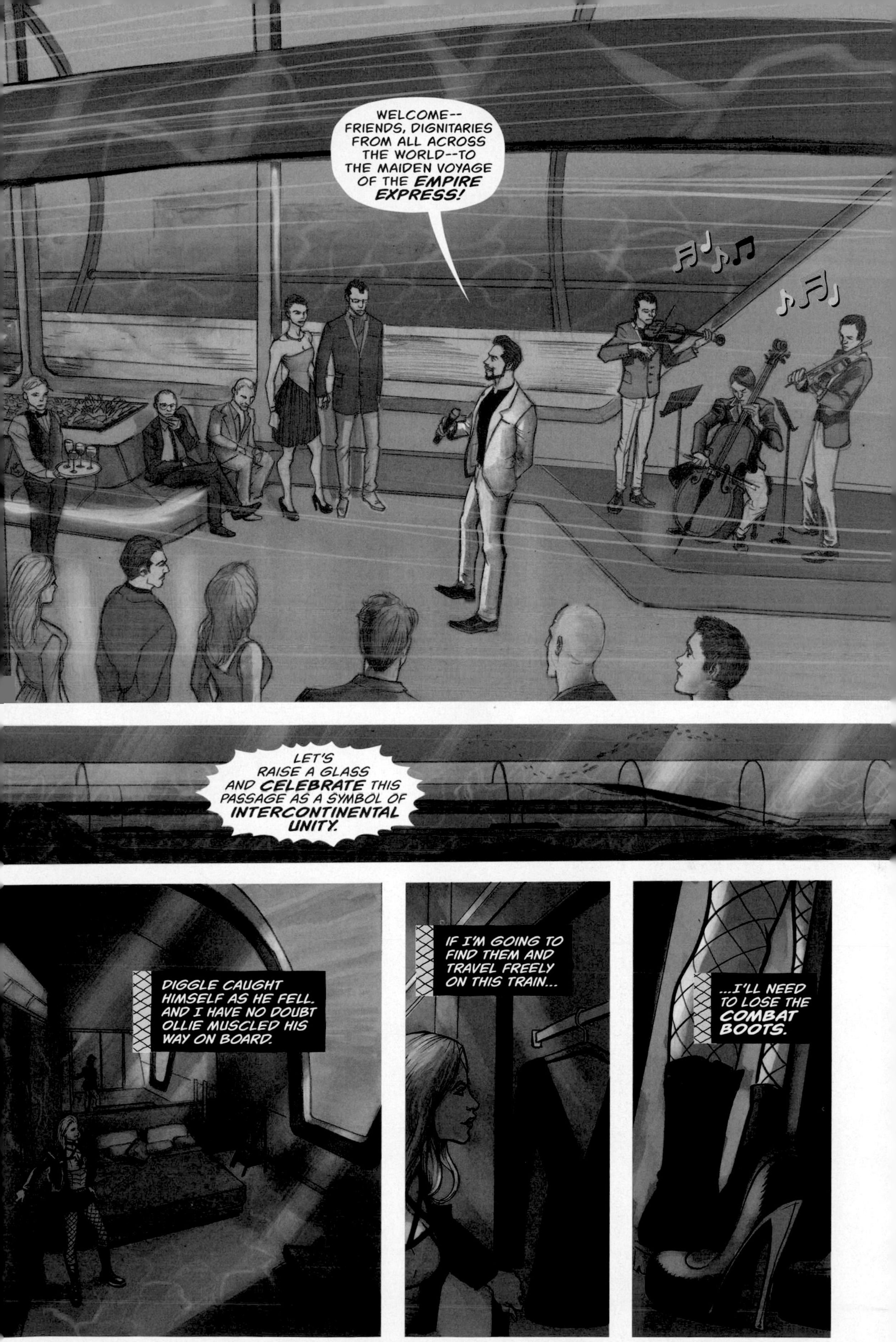
WELCOME-- FRIENDS, DIGNITARIES FROM ALL ACROSS THE WORLD--TO THE MAIDEN VOYAGE OF THE EMPIRE EXPRESS!
LET'S RAISE A GLASS AND CELEBRATE THIS PASSAGE AS A SYMBOL OF INTERCONTINENTAL UNITY.
DIGGLE CAUGHT HIMSELF AS HE FELL. AND I HAVE NO DOUBT OLLIE MUSCLED HIS WAY ON BOARD.
IF I'M GOING TO FIND THEM AND TRAVEL FREELY ON THIS TRAIN...
...I'LL NEED TO LOSE THE COMBAT BOOTS.

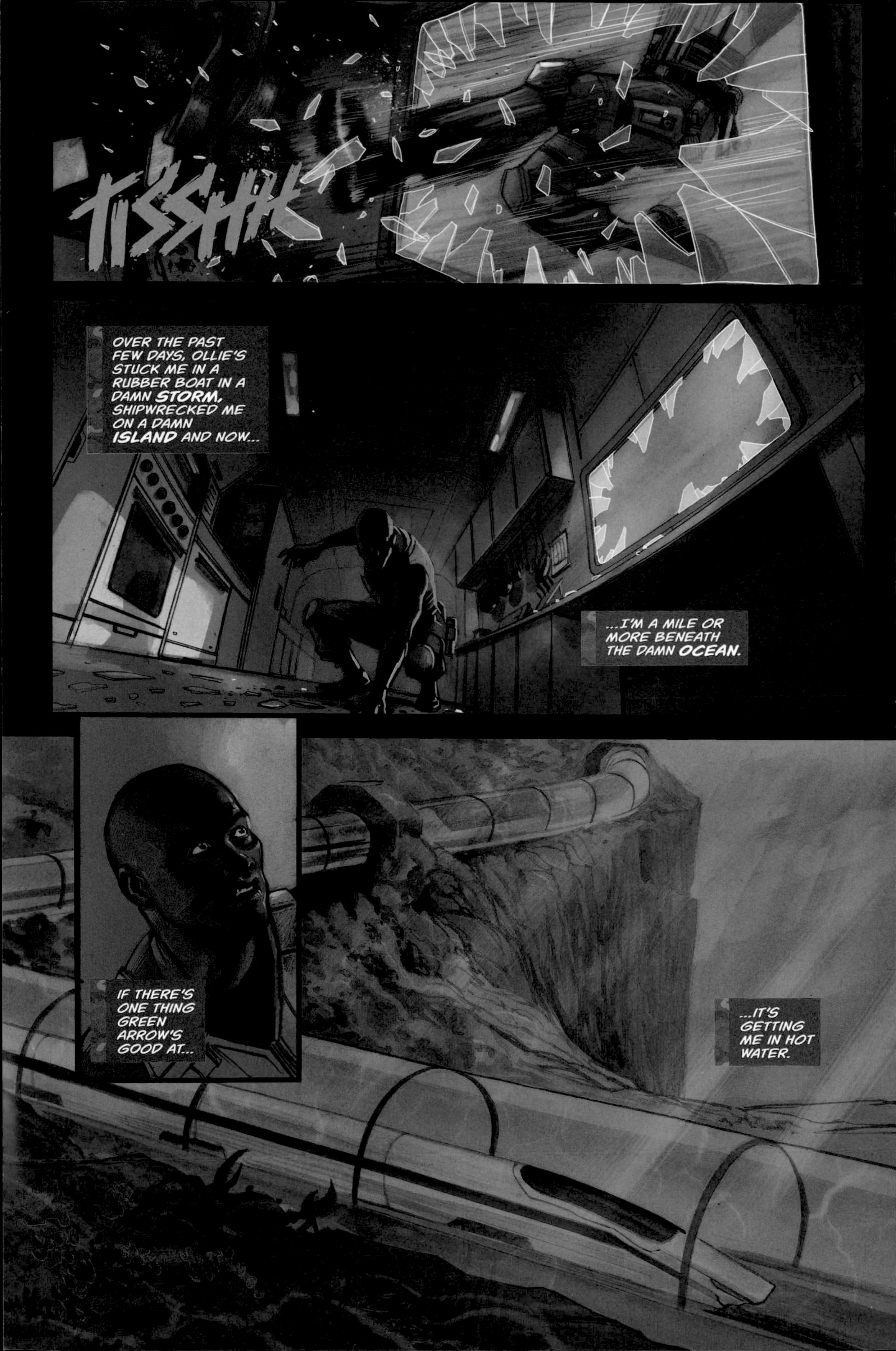
TISSHH
OVER THE PAST FEW DAYS, OLLIE'S STUCK ME IN A RUBBER BOAT IN A DAMN STORM, SHIPWRECKED ME ON A DAMN ISLAND AND NOW...
...I'M A MILE OR MORE BENEATH THE DAMN OCEAN.
IF THERE'S ONE THING GREEN ARROW'S GOOD AT...
...IT'S GETTING ME IN HOT WATER.

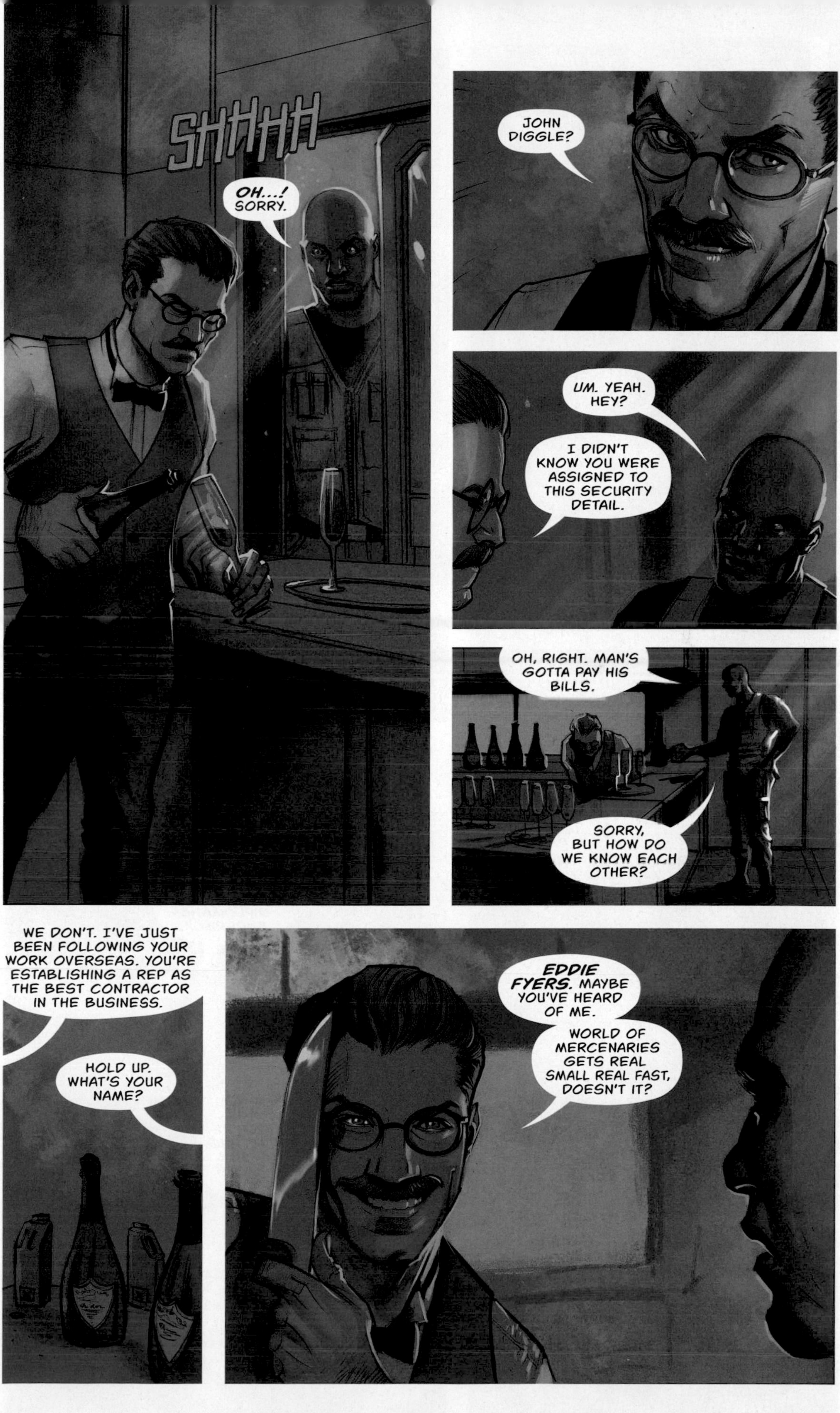
SHHHH
OH...! SORRY.
JOHN DIGGLE?
UM. YEAH. HEY?
I DIDN'T KNOW YOU WERE ASSIGNED TO THIS SECURITY DETAIL.
OH, RIGHT. MAN'S GOTTA PAY HIS BILLS.
SORRY, BUT HOW DO WE KNOW EACH OTHER?
WE DON'T. I'VE JUST BEEN FOLLOWING YOUR WORK OVERSEAS. YOU'RE ESTABLISHING A REP AS THE BEST CONTRACTOR IN THE BUSINESS.
HOLD UP. WHAT'S YOUR NAME?
EDDIE FYERS. MAYBE YOU'VE HEARD OF ME.
WORLD OF MERCENARIES GETS REAL SMALL REAL FAST, DOESN'T IT?

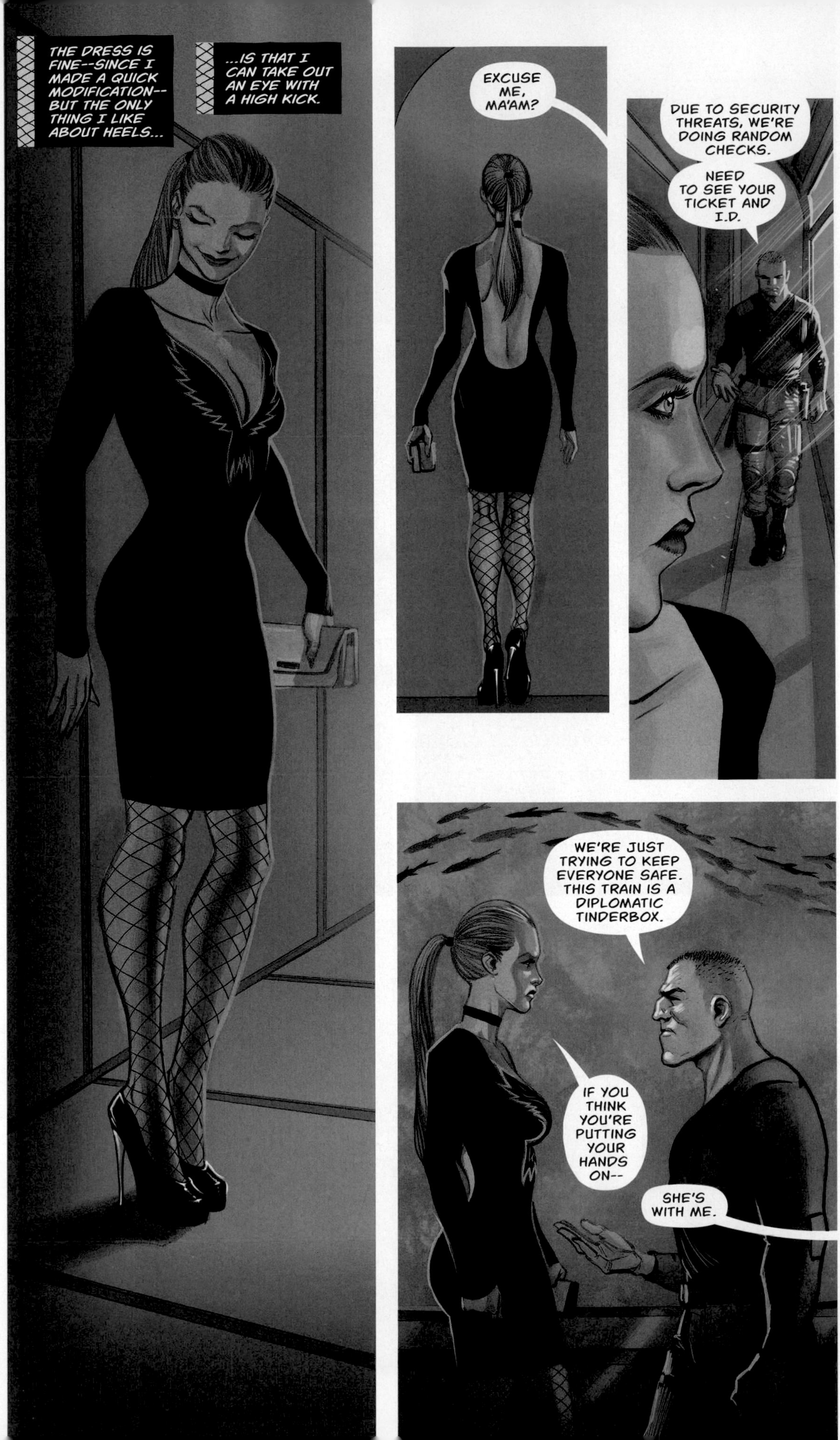
THE DRESS IS FINE--SINCE I MADE A QUICK MODIFICATION--BUT THE ONLY THING I LIKE ABOUT HEELS...
...IS THAT I CAN TAKE OUT AN EYE WITH A HIGH KICK.
EXCUSE ME, MA'AM?
DUE TO SECURITY THREATS, WE'RE DOING RANDOM CHECKS.
NEED TO SEE YOUR TICKET AND I.D.
WE'RE JUST TRYING TO KEEP EVERYONE SAFE. THIS TRAIN IS A DIPLOMATIC TINDERBOX.
IF YOU THINK YOU'RE PUTTING YOUR HANDS ON--
SHE'S WITH ME.

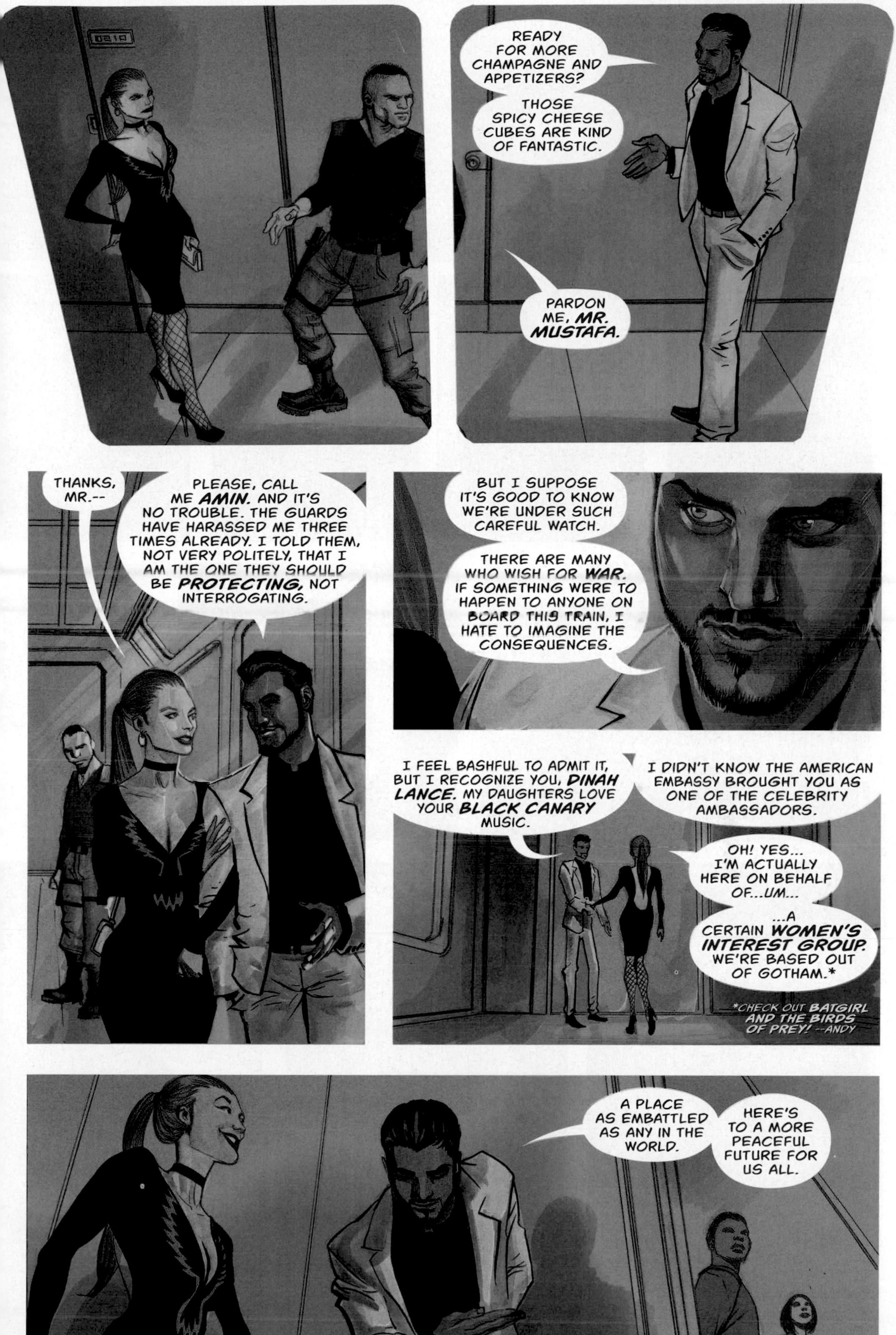
READY FOR MORE CHAMPAGNE AND APPETIZERS?
THOSE SPICY CHEESE CUBES ARE KIND OF FANTASTIC.
PARDON ME, MR. MUSTAFA.
THANKS, MR.--
PLEASE, CALL ME AMIN. AND IT'S NO TROUBLE. THE GUARDS HAVE HARASSED ME THREE TIMES ALREADY. I TOLD THEM, NOT VERY POLITELY, THAT I AM THE ONE THEY SHOULD BE PROTECTING, NOT INTERROGATING.
BUT I SUPPOSE IT'S GOOD TO KNOW WE'RE UNDER SUCH CAREFUL WATCH.
THERE ARE MANY WHO WISH FOR WAR. IF SOMETHING WERE TO HAPPEN TO ANYONE ON BOARD THIS TRAIN, I HATE TO IMAGINE THE CONSEQUENCES.
I FEEL BASHFUL TO ADMIT IT, BUT I RECOGNIZE YOU, DINAH LANCE. MY DAUGHTERS LOVE YOUR BLACK CANARY MUSIC.
I DIDN'T KNOW THE AMERICAN EMBASSY BROUGHT YOU AS ONE OF THE CELEBRITY AMBASSADORS.
OH! YES... I'M ACTUALLY HERE ON BEHALF OF...UM...
...A CERTAIN WOMEN'S INTEREST GROUP. WE'RE BASED OUT OF GOTHAM.*
*CHECK OUT BATGIRL AND THE BIRDS OF PREY! --ANDY
A PLACE AS EMBATTLED AS ANY IN THE WORLD.
HERE'S TO A MORE PEACEFUL FUTURE FOR US ALL.

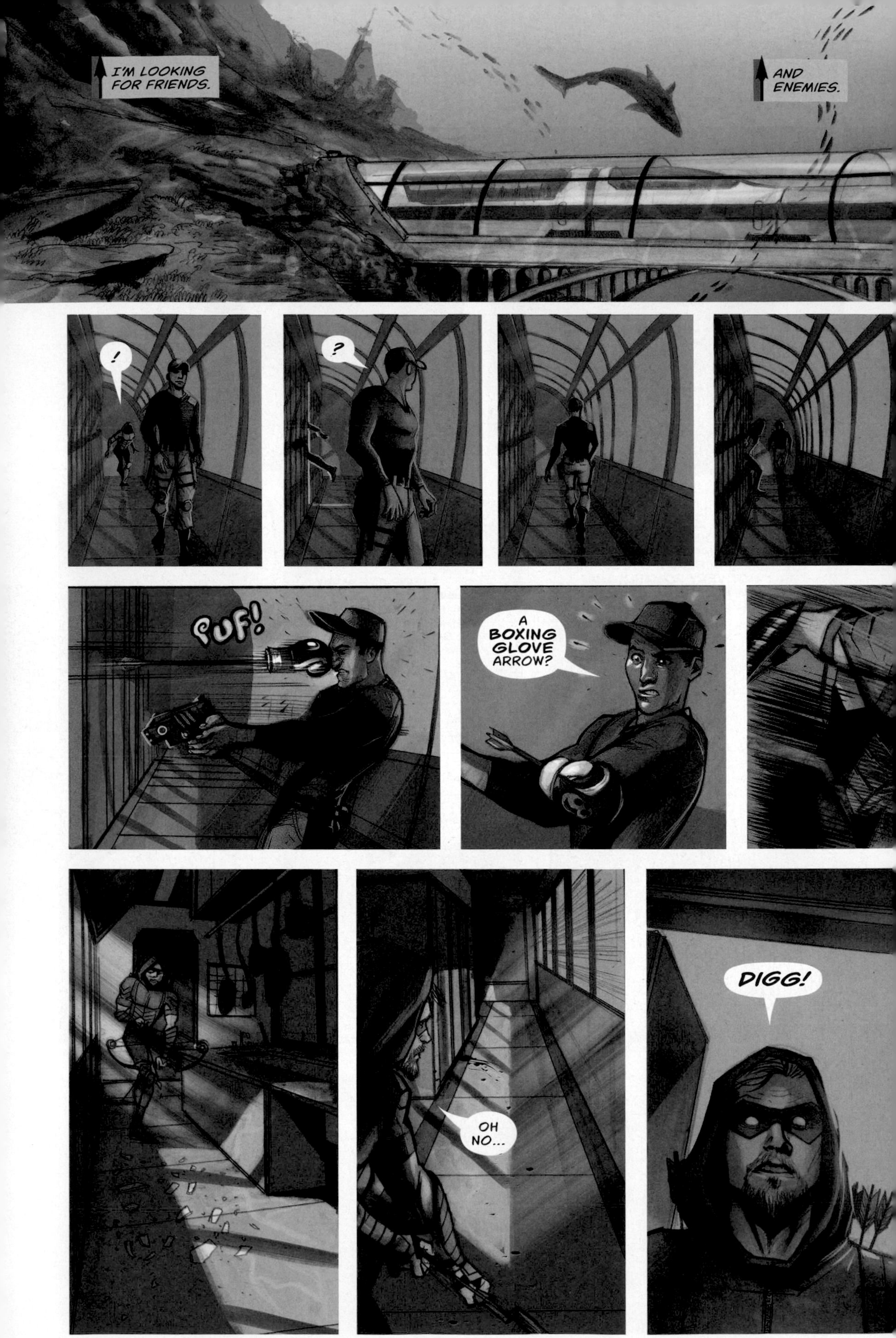
I'M LOOKING FOR FRIENDS.
AND ENEMIES.
!
?
PUF!
A BOXING GLOVE ARROW?
OH NO...
DIGG!

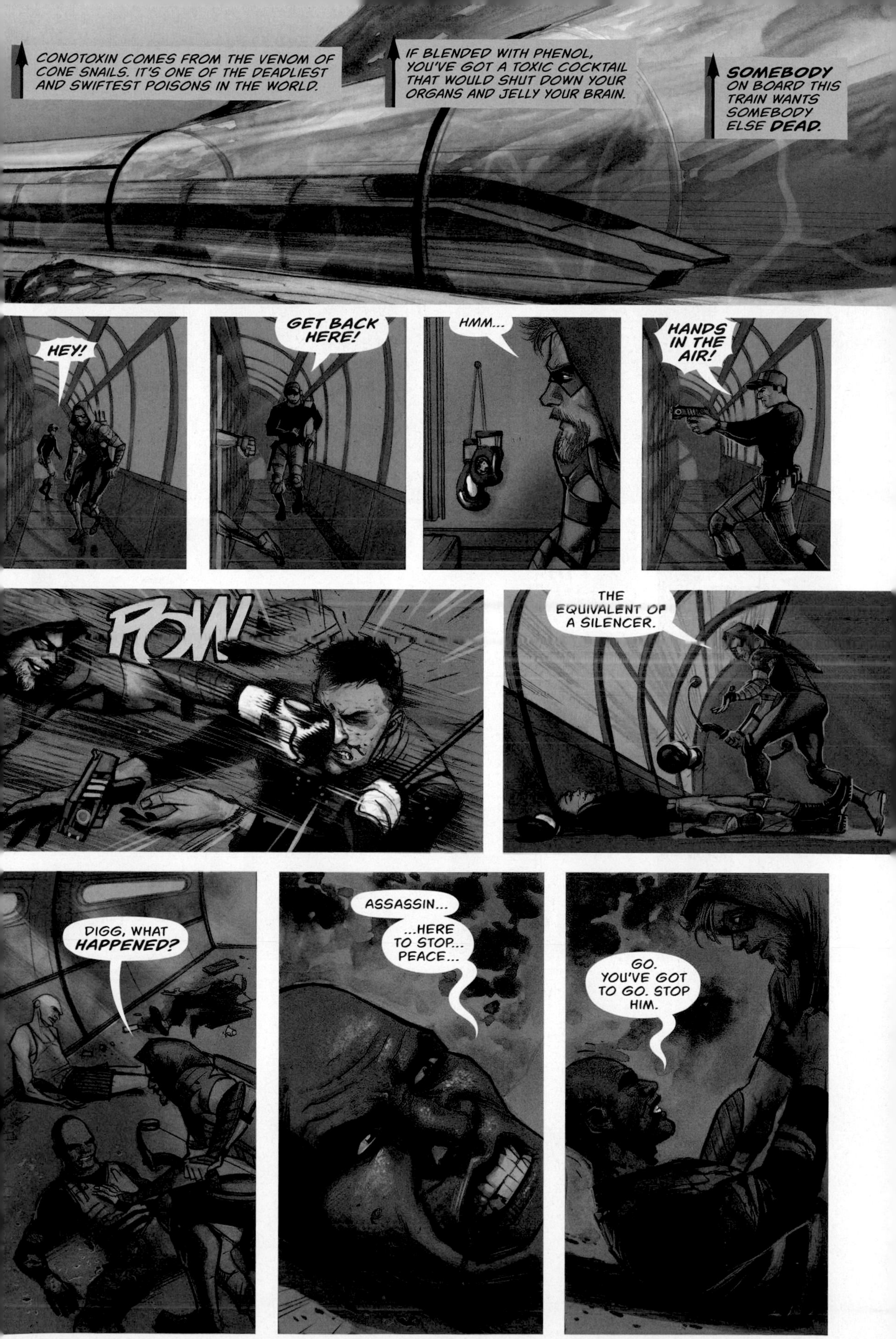
CONOTOXIN COMES FROM THE VENOM OF CONE SNAILS. IT'S ONE OF THE DEADLIEST AND SWIFTEST POISONS IN THE WORLD.
IF BLENDED WITH PHENOL, YOU'VE GOT A TOXIC COCKTAIL THAT WOULD SHUT DOWN YOUR ORGANS AND JELLY YOUR BRAIN.
SOMEBODY ON BOARD THIS TRAIN WANTS SOMEBODY ELSE DEAD.
HEY!
GET BACK HERE!
HMM...
HANDS IN THE AIR!
POW!
THE EQUIVALENT OF A SILENCER.
DIGG, WHAT HAPPENED?
ASSASSIN...
...HERE TO STOP... PEACE...
GO. YOU'VE GOT TO GO. STOP HIM.

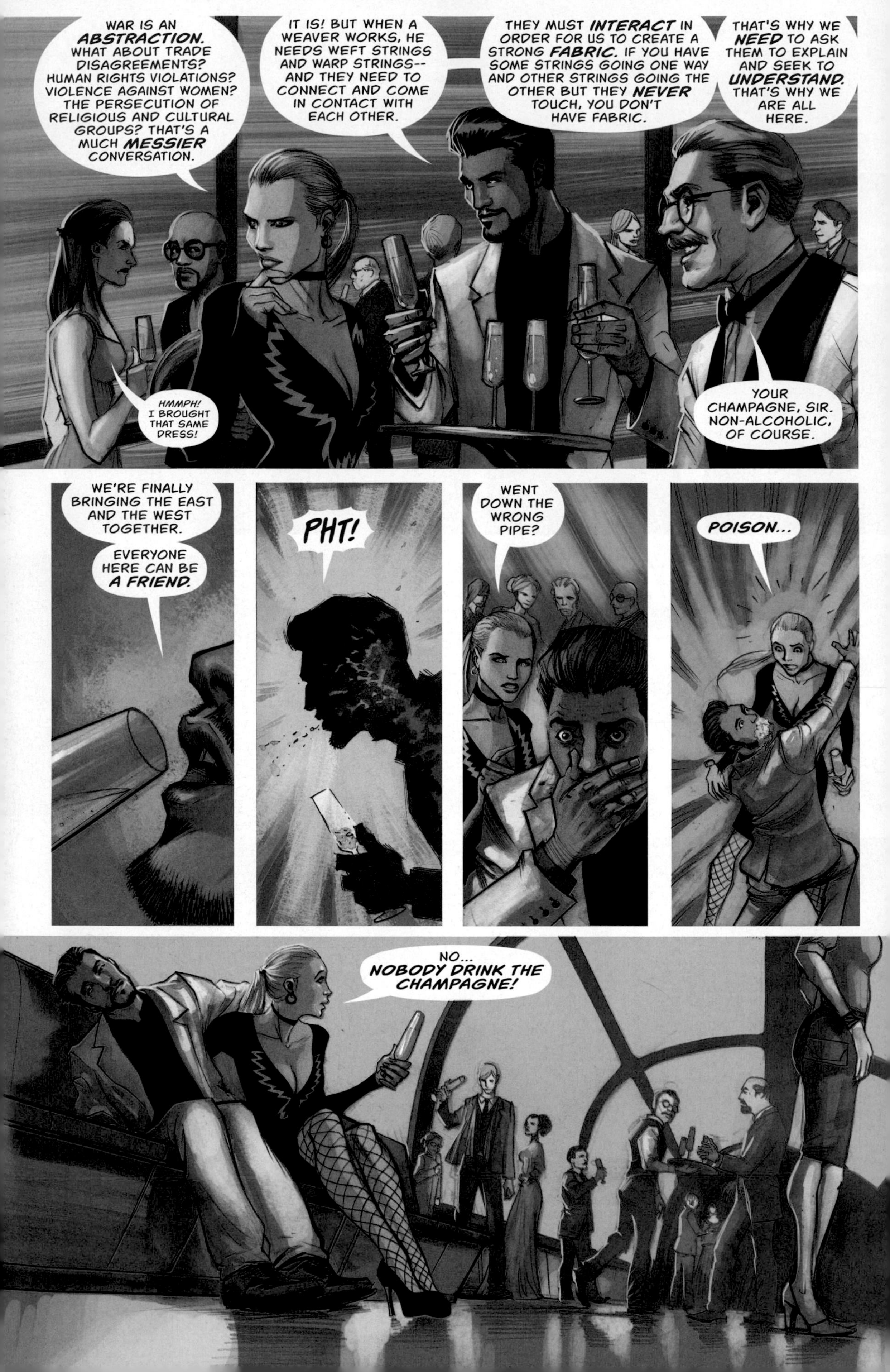
WAR IS AN ABSTRACTION. WHAT ABOUT TRADE DISAGREEMENTS? HUMAN RIGHTS VIOLATIONS? VIOLENCE AGAINST WOMEN? THE PERSECUTION OF RELIGIOUS AND CULTURAL GROUPS? THAT'S A MUCH MESSIER CONVERSATION.
IT IS! BUT WHEN A WEAVER WORKS, HE NEEDS WEFT STRINGS AND WARP STRINGS-- AND THEY NEED TO CONNECT AND COME IN CONTACT WITH EACH OTHER.
THEY MUST INTERACT IN ORDER FOR US TO CREATE A STRONG FABRIC. IF YOU HAVE SOME STRINGS GOING ONE WAY AND OTHER STRINGS GOING THE OTHER BUT THEY NEVER TOUCH, YOU DON'T HAVE FABRIC.
THAT'S WHY WE NEED TO ASK THEM TO EXPLAIN AND SEEK TO UNDERSTAND. THAT'S WHY WE ARE ALL HERE.
HMMPH! I BROUGHT THAT SAME DRESS!
YOUR CHAMPAGNE, SIR. NON-ALCOHOLIC, OF COURSE.
WE'RE FINALLY BRINGING THE EAST AND THE WEST TOGETHER.
EVERYONE HERE CAN BE A FRIEND.
PHT!
WENT DOWN THE WRONG PIPE?
POISON...
NO... NOBODY DRINK THE CHAMPAGNE!

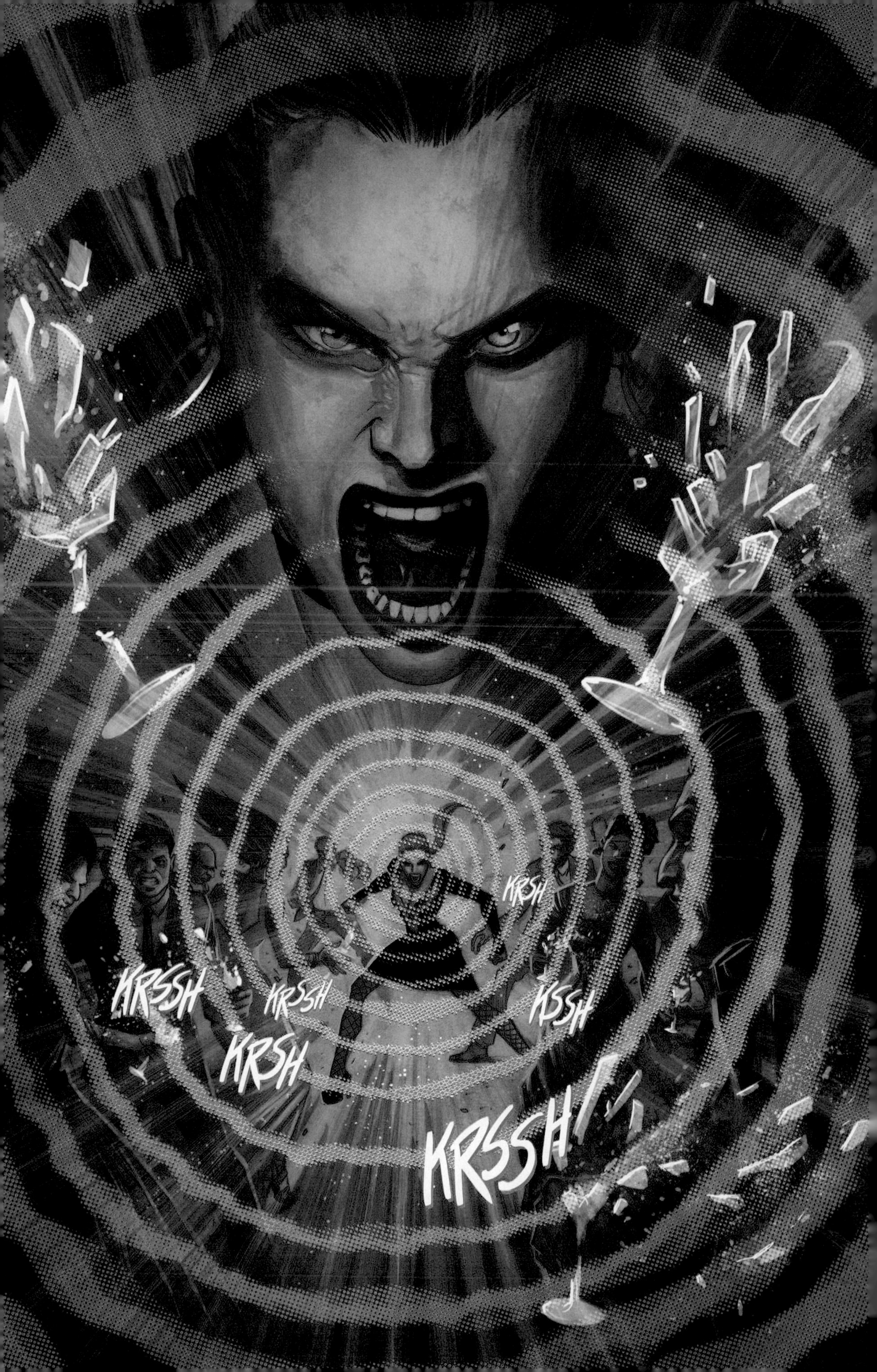
KRSH
KRSSH
KRSSH
KSSH
KRSH
KRSSH

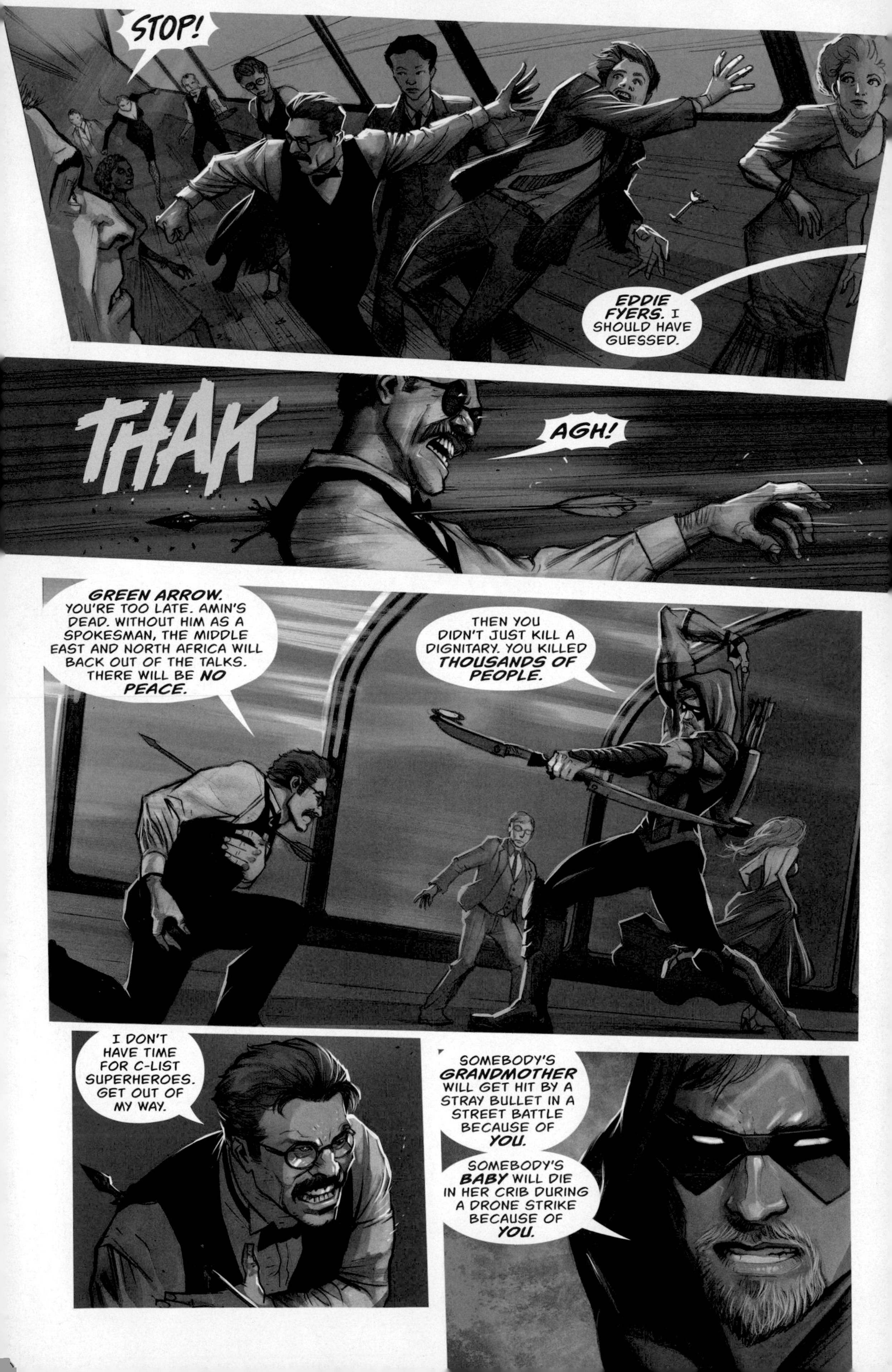

STOP!
EDDIE FYERS. I SHOULD HAVE GUESSED.
THAK
AGH!
GREEN ARROW. YOU'RE TOO LATE. AMIN'S DEAD. WITHOUT HIM AS A SPOKESMAN, THE MIDDLE EAST AND NORTH AFRICA WILL BACK OUT OF THE TALKS. THERE WILL BE NO PEACE.
THEN YOU DIDN'T JUST KILL A DIGNITARY. YOU KILLED THOUSANDS OF PEOPLE.
I DON'T HAVE TIME FOR C-LIST SUPERHEROES. GET OUT OF MY WAY.
SOMEBODY'S GRANDMOTHER WILL GET HIT BY A STRAY BULLET IN A STREET BATTLE BECAUSE OF YOU.
SOMEBODY'S BABY WILL DIE IN HER CRIB DURING A DRONE STRIKE BECAUSE OF YOU.

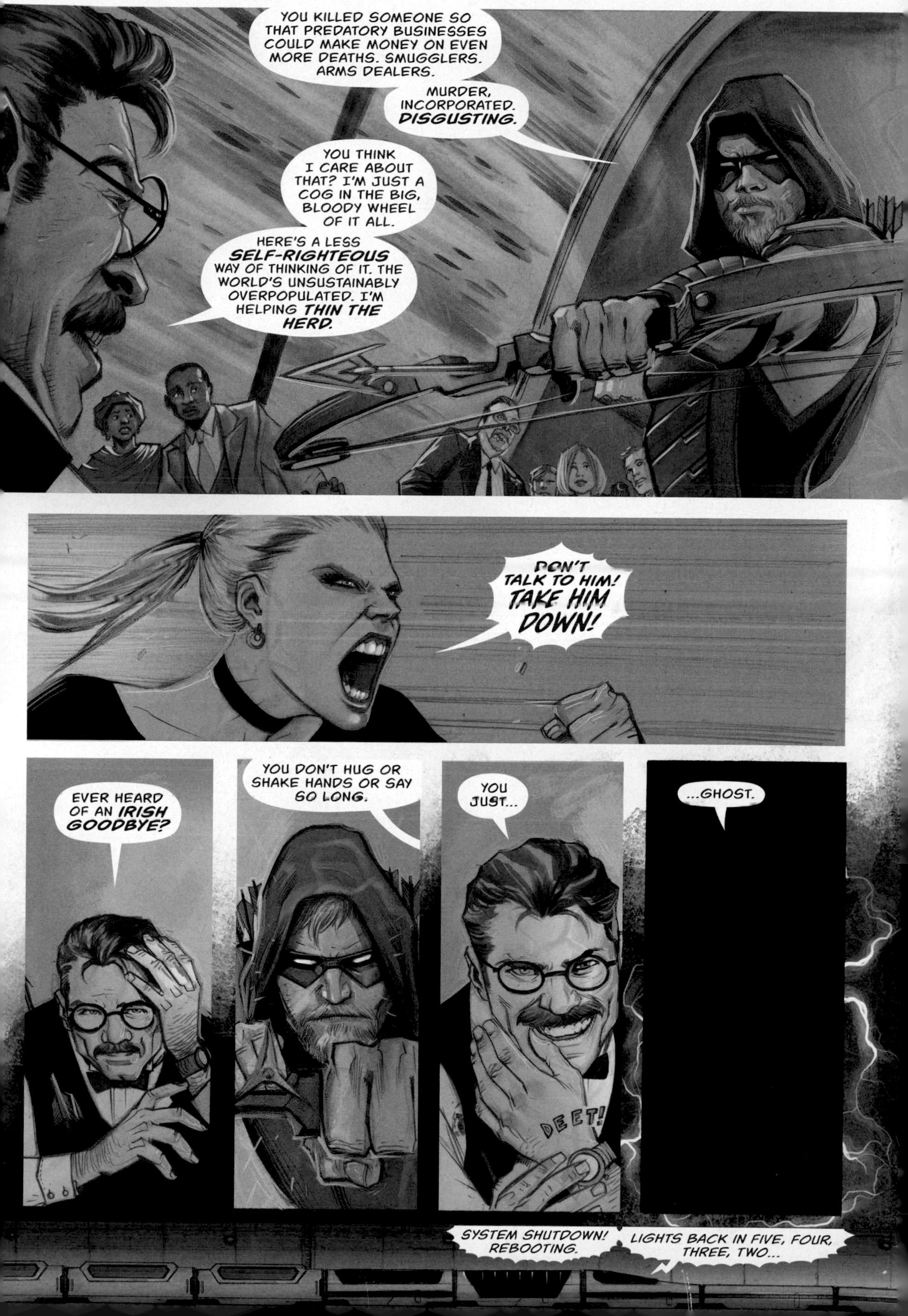
YOU KILLED SOMEONE SO THAT PREDATORY BUSINESSES COULD MAKE MONEY ON EVEN MORE DEATHS. SMUGGLERS. ARMS DEALERS.
MURDER, INCORPORATED. DISGUSTING.
YOU THINK I CARE ABOUT THAT? I'M JUST A COG IN THE BIG, BLOODY WHEEL OF IT ALL.
HERE'S A LESS SELF-RIGHTEOUS WAY OF THINKING OF IT. THE WORLD'S UNSUSTAINABLY OVERPOPULATED. I'M HELPING THIN THE HERD.
DON'T TALK TO HIM! TAKE HIM DOWN!
EVER HEARD OF AN IRISH GOODBYE?
YOU DON'T HUG OR SHAKE HANDS OR SAY SO LONG.
YOU JUST...
...GHOST.
DEET!
SYSTEM SHUTDOWN! REBOOTING.
LIGHTS BACK IN FIVE, FOUR, THREE, TWO...

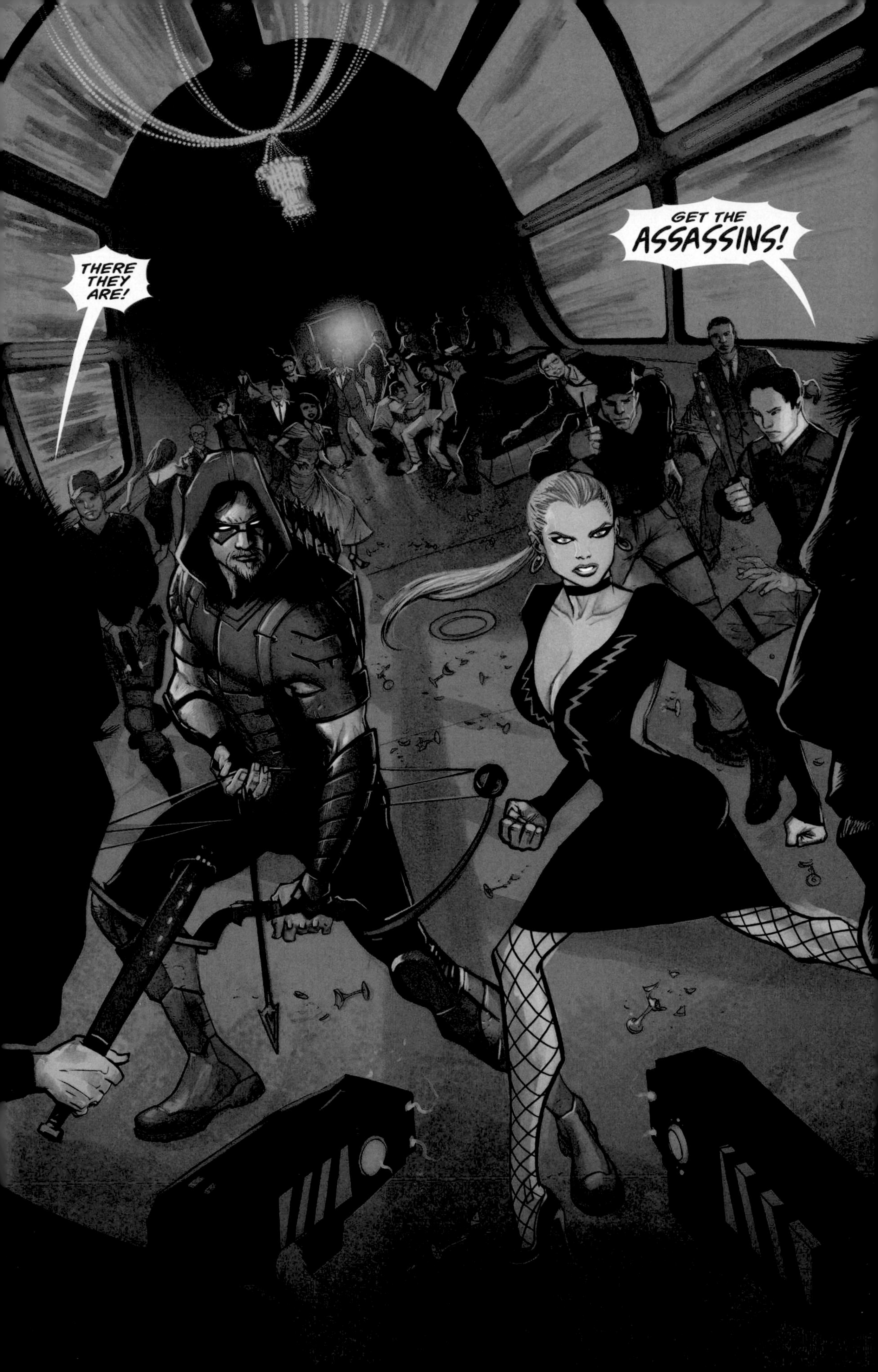
THERE THEY ARE!
GET THE ASSASSINS!

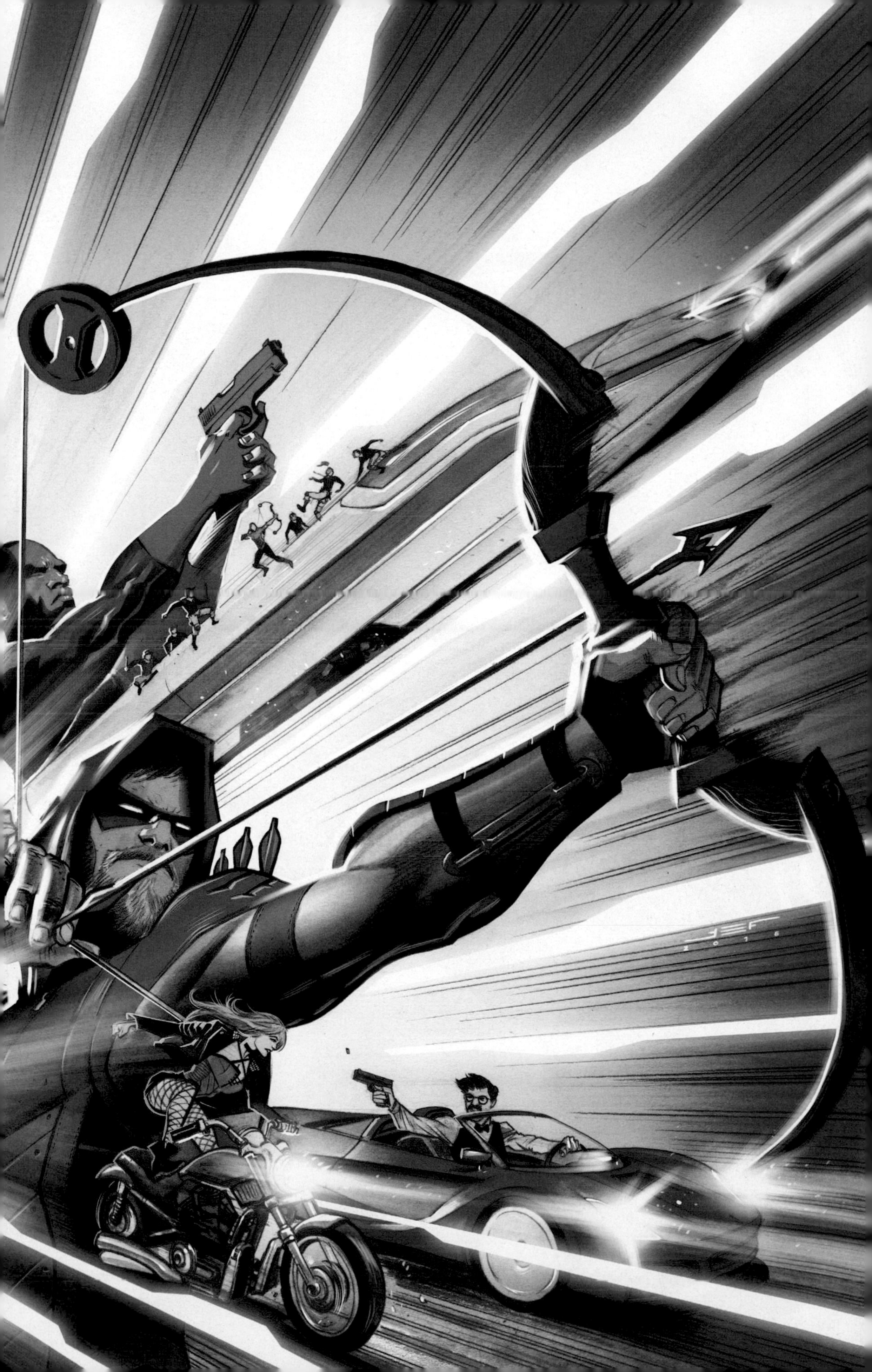

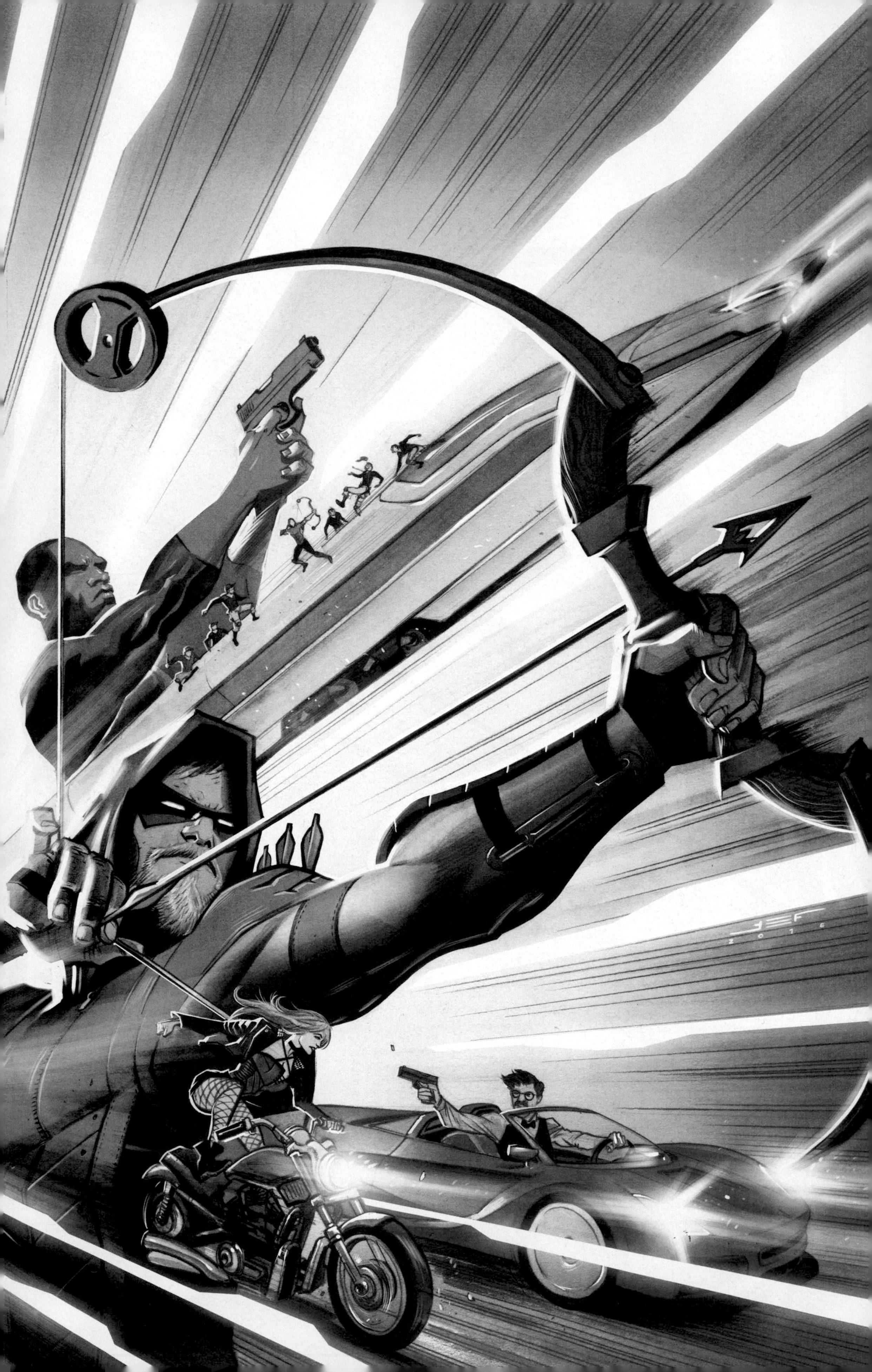

THERE ARE SO MANY REASONS FOR **WAR**.

WATER. LAND.

POLITICS. RELIGION.

LOVE. HATE.

BUT USUALLY IT COMES DOWN TO **MONEY**.

THAT'S WHY AMIN MUSTAFA IS **DEAD**.

THE ARAB DIPLOMAT DID EVERYTHING HE COULD TO BRING ABOUT PEACE BETWEEN THE EAST AND WEST.

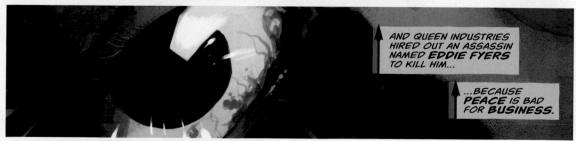

AND QUEEN INDUSTRIES HIRED OUT AN ASSASSIN NAMED **EDDIE FYERS** TO KILL HIM...

...BECAUSE **PEACE** IS BAD FOR **BUSINESS**.

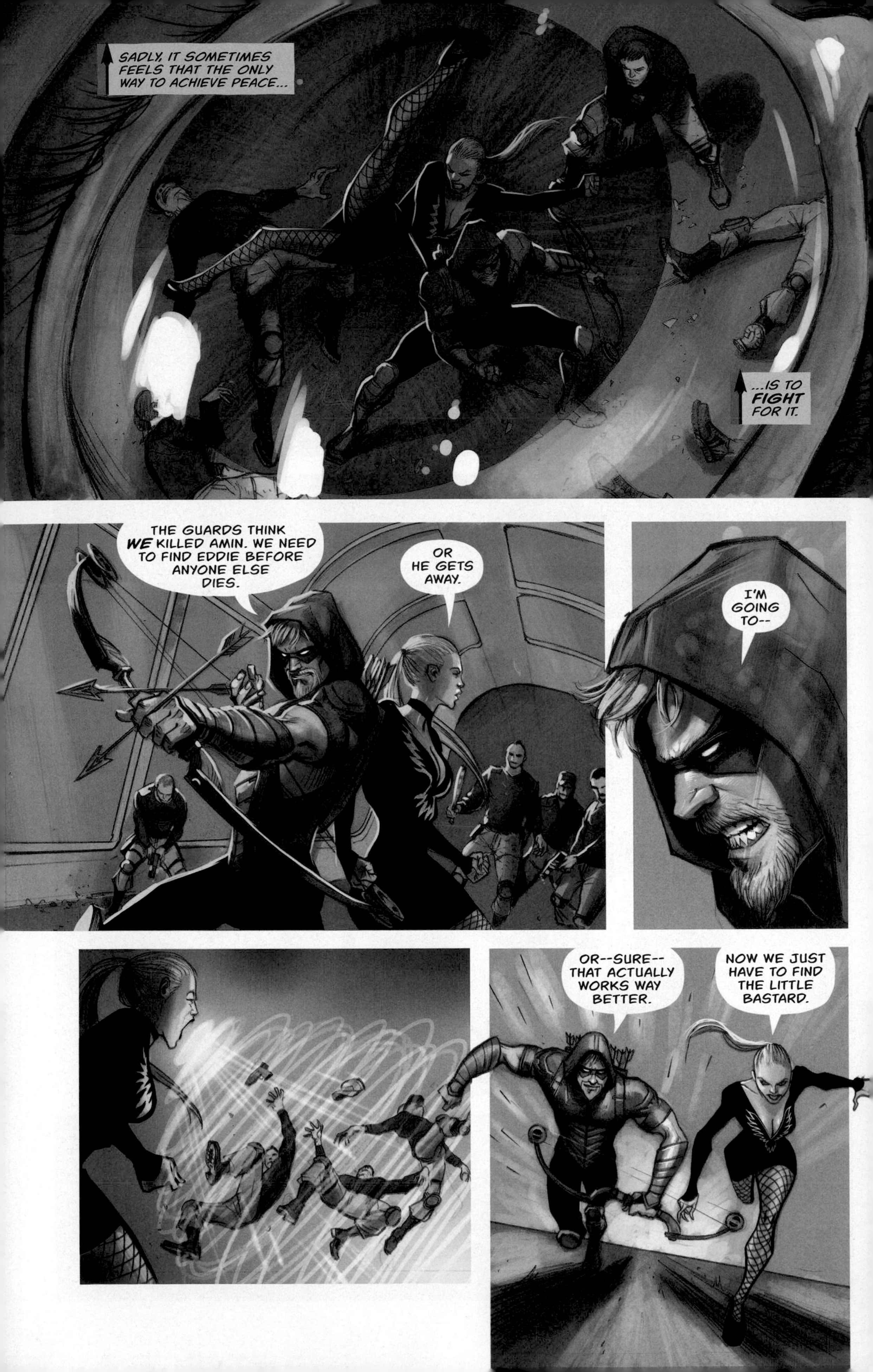
SADLY, IT SOMETIMES FEELS THAT THE ONLY WAY TO ACHIEVE PEACE...
...IS TO FIGHT FOR IT.
THE GUARDS THINK WE KILLED AMIN. WE NEED TO FIND EDDIE BEFORE ANYONE ELSE DIES.
OR HE GETS AWAY.
I'M GOING TO--
OR--SURE--THAT ACTUALLY WORKS WAY BETTER.
NOW WE JUST HAVE TO FIND THE LITTLE BASTARD.

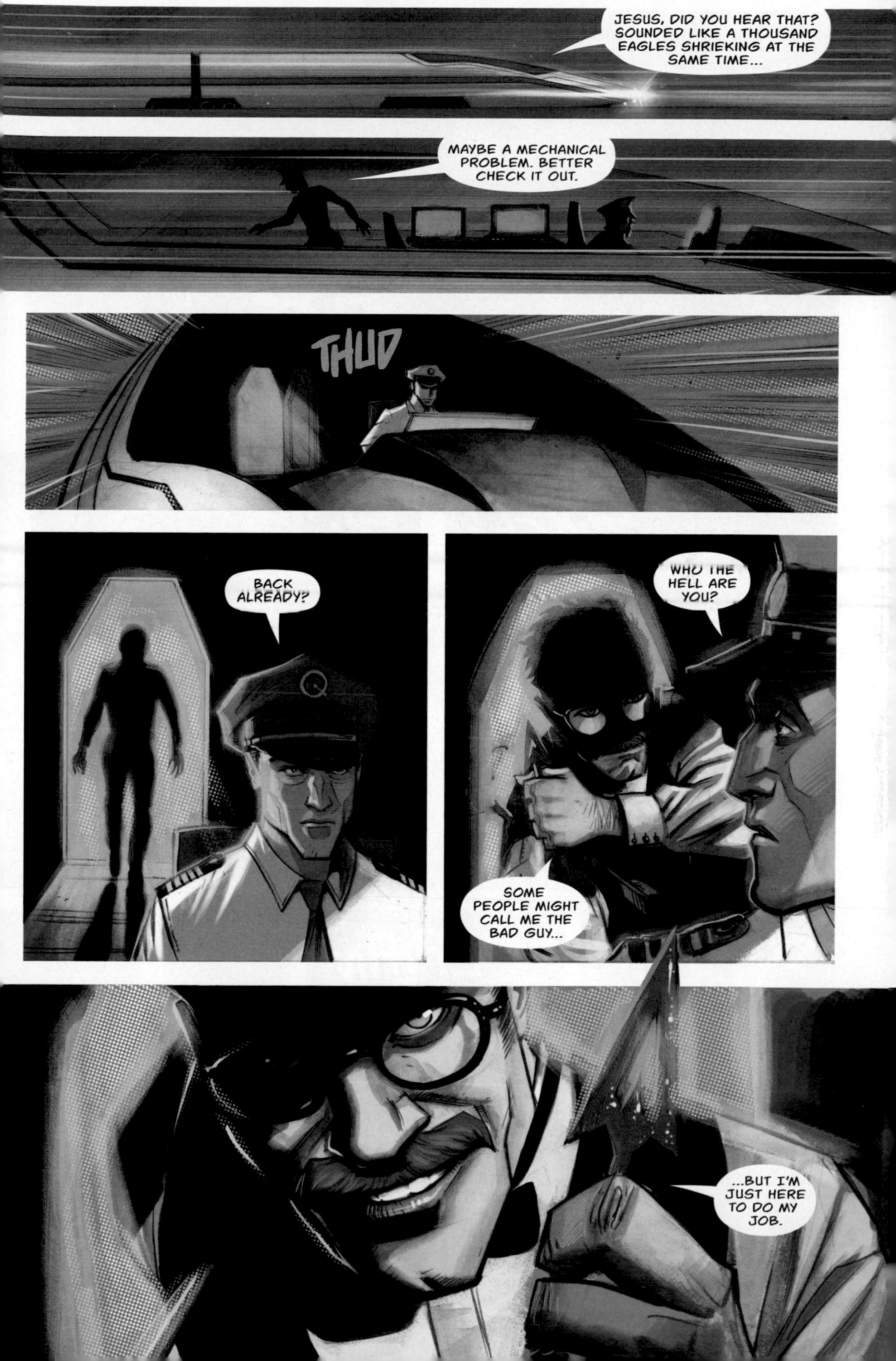
JESUS, DID YOU HEAR THAT? SOUNDED LIKE A THOUSAND EAGLES SHRIEKING AT THE SAME TIME...
MAYBE A MECHANICAL PROBLEM. BETTER CHECK IT OUT.
THUD
BACK ALREADY?
WHO THE HELL ARE YOU?
SOME PEOPLE MIGHT CALL ME THE BAD GUY...
...BUT I'M JUST HERE TO DO MY JOB.

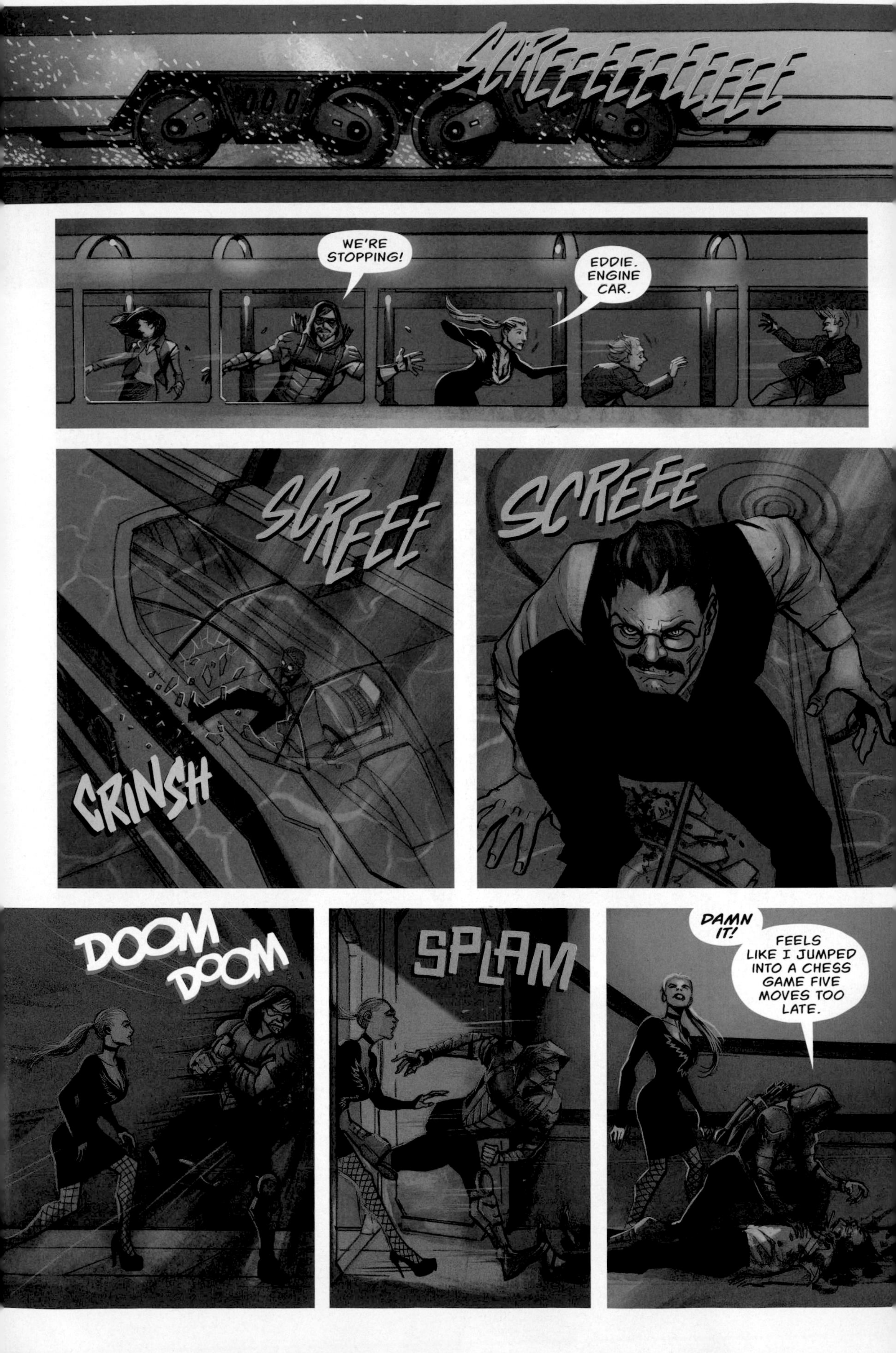
SCREEEEEEEEEEE
WE'RE STOPPING!
EDDIE. ENGINE CAR.
SCREEE
CRINSH
SCREEE
DOOM DOOM
SPLAM
DAMN IT!
FEELS LIKE I JUMPED INTO A CHESS GAME FIVE MOVES TOO LATE.

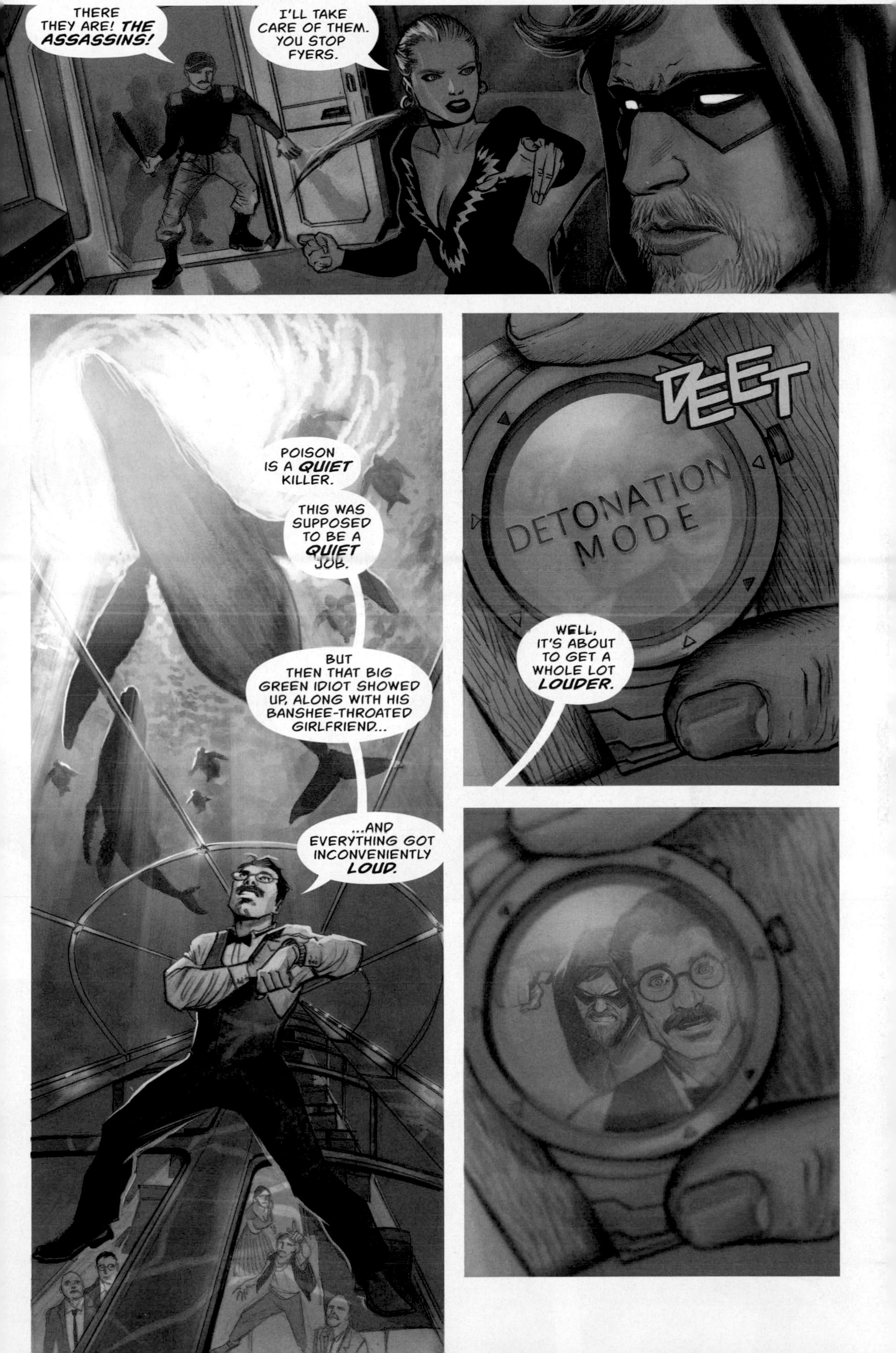
THERE THEY ARE! THE ASSASSINS!
I'LL TAKE CARE OF THEM. YOU STOP FYERS.
POISON IS A QUIET KILLER.
THIS WAS SUPPOSED TO BE A QUIET JOB.
BUT THEN THAT BIG GREEN IDIOT SHOWED UP, ALONG WITH HIS BANSHEE-THROATED GIRLFRIEND...
...AND EVERYTHING GOT INCONVENIENTLY LOUD.
DEET
DETONATION MODE
WELL, IT'S ABOUT TO GET A WHOLE LOT LOUDER.

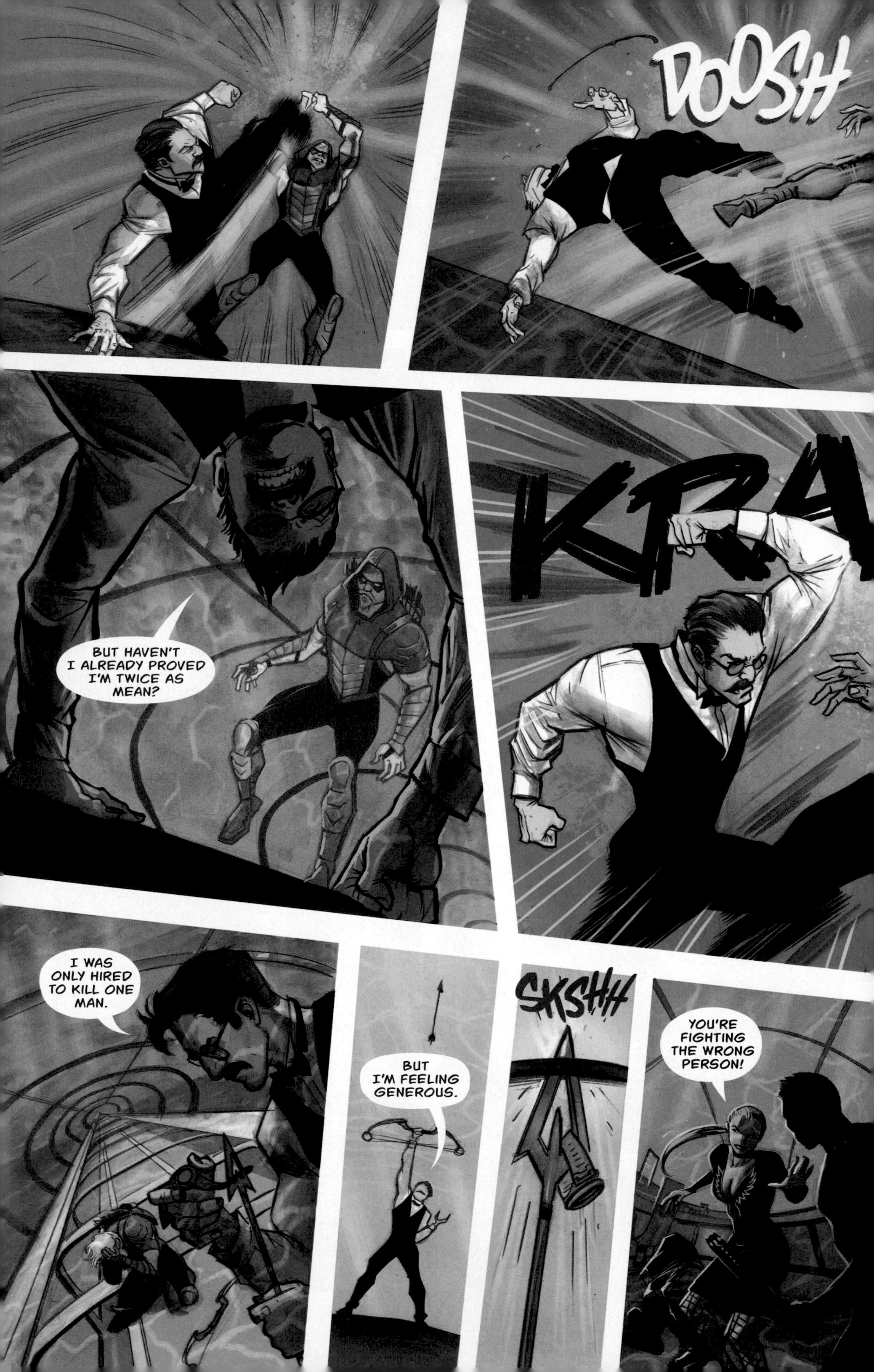
DOOSH
BUT HAVEN'T I ALREADY PROVED I'M TWICE AS MEAN?
KRA
I WAS ONLY HIRED TO KILL ONE MAN.
BUT I'M FEELING GENEROUS.
SKSHH
YOU'RE FIGHTING THE WRONG PERSON!

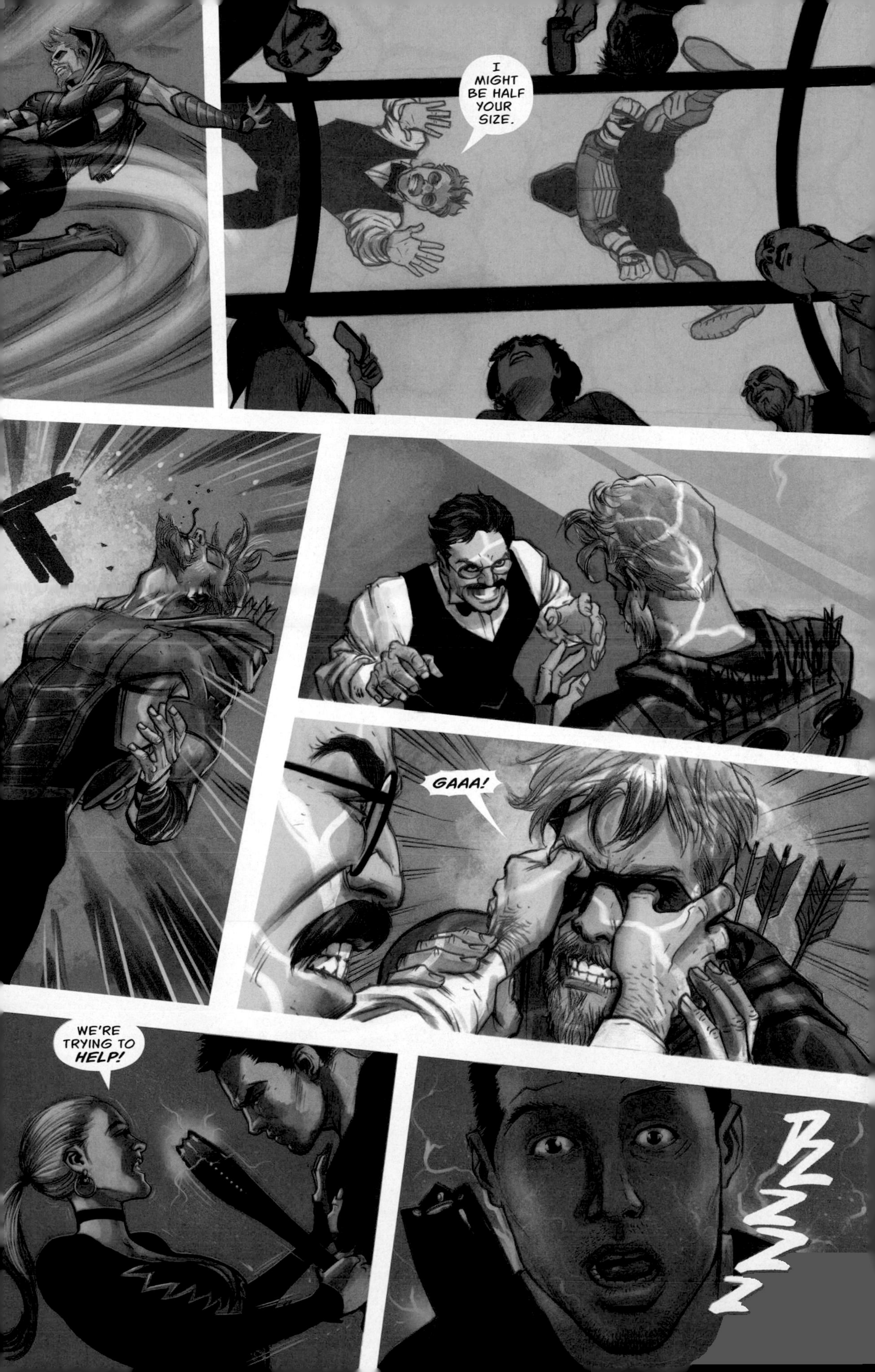
I MIGHT BE HALF YOUR SIZE.
GAAA!
WE'RE TRYING TO HELP!
BZZZZ

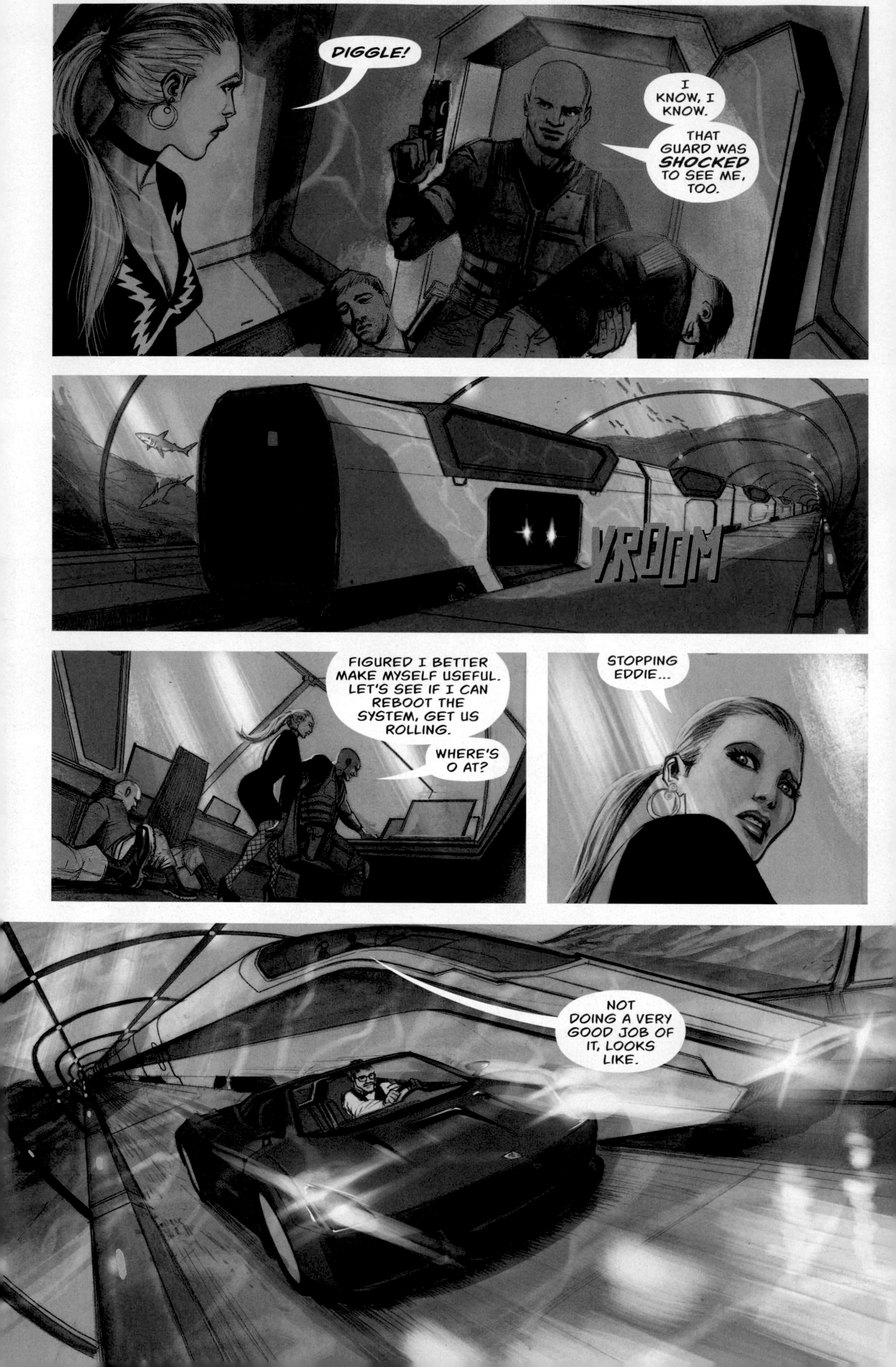
DIGGLE!
I KNOW, I KNOW.
THAT GUARD WAS SHOCKED TO SEE ME, TOO.
VROOM
FIGURED I BETTER MAKE MYSELF USEFUL. LET'S SEE IF I CAN REBOOT THE SYSTEM, GET US ROLLING.
WHERE'S O AT?
STOPPING EDDIE...
NOT DOING A VERY GOOD JOB OF IT, LOOKS LIKE.

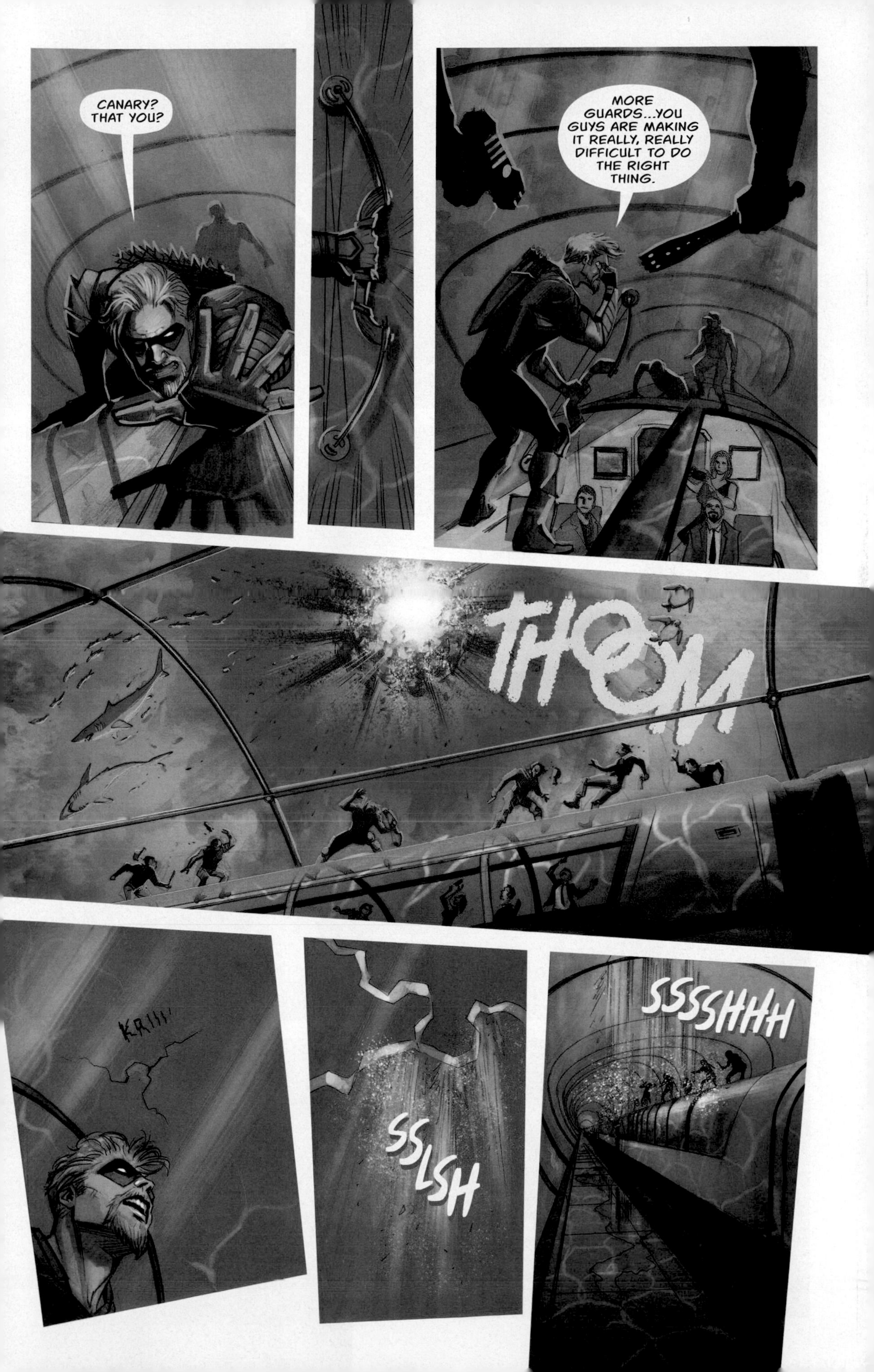
CANARY? THAT YOU?
MORE GUARDS...YOU GUYS ARE MAKING IT REALLY, REALLY DIFFICULT TO DO THE RIGHT THING.
THOOM
KRIII
SSLSH
SSSSHHH

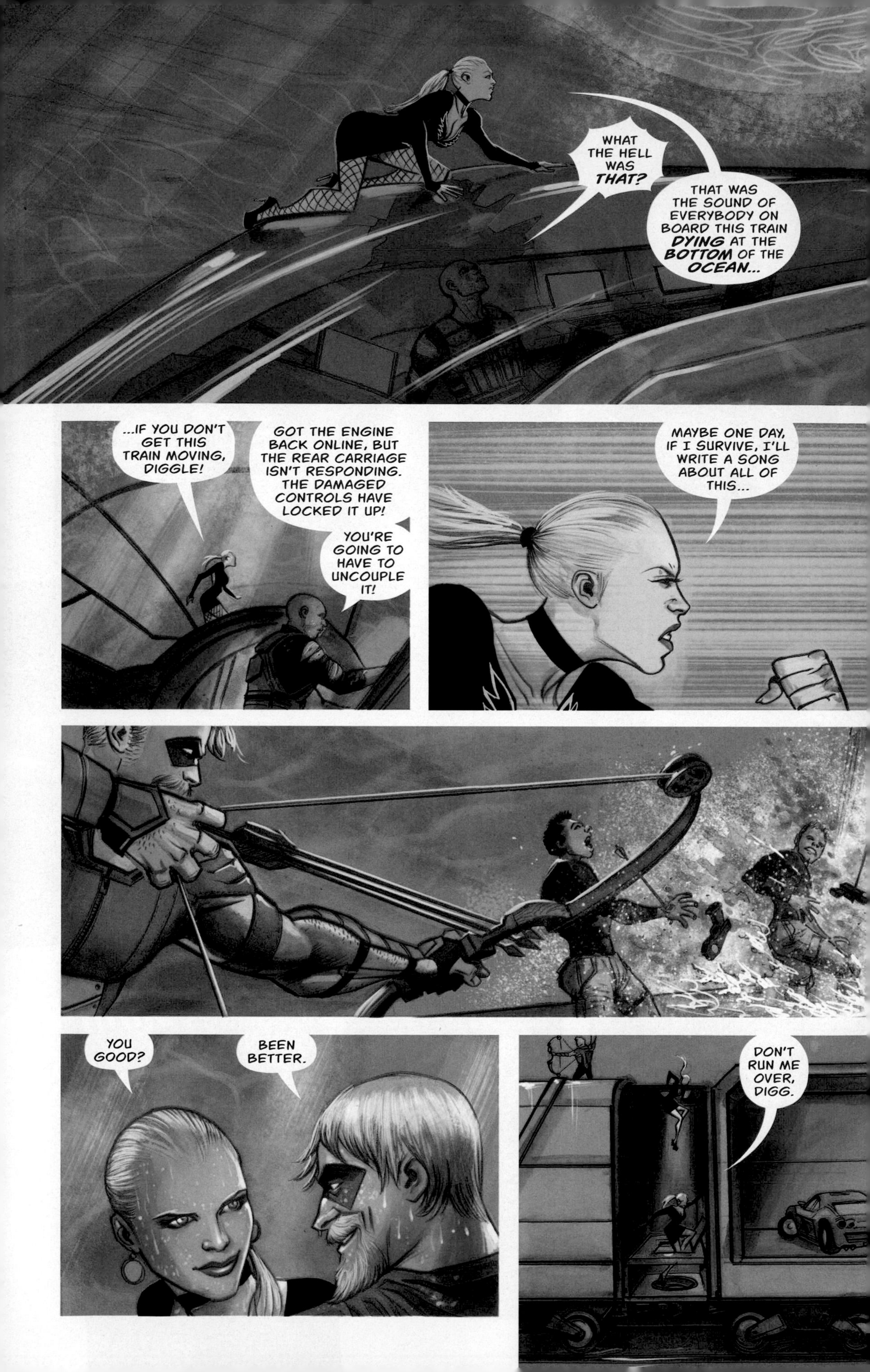
WHAT THE HELL WAS *THAT?*
THAT WAS THE SOUND OF EVERYBODY ON BOARD THIS TRAIN *DYING* AT THE *BOTTOM* OF THE *OCEAN*...
...IF YOU DON'T GET THIS TRAIN MOVING, DIGGLE!
GOT THE ENGINE BACK ONLINE, BUT THE REAR CARRIAGE ISN'T RESPONDING. THE DAMAGED CONTROLS HAVE LOCKED IT UP!
YOU'RE GOING TO HAVE TO UNCOUPLE IT!
MAYBE ONE DAY, IF I SURVIVE, I'LL WRITE A SONG ABOUT ALL OF THIS...
YOU GOOD?
BEEN BETTER.
DON'T RUN ME OVER, DIGG.

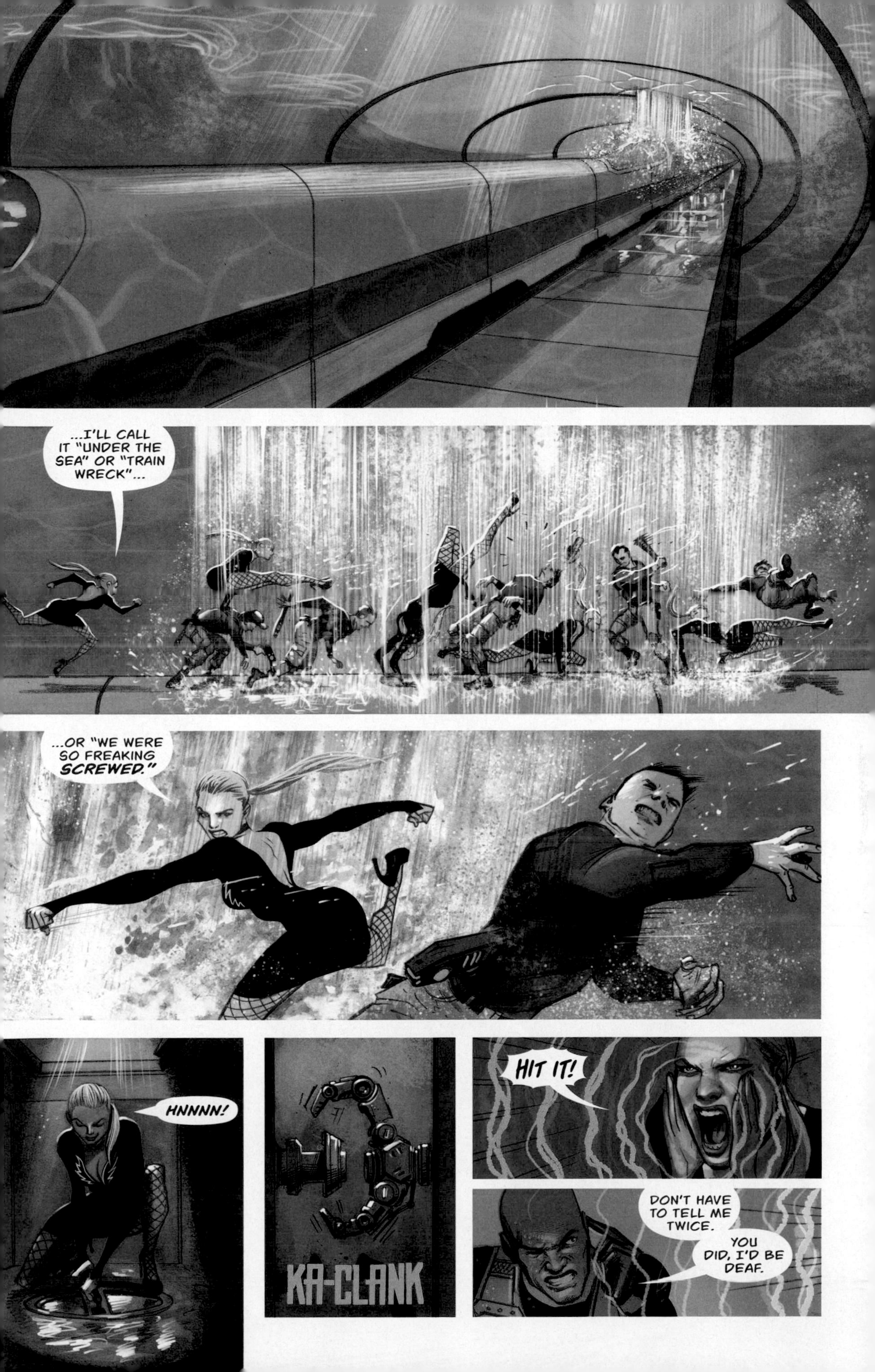

...I'LL CALL IT "UNDER THE SEA" OR "TRAIN WRECK"...
...OR "WE WERE SO FREAKING *SCREWED.*"
HNNNN!
KA-CLANK
HIT IT!
DON'T HAVE TO TELL ME TWICE.
YOU DID, I'D BE DEAF.

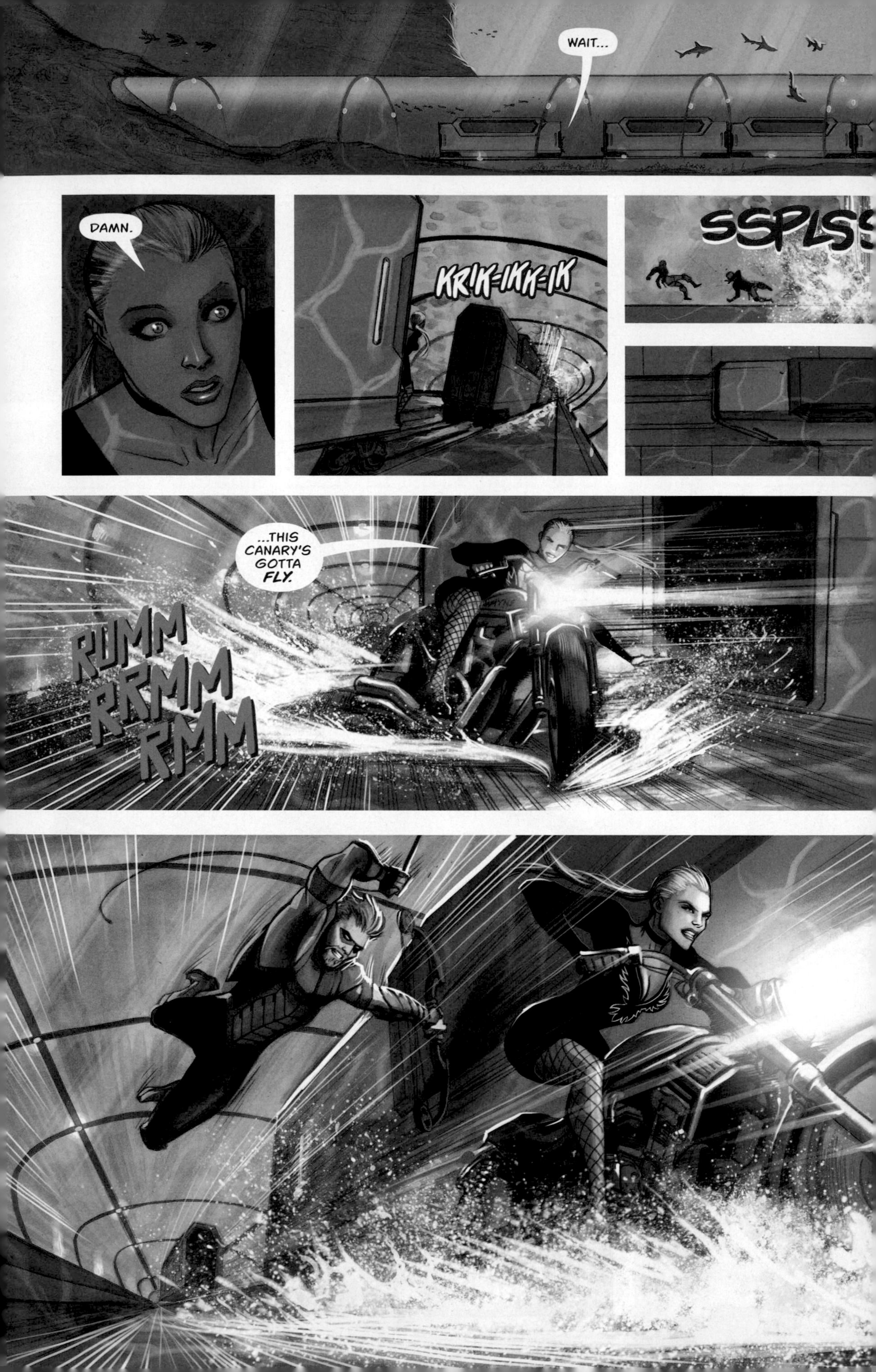

WAIT...
DAMN.
KRIK-IKK-IK
SSPLSS
...THIS CANARY'S GOTTA FLY.
RUMM RRMM RMM

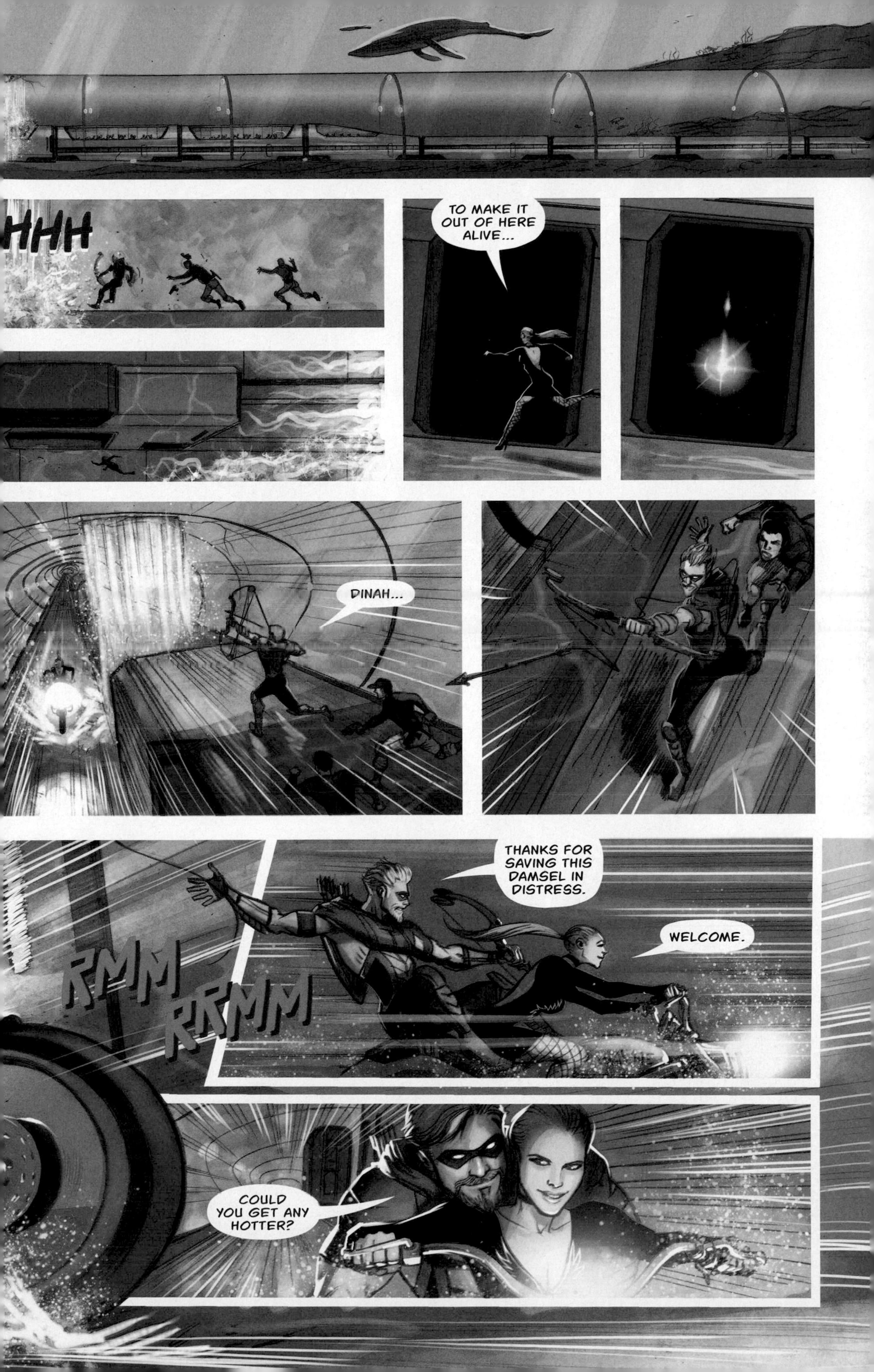
HHH
TO MAKE IT OUT OF HERE ALIVE...
DINAH...
THANKS FOR SAVING THIS DAMSEL IN DISTRESS.
WELCOME.
RMM RRMM
COULD YOU GET ANY HOTTER?

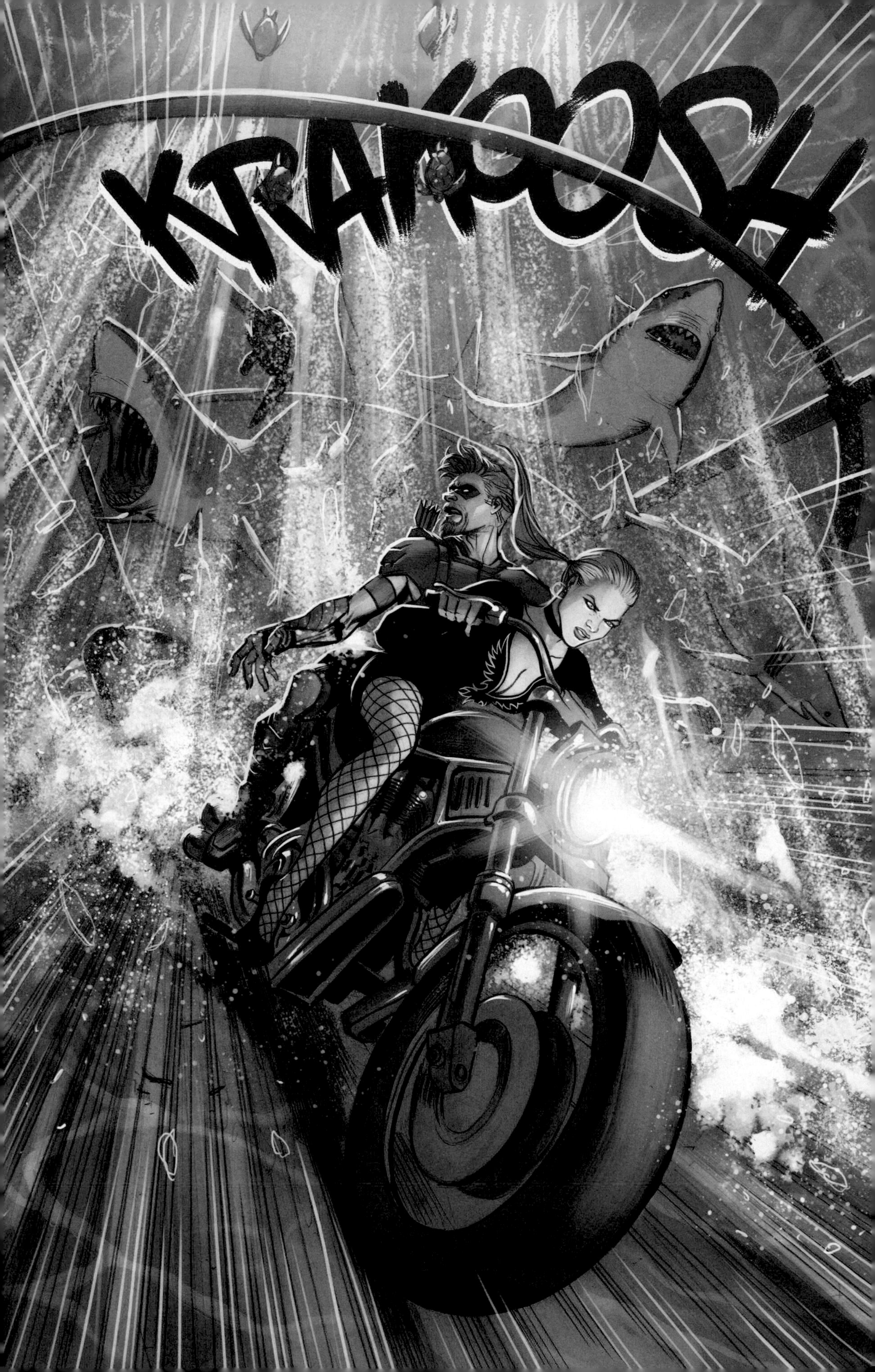
KRAKOOSH

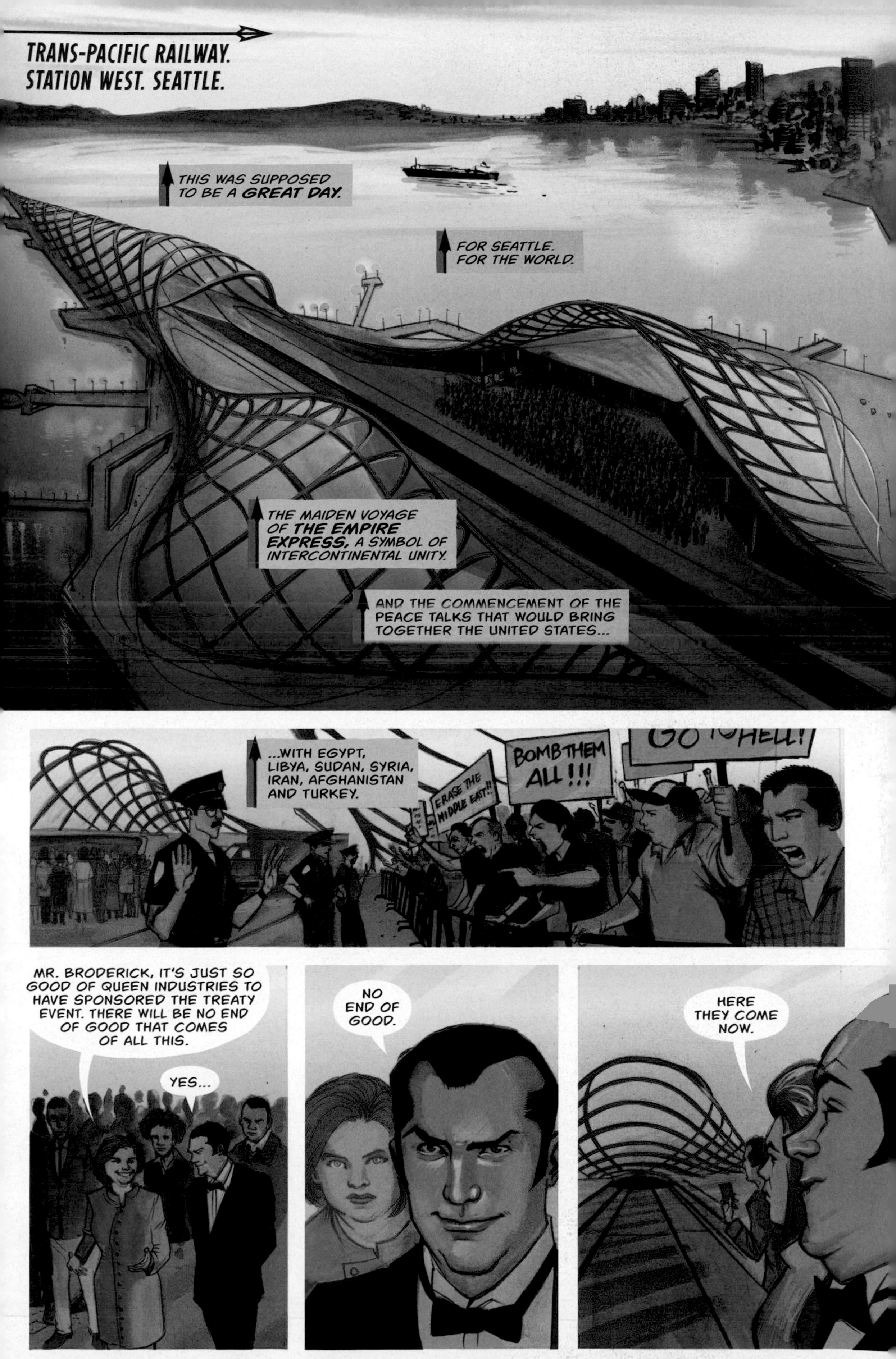
TRANS-PACIFIC RAILWAY.
STATION WEST. SEATTLE.
THIS WAS SUPPOSED TO BE A GREAT DAY.
FOR SEATTLE. FOR THE WORLD.
THE MAIDEN VOYAGE OF THE EMPIRE EXPRESS, A SYMBOL OF INTERCONTINENTAL UNITY.
AND THE COMMENCEMENT OF THE PEACE TALKS THAT WOULD BRING TOGETHER THE UNITED STATES...
...WITH EGYPT, LIBYA, SUDAN, SYRIA, IRAN, AFGHANISTAN AND TURKEY.
ERASE THE MIDDLE EAST!!
BOMB THEM ALL!!!
MR. BRODERICK, IT'S JUST SO GOOD OF QUEEN INDUSTRIES TO HAVE SPONSORED THE TREATY EVENT. THERE WILL BE NO END OF GOOD THAT COMES OF ALL THIS.
YES...
NO END OF GOOD.
HERE THEY COME NOW.

VROOM

WELL, WE'RE NOT GOING TO DROWN...

...BUT I'M NOT SURE THAT'S ANY CONSOLATION!

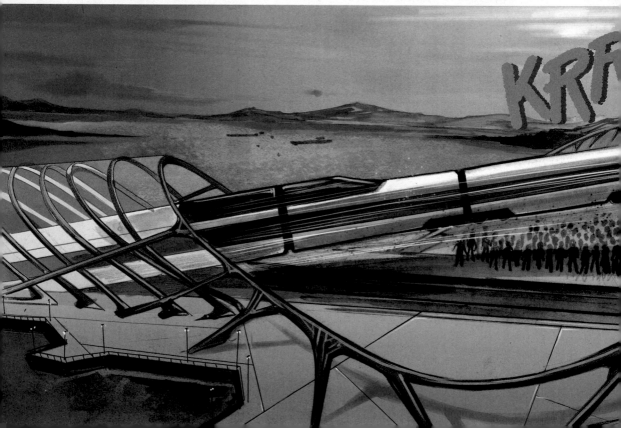

KRF

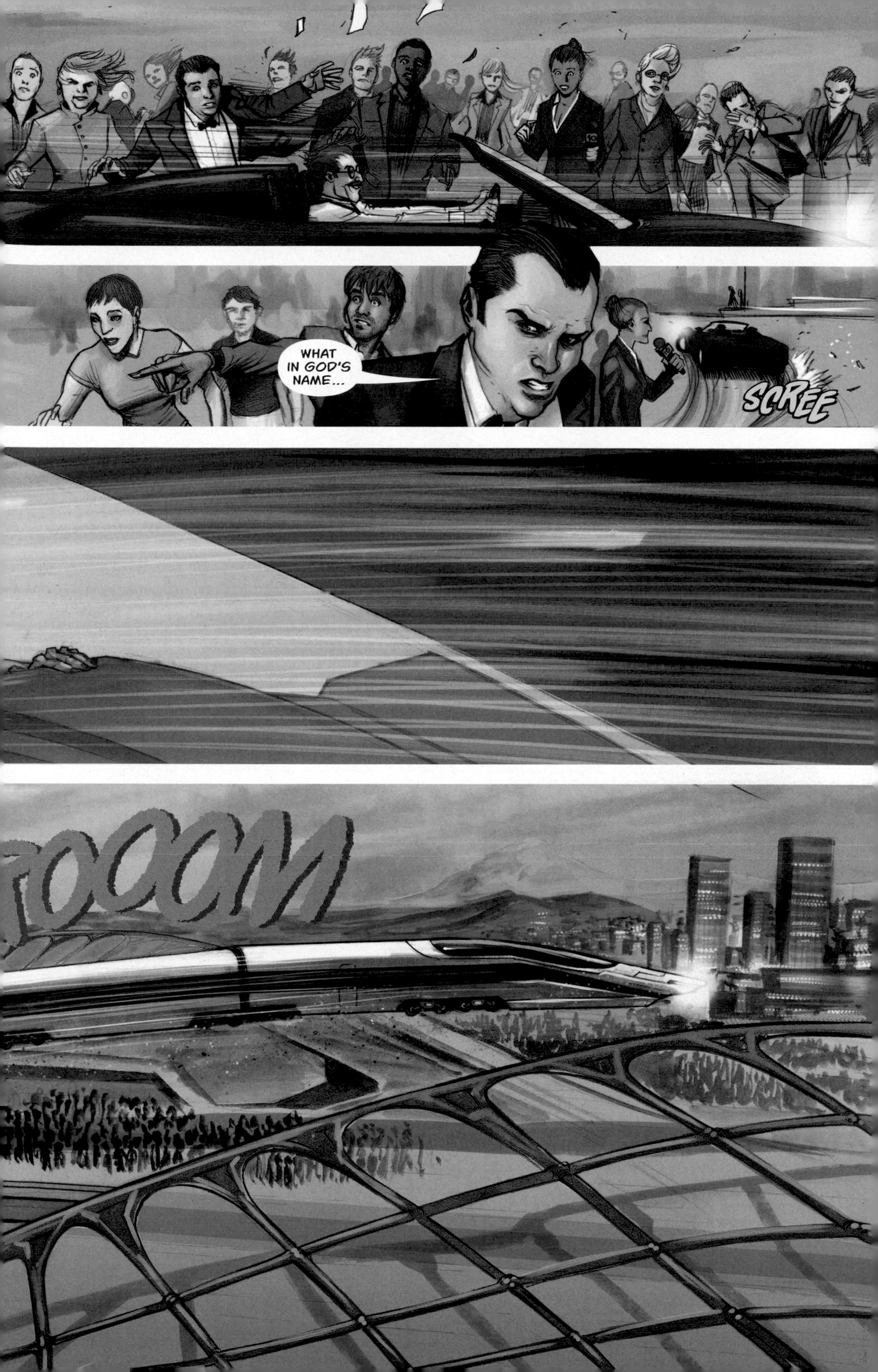
WHAT IN GOD'S NAME...
SCREE
OOOM

CRASHOO
WE'RE ALIVE...
I AM CONVINCED NOW MORE THAN EVER...
...THE PEACE TALKS MUST GO FORWARD.
TO HONOR AMIN'S LEGACY.
WHOEVER TRIED TO STOP US HAS ONLY MADE ME MORE RESOLUTE.

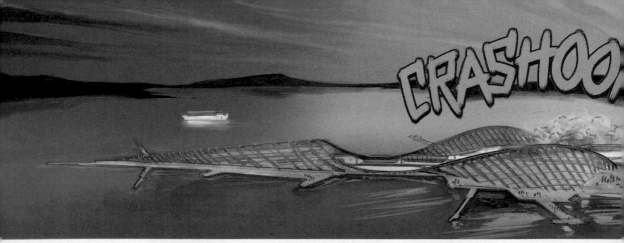

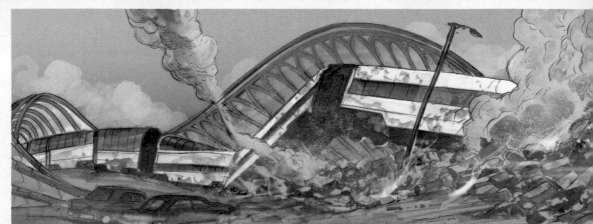

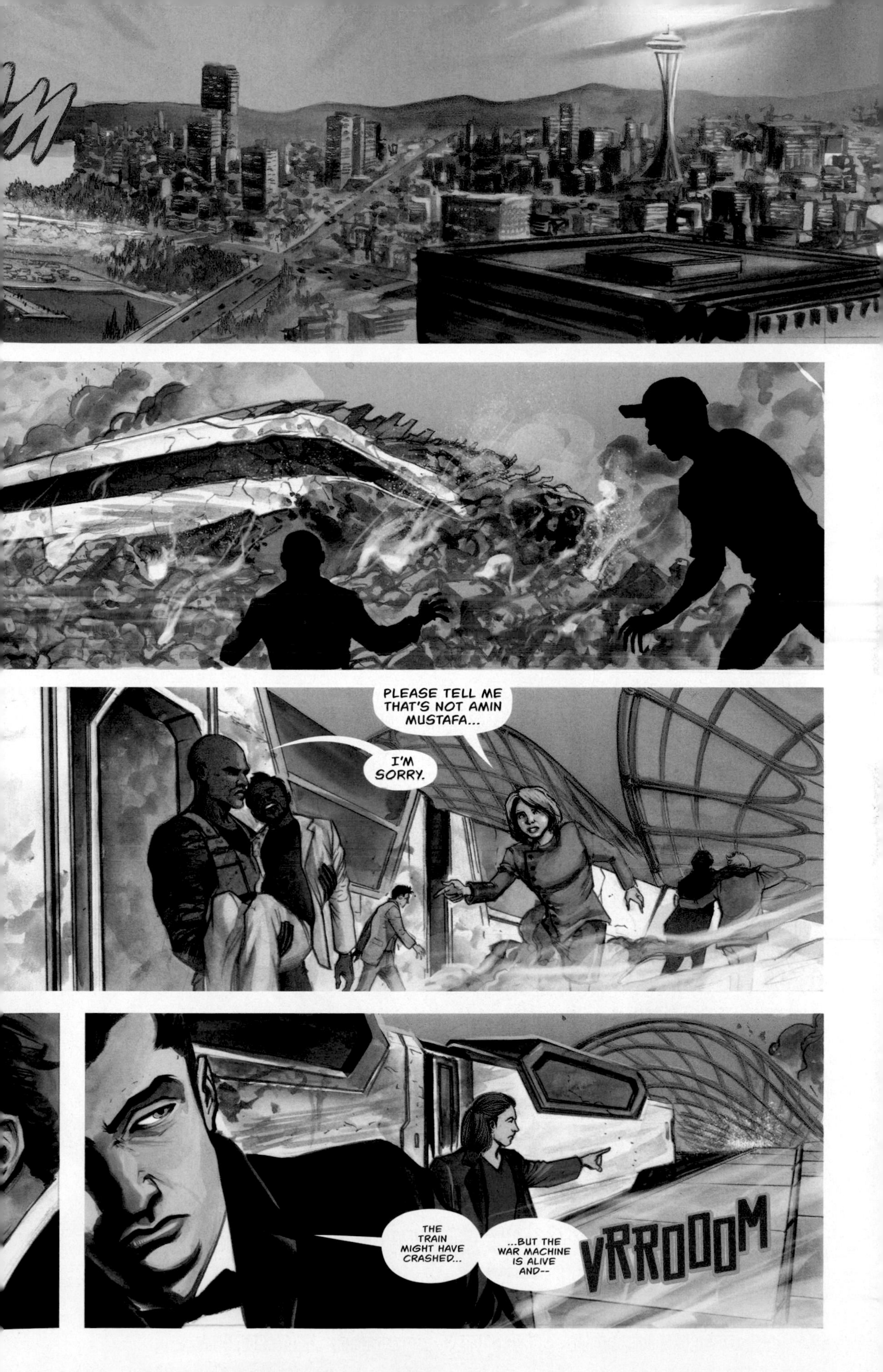
PLEASE TELL ME THAT'S NOT AMIN MUSTAFA...
I'M SORRY.
THE TRAIN MIGHT HAVE CRASHED...
...BUT THE WAR MACHINE IS ALIVE AND--
VRROOOM

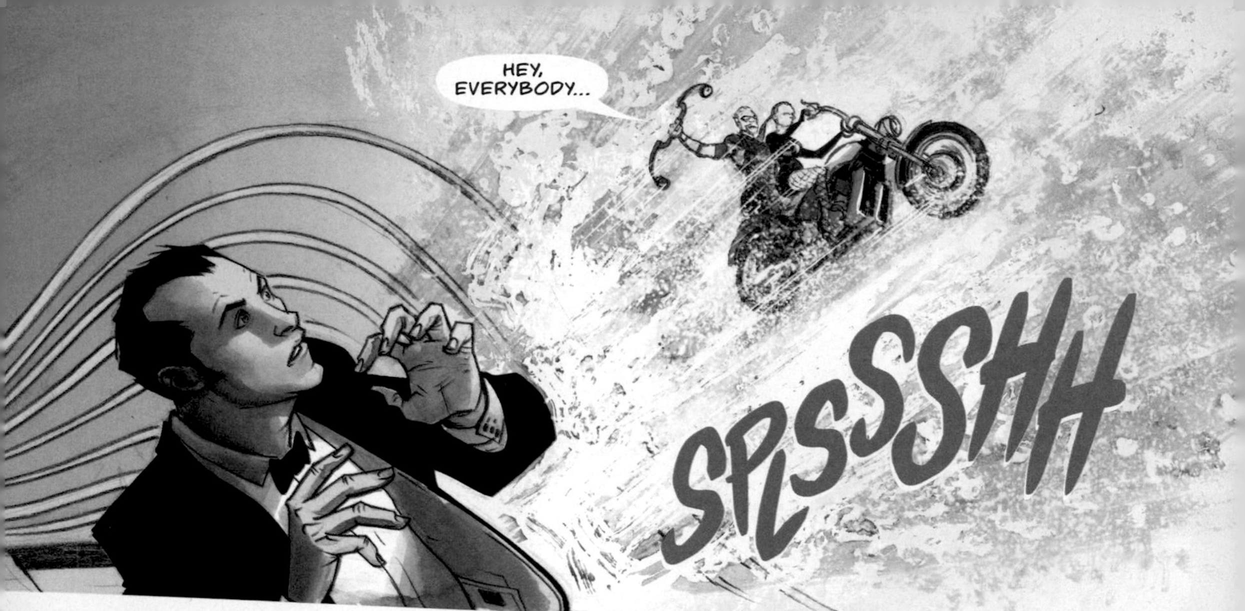
HEY, EVERYBODY...
SPLSSSHH

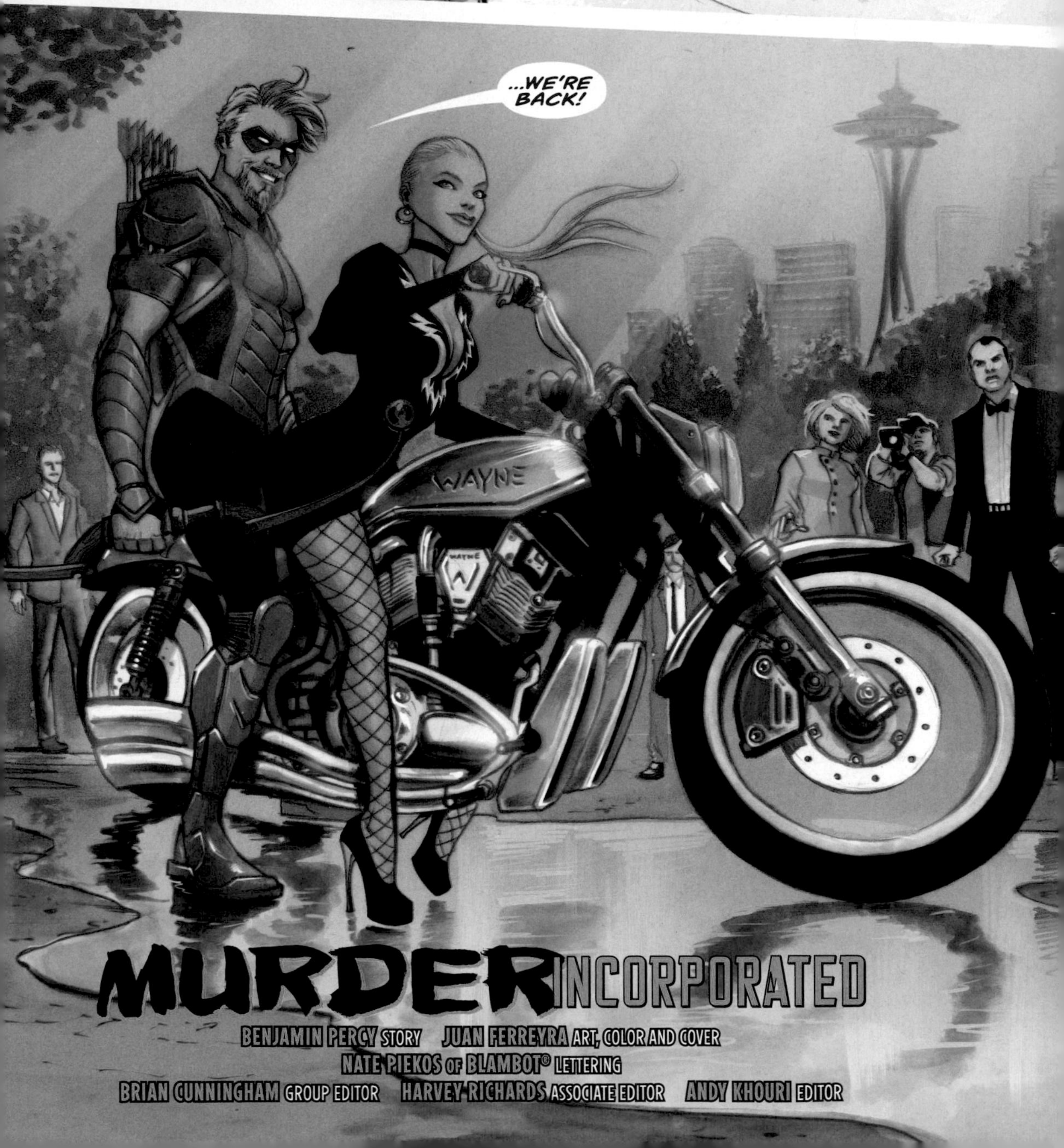
...WE'RE BACK!
WAYNE
MURDER INCORPORATED
BENJAMIN PERCY STORY JUAN FERREYRA ART, COLOR AND COVER
NATE PIEKOS OF BLAMBOT® LETTERING
BRIAN CUNNINGHAM GROUP EDITOR HARVEY RICHARDS ASSOCIATE EDITOR ANDY KHOURI EDITOR

GREEN ARROW

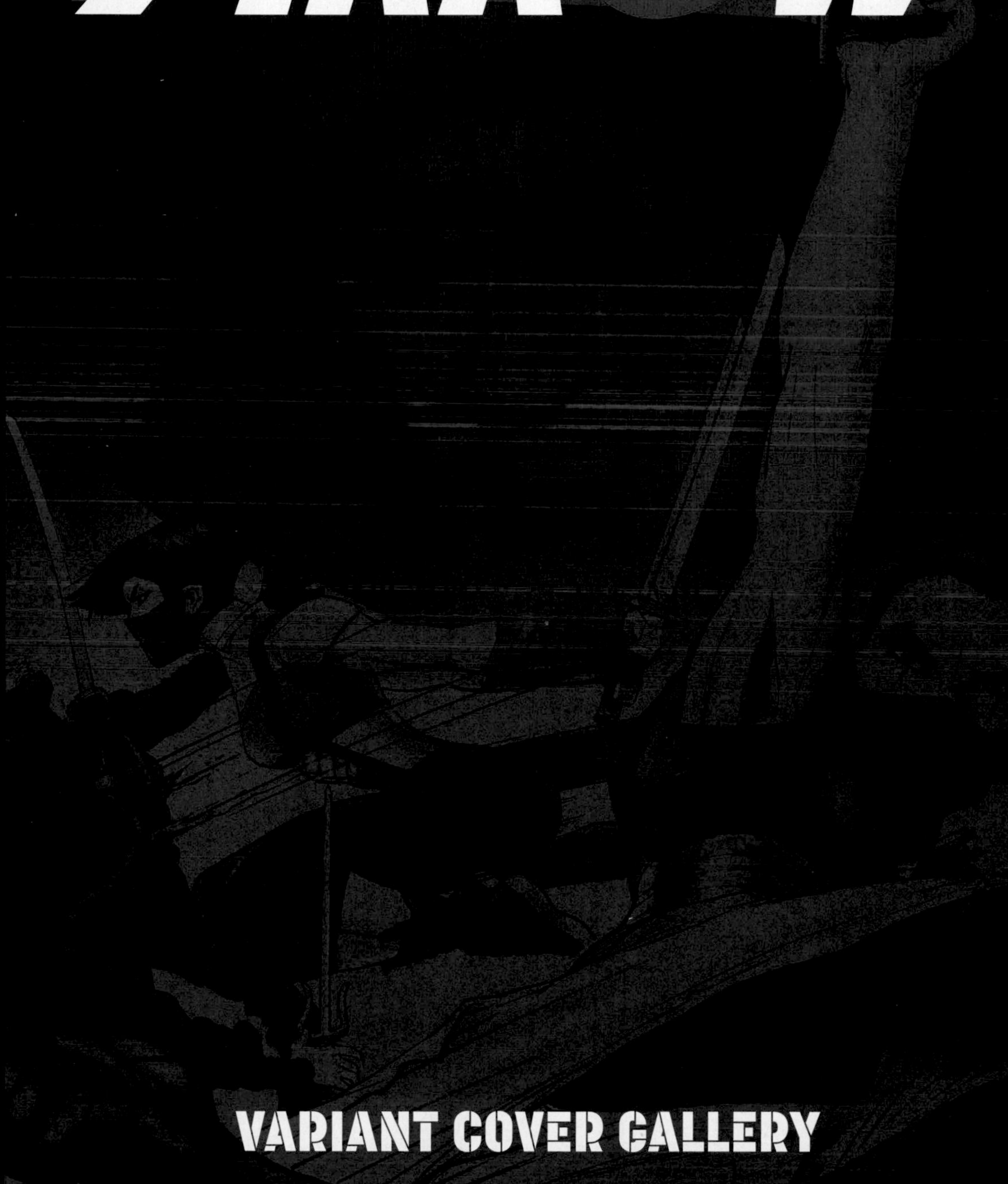

VARIANT COVER GALLERY

GREEN ARROW #6 Variant Cover by NEAL ADAMS and JOSH ADAMS with TIM SHINN

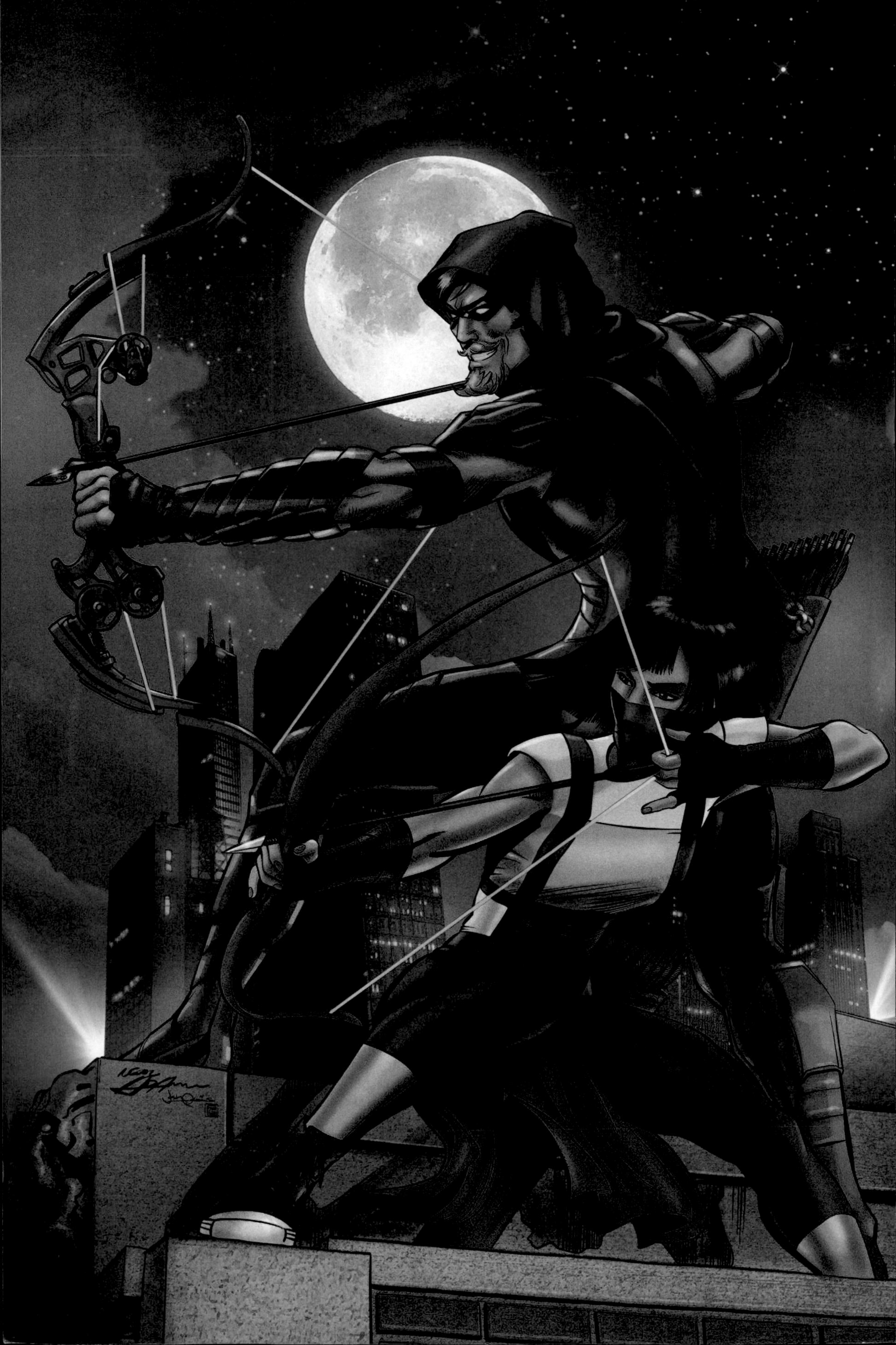

GREEN ARROW #7 Variant Cover by NEAL ADAMS and JOSH ADAMS with TIM SHINN

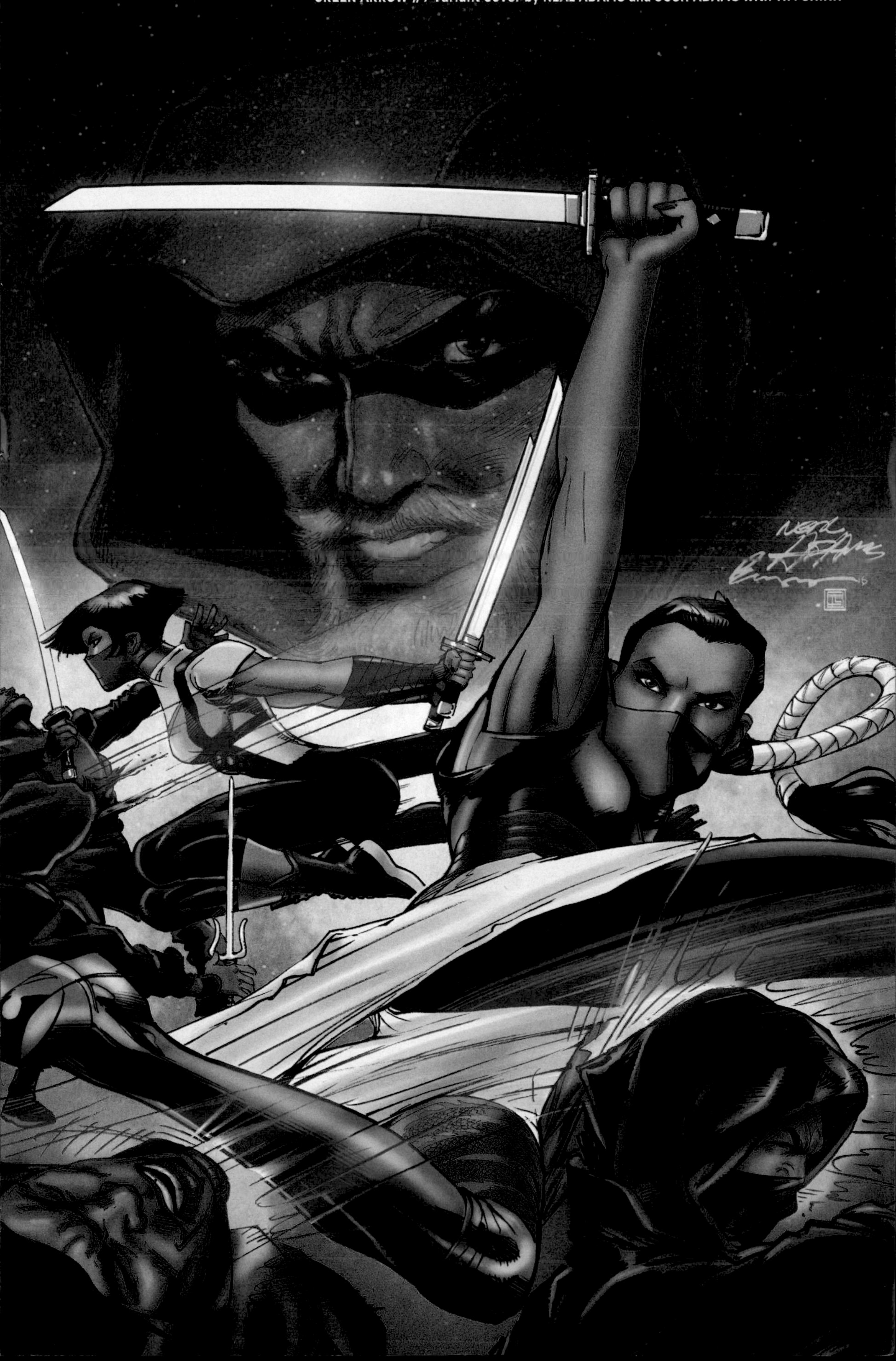

GREEN ARROW #8 Variant Cover by NEAL ADAMS with JEROMY COX

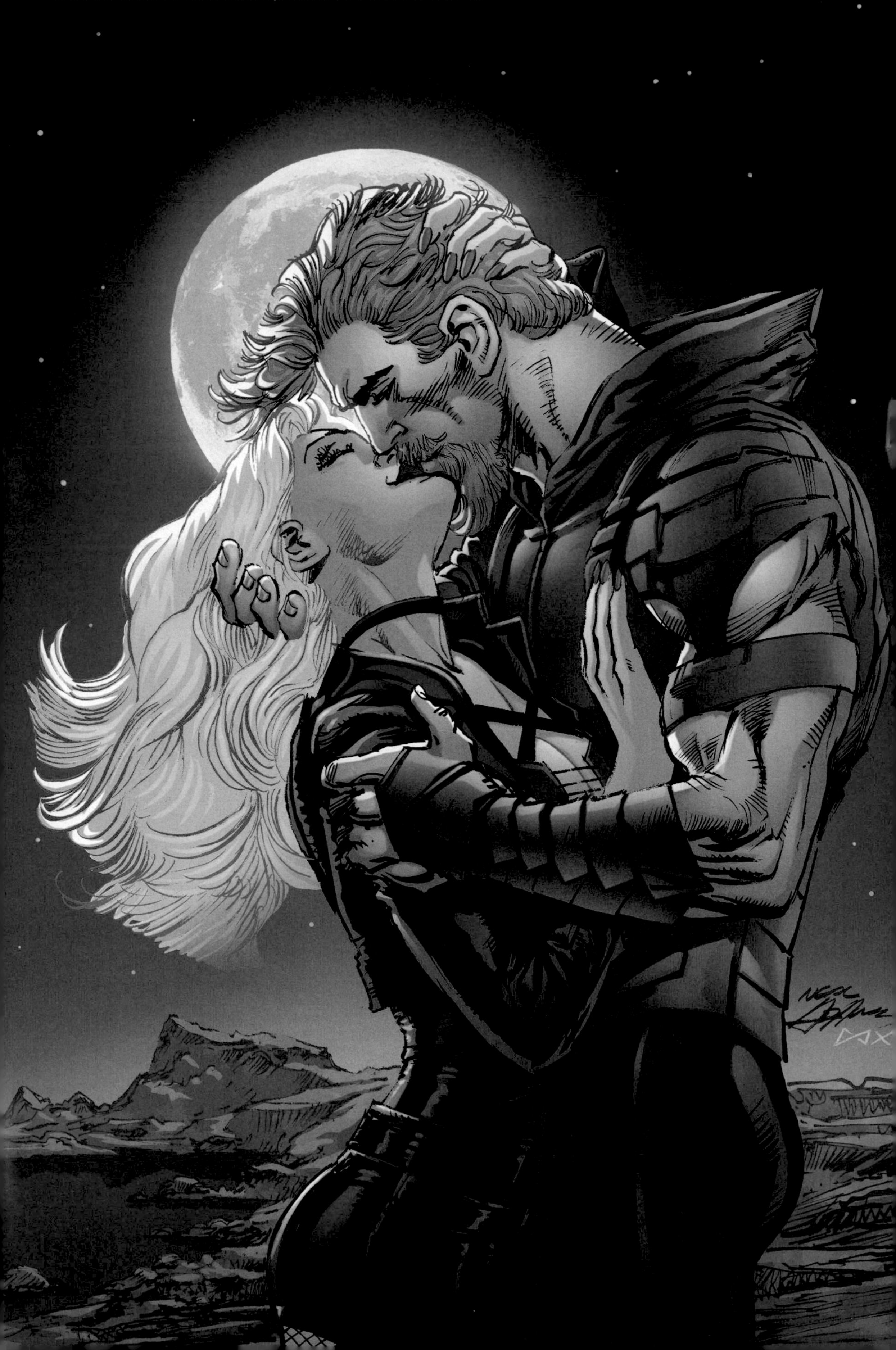

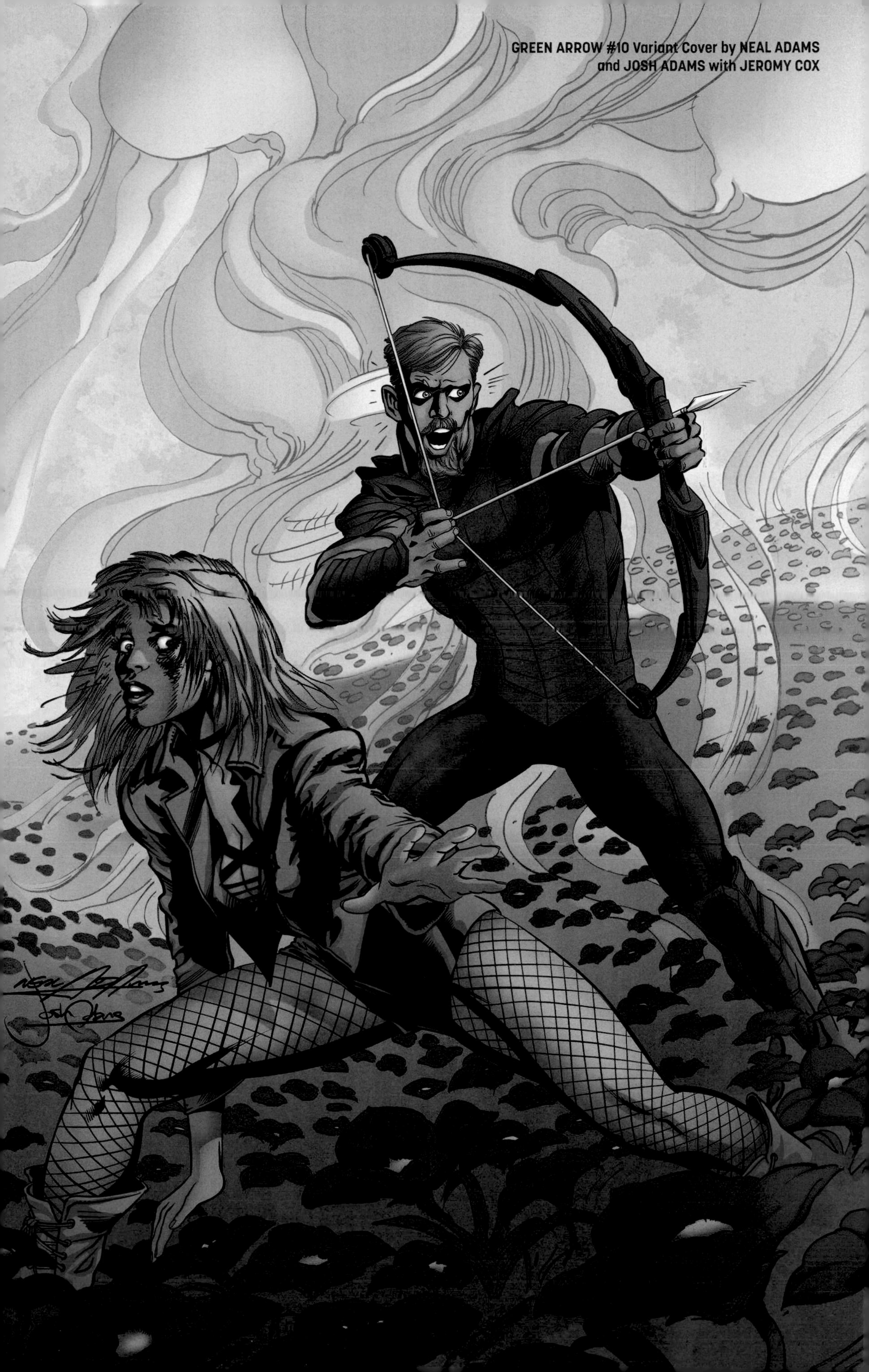

GREEN ARROW #10 Variant Cover by NEAL ADAMS
and JOSH ADAMS with JEROMY COX

GREEN ARROW #10 Variant Cover by NEAL ADAMS with ALEX SINCLAIR

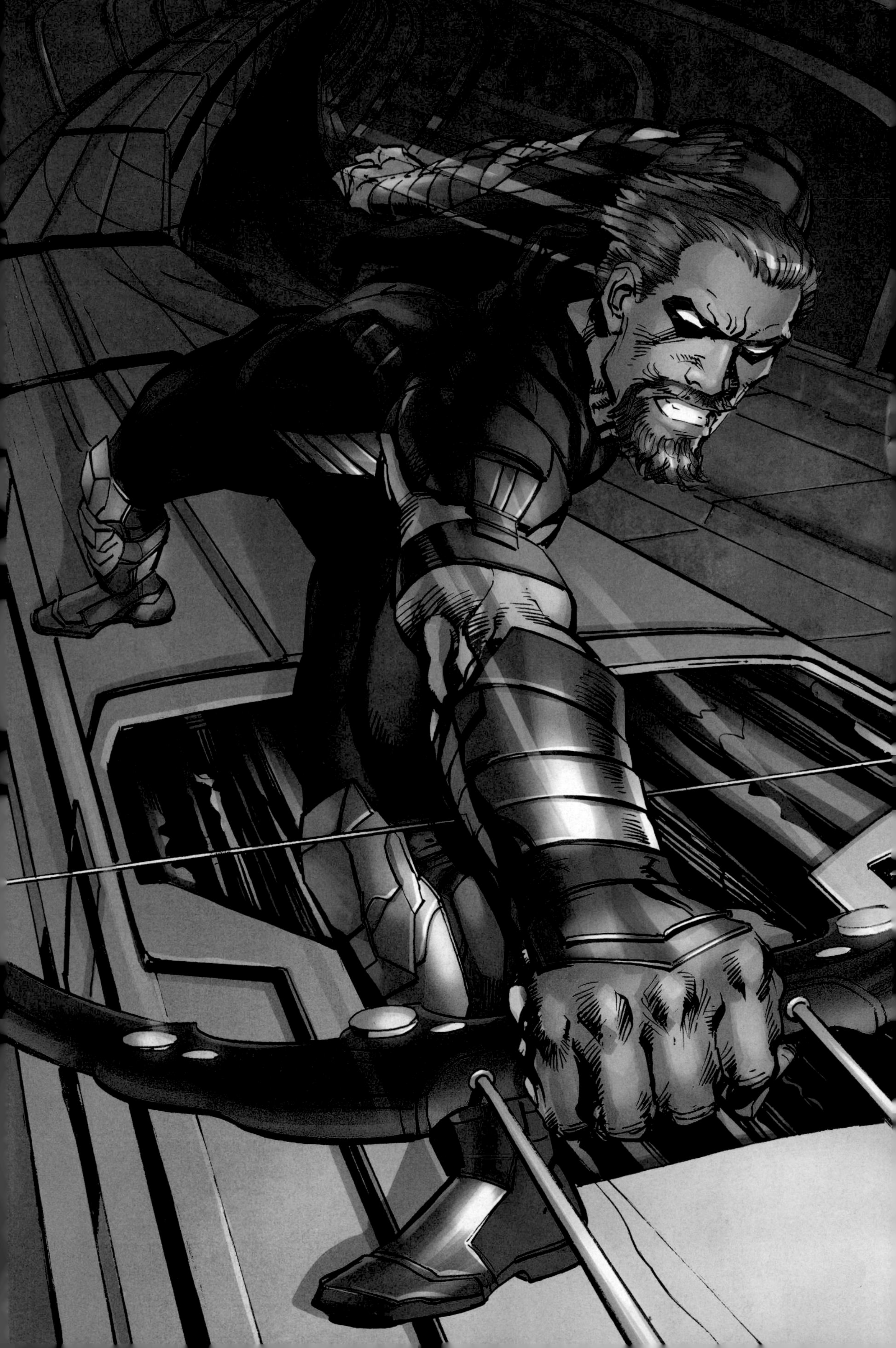

GREEN ARROW #11 Variant Cover by NEAL ADAMS with ALEX SINCLAIR

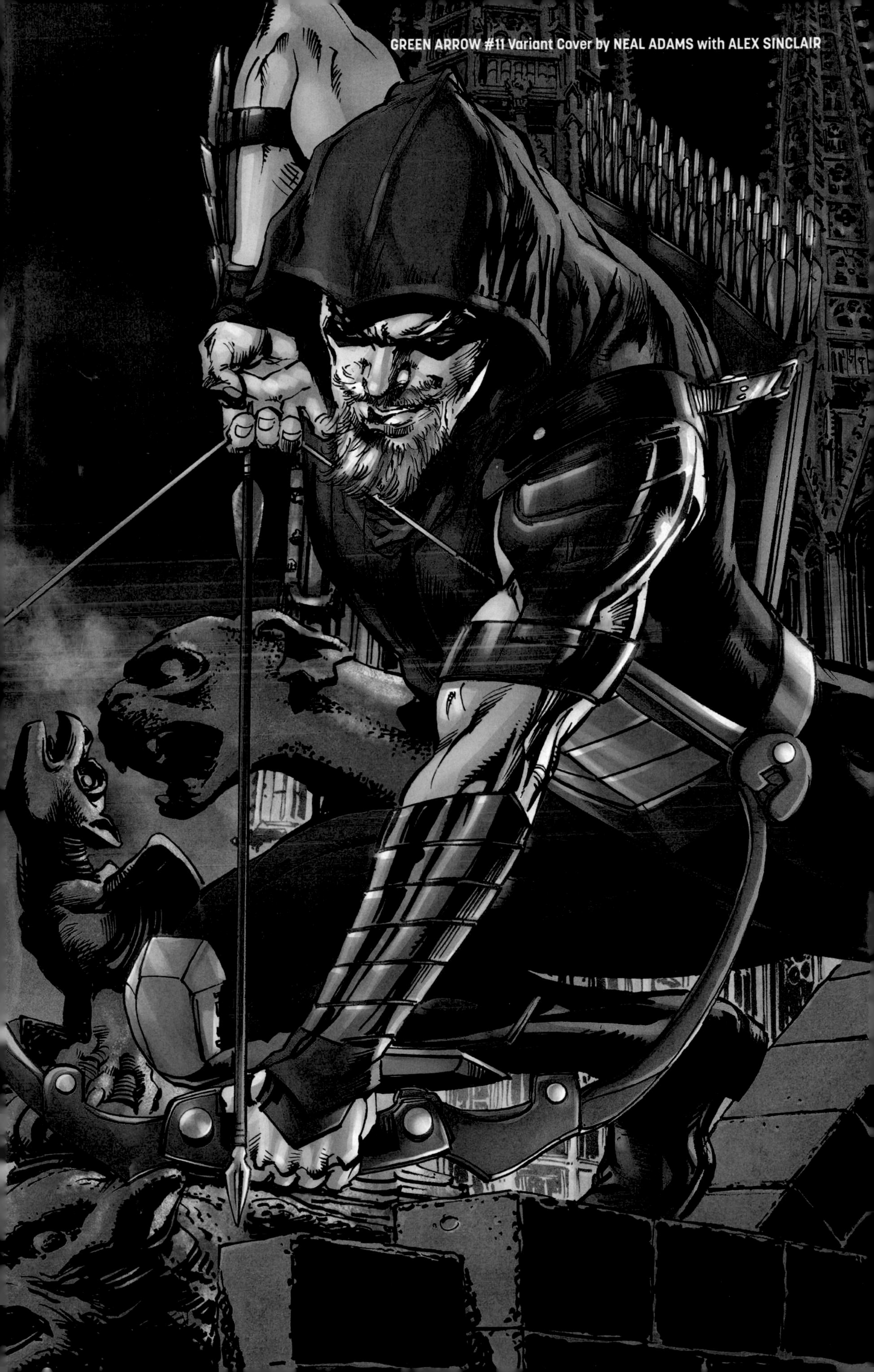

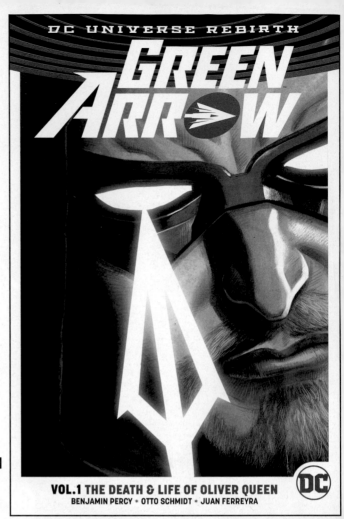

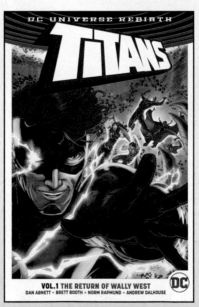

 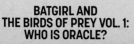